The Rental Property Manager's Toolbox

*A Complete Guide Including
Pre-Written Forms, Agreements,
Letters, and Legal Notices:
With Companion CD-ROM*

By Jamaine Burrell

The Rental Property Manager's Toolbox—A Complete Guide Including Pre-Written Forms, Agreements, Letters, and Legal Notices: With Companion CD-ROM

ISBN-13: 978-0-910627-71-9   ISBN-10: 0-910627-71-1

Library of Congress Cataloging-in-Publication Data
Burrell, Jamaine, 1958-
The rental property manager's toolbox : a complete guide including pre-written forms, agreements, letters, and legal notices : with companion CD-ROM / Jamaine Burrell. p. cm.
The accompanying CD-ROM contains dozens of forms, sample contracts, letters, notices, rental applications, agreements, and checklists.
Includes bibliographical references and index.
ISBN-13: 978-0-910627-71-9 (alk. paper)   ISBN-10: 0-910627-71-1
1. Real estate management--United States--Handbooks, manuals, etc. 2. Rental housing--United States--Handbooks, manuals, etc. 3. Real estate management--United States--Forms. 4. Real estate management--Law and legislation--United States--Forms. I. Title: Property manager's toolbox. II. Title.

HD1394.5.U6B87 2006
333.5068--dc22
                              2006003915

EDITOR: Jackie Ness • jackie_ness@charter.net
ART DIRECTION & INTERIOR DESIGN: Meg Buchner • megadesn@mchsi.com
FRONT COVER & BOOK PRODUCTION DESIGN: Lisa Peterson, Michael Meister • info@6sense.net
GLOSSARY COMPILED BY: Christina Mohammed

Printed in the United States

Contents

CHAPTER THREE: Financial, Legal & Advertising Skills of a Good Property Manager   45

CHAPTER SEVEN: Establishing Good Relationships   173

CHAPTER EIGHT: Tenants   187

CHAPTER NINE: Tenant Problems and Complaints 229

CHAPTER TEN: Selling Management Property   267

Bibliography   285

Index   286

Glossary   293

Resources   355

About the Author   367

Forms   368

Foreword

People have hoped, dreamed and planned for it, saved for it, worked for it, fought over it, died for it—real property.

At the top of most people's acquisition list is their own land with a home on it. I call that the white picket fence syndrome.

Whether or not we own our land and home, eventually the allure of reaping financial rewards from owning real estate leads many to take that leap into the real estate world.

An investor entrepreneur may want to include real property in his or her portfolio. Another individual may see the career advantages of assisting others in buying, selling and/or managing real estate. Both persons wish for a successful financial outcome with real estate as the vehicle. However, in the beginning of their endeavor, they need backbone rather than wishbone. They need the tools to make their dreams come to fruition.

Taking the first steps toward investment property acquisition for oneself or entering into a property management career may seem like a grand idea. Just as a rock climber wouldn't think of throwing himself off a cliff to rappel down a 500 foot granite face without having procured the right equipment and trained for the arduous task, so too, anyone contemplating venturing down the path of real estate investment and property management needs the tools of developed skills and on-going training.

Twenty years ago, resources for the landlord or property manager were hard to find. For the most part, applicable and relevant education and resources were non-existent. Resources were on the "wishin' and hoping" list. The IREM® (Institute of Real Estate Management) offered through NAR® (National Association of Realtors) did a fine job of preparing and supporting those who were preparing for commercial real estate management. However, there was a giant void for those who wanted to develop skills and expertise in managing their own or other's residential properties.

In the late 1980's a few landlords working in the trenches began writing about the field and offering "how-to" suggestions via newsletters and books. A group of professional property managers formed a trade association with the goals of developing education, credentials, support, and networking opportunities. Known as the National Association of Residential Property Managers, NARPM®, this trade association has grown to support residential property managers in the United States mainland, Hawaii, and abroad. Today there are numerous resources for landlords and professional property managers. *The Rental Property Manager's Toolbox* highlights major institutions and entities that offer education and assistance for landlords and property managers. It is a welcomed asset to property management development.

If you are a person who is contemplating purchasing that first investment property or who is a relatively new landlord, you will find *The Rental Property Manager's Toolbox* to be invaluable. It offers quality tools to help build a sound foundation that will lead to a more successful outcome and avoid the pitfalls that result from poor planning and inadequate knowledge. Property management is a complex field fraught with exponentially expanding information and changes that can be a source of risk to the landlord or property manager. Ongoing education about current trends, technology, laws and statutes is essential.

If you are an investor, this book can assist you in deciding if you have the skills, temperament and time to be a landlord.

After reading this book and familiarizing yourself with the requirements of property management, you can evaluate and choose the best professional property manager for your portfolio should you decide being a landlord is not for you.

If you manage real estate for a fee, *The Rental Property Manager's Toolbox* is a two-tiered toolbox. The book is a comprehensive primer on all the facets of property management and offers many resources for the property manager. If you have mastered the basic tools, you can use this book to assess and evaluate your current skill level, knowledge and expertise and become aware of systems and procedures you need to fine tune.

The Rental Property Manager's Toolbox with its detailed guidelines, pre-written forms, agreements, letters, legal notices and companion CD-ROM can be the backbone that replaces the "wishbone" for the investor and property manager. If you are reading this book, you are taking a commanding step towards more cutting edge professionalism. This book can be your tool for achieving personal and financial success.

Karen Ebert, MPM, RMP, Realtor

A founding member of the NARPM® (National Association of Residential Property Managers), Karen Ebert, MPM, RMP, is a Realtor and served as an officer, director, and first editor of the "Residential Resource", newsletter of the NARPM® and was given the NARPM® President's award in 1998. She wrote and presented several education workshops for the NARPM® annual conventions. Karen holds the e-Pro designation from the NAR®. She has been president and director of operations of Austin Landmark Property Services, ALPS, Inc. in Austin, Texas since 1986. ALPS earned the designation of CRMC (Certified Residential Management Company) provided by the NARPM®. Karen and Rick Ebert, MPM manage close to 500 rental units.

Author Dedication

My writing is dedicated to both my biological family and my street family. A special dedication is reserved for my single mother, who lost the battle with cancer, the many, many neighborhood youth of Baltimore City who were murdered before we were ever privileged to see their adult faces and those who had their adulthood abruptly shortened. R.I.P.

CHAPTER ONE

What Is Property Management?

Property management is the care and maintenance of leased or rental property by or on behalf of the property owner. Property management requires a number of skills, including finance, insurance, research, marketing, communication, problem solving, people skills, and, of course, management. A property manager takes on a number of responsibilities, with the overall goal of maintaining rental property sufficient to collect rental payments as prescribed by a lease or rental agreement. A property manager may maintain residential, commercial, or industrial properties. In all properties, the property manager must meet the needs of the tenant as well as of the property owner. Management activities usually require the skills or services of more than one individual for maintenance, repairs, and other necessary assistance. A property manager must delegate and coordinate these types of services.

The Owner as Property Manager

The property owner may serve as the property manager for his or her own property. Owners are quite successful in managing their own properties when they have the skill set necessary to accomplish the job. Owner-managers usually have a small number of properties to manage and are located within close proximity to their properties. Also, owners that extend their budgets to rehabilitate or modify rental property may fall short of funds and take on the responsibility of managing their own property as a cost-savings measure.

Owner-management offers cost effectiveness, saving both monthly management fees and maintenance costs. If, however, the cost savings are swallowed up by poor workmanship, poor time management, or poor management skills, it may be more advantageous for the owner to take on the additional expense of professional management services. The owner-manager who performs a poor plumbing repair and has to take time from his or her normal job to repair the plumbing a second time around, and also replace and repair furniture and structures damaged by the water, loses profits that could have been more effectively invested in professional management services. Should such damage be so severe that it causes tenants to be displaced, additional losses and expenses are incurred. Cash flow may be disrupted for many months to come.

Hiring a Professional Property Manager

Owners who lack the necessary skills and required time or those who have a large number of properties should make use of professional property managers. The chosen professional assumes responsibility for the management of property for a fee, usually collected on a monthly basis. The monthly management fee entitles the owner to a commitment to manage the needs of the property. The costs to actually perform services such as repairs and legal filings are incurred by the owner. Though the property manager assumes responsibility for maintaining the property, the owner has the final say about the treatment of his or her property. The owner should be clear on the expectations of the management company and select a company that allows owners to choose their level of participation in the management process. Generally, professional property managers are expected to:

- Screen prospective tenants.

- Collect lease payments (rent) from the tenants.

- Make or coordinate repairs to the property.

- Enforce rules as specified in the rent agreement and established by law.

- Satisfy tenant complaints and provide problem resolution.

- Inspect the property on a regular basis.

- Provide monthly or agreed-upon schedules of accounting for the property.

- Advertise and show vacant properties to prospective tenants.

The owner should have the option of taking control over any of these functions if it is found to be more cost effective than having the management company perform the same function. If, for example, the owner lives in close proximity to the property and is able to mow the lawn of the property, there is no need to pay the management company's fee for this service. Likewise, if the owner is associated with a gardener that he or she feels comfortable with and charges a lower cost than the management firm for the same work, the owner may intervene in the professional management process and insist that his or her chosen gardener be used to perform the work instead.

Property-management companies may have more than one property manager. Property owners should interview the individual who will be responsible and accountable for the management of their particular property. An appropriate manager will be able to provide references, such as previous clients, to contact with regard to the quality of service. It is important to understand the difference between an exclusive property-management firm and a real estate broker that offers property-management services. Real estate brokers and their salespersons have a direct responsibility to assist their clients in the sale of properties. They offer property-management services, in most cases, at reasonable fees in hopes that the owner will eventually sell the property. The real estate agent's expertise and experience in the sale of property is not necessarily the expertise necessary to properly manage property.

The Role of the Professional Property Manager

The professional property manager offers expertise in the laws and regulations applicable to the particular property. Most states require that property managers be licensed in either real estate or property management. The Institute of Real Estate Management (IREM) is an organization of property managers that certifies and accredits property-management firms based on excellence and dedication. Its ratings, from the most to the least prestigious, are as follows:

- **AMO** — Accredited Management Organization

- **ARM** — Accredited Residential Manager

- **CPM** — Certified Property Manager

A good management company will combine its experiences and expertise in maintaining property to seek better tenants, higher rents, and lower costs, as well as to generate a satisfactory cash flow. The professional-management company should:

- Be insured for general, automobile, and professional liability as well as workers' compensation.

- Hold a fidelity bond to protect against the theft of money collected on behalf of the owner.

- Be able to handle the financial aspects of the business to include bookkeeping and rent collection. The responsibility for taxes associated with the particular property belongs to the owner.

- Offer the necessary people skills to assess and resolve tenant issues.

- Provide for the screening of applicants.

- Establish an effective method of two-way communication with the tenant.

- Establish relationships with maintenance and repair workers, who may offer more timely services at preferential pricing.

There are, however, those property managers who are unethical and will mismanage property. Their practices often result in careless tenants who cause damage. Typical circumstances of mismanagement practices include the following:

- Employing maintenance personnel who inflate the cost of supplies and labor.

- Accounting for repairs that are unnecessary or of no value.

- Ignoring needed repairs until small problems increase to larger, more expensive repairs.

- Implementing complicated rent-collection schemes to create an abundance of late fees, particularly when the management company is contracted to keep such fees.

- Overcharging to fill vacancies or purposely delaying the filling of vacancies to increase fees.

Continuing Development

Property management requires continuing career development, advice, and counsel. There are a number of resources available to property managers that will keep them in touch with trends, advances, and changes in the real estate and property-management market. The Internet provides a wealth of available resources. Likewise, family, friends, and associates involved in real estate or real estate-related businesses are a source of valuable information. The real estate professional needs to have a network of professionals with whom to share ideas and information. They have the option of membership or participation in a number of community groups and professional associations.

Networks of real estate professionals usually require its members to pay a fee. As such, some groups entertain anyone willing to pay the associated fee regardless of their value to the group as a whole. The property manager must research potential networks and groups to be sure that the groups provide the needs of his or her business. Property managers are encouraged to attend group meetings and to talk to members before joining an organization. The property manager needs to assess whether the group or individuals in the group are able to enhance his or her development.

Colleges, universities, and trade schools offer courses and seminars that property managers may attend not only to increase their knowledge base, but also to meet and network with other individuals in the field. The local newspaper may also provide valuable information about current and future trends, market fluctuations, and other avenues of the real estate market in the local area. The newspaper may introduce property managers to names and businesses to watch for in the market. The Internet provides news for any particular market of interest, networking information, and online courses. Many online courses are provided for a nonrefundable fee; as such, property managers must do some research into the many online companies to determine those that are legitimate and offer accurate and substantiated information. The Internet also provides information about real estate brokers. Real estate brokers are familiar with the local community in which they are located and they are able to provide valuable and useful information.

The real estate industry has a wealth of professional organizations, and property managers should investigate and explore the possibility of becoming a member of such organizations. Some of the prominent real estate organizations include the following:

Counselors of Real Estate (CRE)

The CRE is an organization of real estate professionals that support leaders in the real estate industry. Membership in the CRE is by invitation only. The CRE promotes a strict code of ethics and standards to which members must adhere. Members are judged by established criteria, and membership equates to recognition for outstanding performance in the real estate industry. Members must have at least ten years of experience in real estate, at least three years of counseling, and other qualities that represent excellence, knowledge, integrity, and judgment in the practice of real estate.

Society of Industrial and Office Realtors (SIOR)

The SIOR is a membership of Realtors who specializes in industrial, office sales management, and advisory functions. Members number more than two thousand in 25 countries on six continents around the world. The prestigious SIOR designation signifies a high level of competence and achievement. The organization offers educational programs for members which include courses, seminars, and conventions as well as publications and a quarterly magazine. The SIOR Web site (**www.sior.com**) provides members with comparative statistics for more than 130 different markets. In addition to providing educational opportunities, the SIOR provides its members with assistance in public relations; mediation and arbitration services; networking opportunities; and the SIOR designation of high competence and achievement.

Realtors Land Institute (RLI)

The RLI is an affiliate organization of the National Association of Realtors that exists to network real estate professionals interested in raw land. Land interests include land development, management, planning, development appraisals, acquisitions, agribusiness, and other areas that pertain to land. Members may earn the RLI designation, Accredited Land Consultant (ALC), by meeting established requirements for consultation services. The RLI has five primary focus areas:

1. Undeveloped land

2. Farms and ranches

3. Transitional and development land

4. Site selection and land assemblages

5. Subdivisions and wholesale lots

The RLI provides continuing education to promote professional expertise. In addition, the organization performs the following functions with respect to raw land:

- Identifies members as land specialists.

- Markets members' businesses.

- Makes recommendations on public policy affecting land use.

- Develops and maintains professional standards.

- Advocates the wise use of land.

- Advocates reasonable rights and privileges for private land ownership.

The National Association of Residential Property Managers (NARPM)

The NARPM exists to promote professional and ethical practices in the management of residential properties. Members of NARPM include residential property managers, property management companies, and their associated support staff. The NARPM is unique in that it focuses solely on the management of single-family rental homes and other small residential properties. In an effort to provide support to professionals in all aspects of residential property management, the NARPM offers three differing types of membership:

1. Professional Memberships are designed for individuals who act in the role of property manager and are licensed in states that require property managers to be licensed. Over 75 percent of NARPM Professional Members are either full or partial owners of the companies in which they are employed.

2. Support Specialist Memberships are designed for individuals who provide support services to property managers and property-management companies. Support Specialist Members perform property-management functions but do not operate in a capacity that requires licensing.

3. Affiliate Memberships are designed for individuals who act as vendors in the property management industry. Affiliate Members are required to comply with established professional ethics in providing products and services.

With member chapters in 24 states across the country, the NARPM provides professional training and accreditation for residential property management by top industry leaders. These leaders are not only poised to teach coursework, but also to share personal and professional experiences. In addition, NARPM members are provided the following resources and services to assist in their professional development:

- The NARPM newsletter, Residential Resource

- Special publications that address legislative issues and product innovations that are only available to members

- A national annual convention and trade show

- Regional and state conferences

- Discounted rates for professional courses

The NARPM recognizes members who demonstrate knowledge, commitment, and dedication in residential property management by awarding such members with its nationally recognized designations:

- RMP—Residential Management Professional

- MPM—Master Property Manager

- CSS—Certified Support Specialist

- CRMC—Certified Residential Management Company

These designations symbolize achievement in coursework, property management experiences, and volunteer activities. A member who holds the MPM designation must head a company designated as a CRMC. Likewise, a company must have either a designated RMP or MPM member in order for individuals on its support staff to obtain the CSS designation.

Institute of Real Estate Management (IREM)

The IREM is a professional organization that provides nationwide educational, marketing, and advocacy needs to property managers. The IREM exists to enhance and support its members' competence in gaining access to new clients, tenants, and markets. Members are taught skills that allow them to offer quality service that retains clients, tenants, and newly acquired markets. Members who are able to demonstrate extra effort in their commitment to professionalism may earn the IREM designations: CPM, ARM, and AMO. The designations signify real estate professionals who are able to abide by high standards of business conduct. The CPM designation, the lowest level of designation provided by the IREM, allows licensed real estate recipients to attend professional classes, seminars, and lectures that target their particular business needs.

The organization assists property managers, property management companies, and other real estate professionals to include managers and owners of:

- Retail properties

- Office buildings

- Industrial properties

- Corporate real estate holdings

- Conventionally financed multi-family units

- Government-assisted multi-family units

- Homeowner associations

- Mobile home parks

- Single-family units

The IREM provides the following services to assist these individuals and companies:

- Education

- Research

- Analysis

- Publications

- Career development

- Networking opportunities

Classroom courses, online courses, and home-study courses are used to stress real-world skills. Courses are taught and developed by professionals in the field, with real-world experience. Course topics include the following:

- Ethics

- Maintenance and operations

- Marketing

- Asset management

- Legal issues

- Leasing

- Financial management

- Accounting

- Human resources management

- Risk management

- Business development

The IREM also provides customized online training for government entities, corporations, and other organizations.

Certified Commercial Investor Member (CCIM) Institute

The CCIM Institute exists to promote commercial real estate professionals who have both coursework knowledge and real-world experience. The CCIM Institute offers both opportunities for members to network and specialized courses for certifying professionals and continuing education. The NAR designates a CCIM as a part of an organization of thousands that own, use, or invest in commercial real estate. The CCIM designation is considered the doctorate of commercial real estate. Only 6 percent of commercial real estate professionals have earned this designation. To achieve such a designation, the commercial real estate professional must do the following:

- Complete coursework in investment, financial, market, and decision analysis.

- Submit a professional résumé to the CCIM Institute for an evaluation of closed transactions and consultations in commercial real estate.

- Pass a comprehensive exam in commercial real estate.

The CCIM Institute is organized into regions and local chapters throughout the United States and Canada. The institute has ties with other national and international real estate organizations, including the International Property Market (MIPIM) and the

International Real Estate Federation (FIABCI).

Economic Models

Property acquisition offers three economic models. The first model is based on property retention, the second model is based on cash flow, and the third model is based on property appreciation. People invest in residential, commercial, and industrial real estate for a number of reasons. Some investors use the acquired property to provide shelter and living space for their family (homeowners) or they use the property to house a personal business. The investment is intended to sustain the growth and livelihood of the family unit or business. Others invest in real estate strictly for business purposes. The business of investing in either developed or undeveloped real estate has proven to be a very lucrative business venture. The intended purpose is either to generate cash flow or to allow the property to appreciate. Whether property is used for personal space, cash flow, or appreciation, property must be properly managed to maintain or increase its value or worth.

The list of developed and undeveloped properties that require property management extends to the extent of one's imagination. Some common properties include the following:

- Apartments

- Townhouses

- Single-family houses

- Duplexes

- Condominiums

- Shopping centers

- Retail stores

- Parking lots

- Parks

- Golf courses

- Resorts

- Warehouse space

- Hardwood lots

- Deteriorated lots

- Demolished housing

- Hotels and motels

- Cemeteries

The best choice of economic models to implement is dependent upon the anticipated outcome. The investor must evaluate the potential for success with thorough research in market trends, demographics, and the potential for profit.

Property Retention

When property acquisition is intended to provide personal space, the occupants, who are also the owners, are responsible for the management and care of the property. If the owner is successful in maintaining the property, the property can be sold when the owner no longer wants or needs to occupy the space.

The sale price of the property is expected to sell for more than the amount invested. In instances where the owner/occupants move to another location but want to retain ownership of the property, the owner may rent or lease the property to others. The investor/owner engages in the economic model of property management based on property retention (the owner wants to retain and maintain the property for future occupancy or use). The leased property must be properly maintained in order to be of value in the future. The owner may choose to manage the property on his or her own or hire a professional management firm to manage the property.

Appreciation

Managed property consists of either developed or undeveloped properties. An undeveloped property, usually raw land, is oftentimes purchased for the purpose of allowing it to sit idle and appreciate over time. Time allows the property to increase in value. The appreciated property can then be resold, leased for others to develop, or developed by the owner. This economic model, based on appreciation, offers two advantages: 1) the sale value of the property is expected to be much more than the purchase value, 2) and zoning, redistricting, and demographics may allow for the development of more profit-producing properties than would have been allowed at the time of purchase.

Cash Flow

The economic model of property management based on cash flow occurs when the investor invests in existing property for the purpose of either leasing as is or rehabbing the property for lease or sale. The investor may seek developed and occupied properties that are capable of producing immediate cash flow. On the other hand, the investor may seek unoccupied and/or undeveloped properties because he or she envisions the potential to produce cash flow in the future.

Keli Demland
American Realty
104 Circle Way, Ste. C
Lake Jackson, TX 77566
979-297-7700

My career in real estate began when I started working as a part-time assistant to a property manager. I was also working to get my real estate license at the time. She quit a few months after I got my license, so here I am 12 years later. I now manage mostly residential properties, of which I have 50, but I also have a professional complex with approximately 12 offices.

Managing rental properties is pretty much my full-time job; in addition, I list and sell properties. To determine rental rates for my rental properties, I do comparable analysis. My goal as a property manager is to ensure customer satisfaction by answering all calls and taking care of any problems or issues as soon as possible. We get some requests for repairs but not too many.

When I first started in real estate, I faced problems mainly dealing with poor maintenance and low rent properties. I learned quickly to only take properties that owners are willing to keep maintained and who will thoroughly screen tenants.

I minimize my risk by strictly adhering to the law and to contracts while I maximize my profits by ensuring the management company has a good reputation, and we're competitive.

Our company has a CPA who does our accounting. If the taxes increase for the commercial property, the tenants pay the increase. The owners pay the increase for taxes on residential properties.

2

CHAPTER TWO

Management Properties

Management properties are properties, owned by either an individual or group of individuals, that are either empty or occupied by others. All properties, including private homes and vacant lots, require some type of property maintenance. Owners are usually responsible to maintain private homes and businesses. When an investor acquires property to rent or lease as residential, commercial, or industrial space, the owner creates management property. Residential properties usually offer living space while commercial and industrial properties serve one or more of the following purposes:

- To house businesses operations.

- To provide space for future development.

- To hold title to property that will appreciate over time.

Residential Properties

Residential properties are usually acquired to provide living space for individuals over time. The needs for residential properties differ from the needs of commercial and industrial properties. Tenants of commercial and industrial properties expect to be able to make adjustments to suit their individual needs. Tenants of residential properties, on the other hand, expect to make use of the existing rental space and to be able to make use of all amenities located within or on the property.

Older homes may not have the types of amenities that are offered in newer homes. As such, older homes can often be purchased more cheaply than newer homes, and older homes usually require more maintenance and upkeep than newer homes. However, many older homes have been well maintained with add-ons and capital improvements from previous homeowners. Older homes offer the benefit of having been tried and tested as living space. Structural deficiencies and defects, resulting from poor construction, are more likely to be visible or to have been addressed in older homes. Structural deficiencies in newer homes, particularly the newest of homes, may not be obvious. The costs for unexpected capital improvements or constant repairs may be forthcoming during the investor's ownership.

Financing

The financing of residential properties typically requires an investment of 10 to 20 percent of the selling price of the property. Those investors who have never owned a residential property are privy to first-time homeowner benefits. Lenders may offer as much as 100 percent of the first-time buyer's financing, but this applies to a single home and requires that the new homeowner commit to some tenure in the home. A homeowner, first-time or otherwise, with established equity in a home may use the equity to refinance the home and acquire capital for additional investments. A homeowner interested in investing in residential properties may apply the capital to the down payment on one or more rental properties. The mortgage and expenses of any newly acquired property could then be paid from the received rents.

Renting and Leasing

Various governments have established laws and regulations with regard to renting residential property. The investor must be careful to have legal expertise in federal, state, and local laws, applicable to the particular property, when drafting tenant agreements and leases. The property manager must be contracted to invest time in explaining agreements, and all of their specific clauses, to potential tenants before the signing of agreements. Residential properties are usually rented under one of two agreements: month-to-month agreements or leases.

Month-to-month agreements are renewed every month unless the tenant or landlord gives notice to terminate the agreement. Generally, either party must submit notice of termination at least 30 days before the agreement is to end. Month-to-month agreements provide flexibility for both the landlord and the tenant. The landlord, with 30 days' notice, may increase the rent or change other terms of the agreement. The tenant may vacate the property with 30 days' notice, without repercussions.

Leases are fixed-term agreements, usually offered for terms of 6 or 12 months. Some leases automatically renew at the end of the term; others are written so that they convert to month-to-month at the end of the initial term, and still others must be renegotiated at the expiration of the initial terms. In any case, the rent payment cannot be increased and the terms of the lease cannot be changed during the initial term of the lease. The landlord may terminate a lease at his or her discretion when a tenant violates the terms of the lease. However, the burden of proof falls upon the landlord to prove to a court that he or she was justified in terminating a lease. Unless the tenant poses an extreme threat or creates extensive damage, the landlord should employ systematic methods of terminating leases and getting tenants to move.

Configurations

Residential properties consist of single-family units such as town homes, row homes, and single-family homes, or multiple-family units such as duplexes, condominiums, and apartments. In some states, rent-control laws, which place limitations on the amount of rent that may be charged to occupy a given space, govern residential properties. Rent control was initiated to prevent landlords from raising rents beyond the means of established tenants, forcing them to relocate. Many residential properties under rent control, however, become neglected when maintenance and repair expenses exceed the amount allowed for rent. An investor should research investment properties before acquisition to determine the limitations of rent control, if any, that apply. This becomes particularly important when an investor is interested in acquiring previously managed residential property. The investor may rehab and upgrade a housing unit only to find that the established limits on rent are not sufficient to cover the costs that the investor had hoped to charge for the newly renovated unit.

Single-Family Homes

Single-family homes are easiest to manage, particularly for the inexperienced investor or property manager. A leak in the bathroom plumbing of a single-family home may cause damage in one or more rooms in the unit; however, a plumbing leak in an apartment building may damage one or more rooms for one or more family units. Should displacement occur, several expected rents will be lost as opposed to the rent payment loss for a single-family home. Single-family homes also offer the benefit of being the preferred choice for housing. As such, they are plentiful, easy to purchase, and easy to sell. Some single-family homes are part of homeowner associations, which are responsible for the exterior maintenance of properties. Most homeowner associations impose limitations on the amount and extent of their services, but their services always mean less maintenance for the property owner. The disadvantage to investors occurs when investment homes are located in different areas, requiring either more travel time to manage the properties or the need to employ more than one property-management firm to manage the properties. Another challenge for single-family homes lies in keeping the properties occupied. In the competitive rental-housing market, single-family homes are plentiful. The investor must be financially able to withstand the loss of rent during the vacancies.

Multiple-Family Units

Multiple-family units offer some of the same challenges as single-family units; however, the rents for multiple-family units can be established so that income from the occupied properties is sufficient to maintain a positive cash flow during vacancies. Even with the loss of multiple tenants, carefully structured rents will ensure that basic expenses are met, though it may cause temporary disruptions to cash flow.

Commercial Properties

Financing

The financing of commercial properties requires more out-of-pocket capital than residential properties. Typically, a lender will require 25 to 35 percent upfront financing for commercial property. This is in contrast to the, typical, 10 to 20 percent required for residential properties

Leasing

Unlike leases for residential properties, commercial leases may be held for five, ten, or more years. Only under special circumstances are commercial properties leased for month-to-month, bi-annual, and annual terms. Commercial leases take on one of three forms:

1. Gross lease — The landlord is responsible to pay all expenses with the exception of utilities.

2. Net lease — The tenant and landlord share predetermined expenses that are specified in the lease or rental agreement.

3. Triple net lease — The tenant pays all repair and maintenance expenses of the business. The tenant also pays the taxes of the property. Usually, one-twelfth of the total tax is paid into escrow each month. The lease must be defined as a triple net lease with the payment arrangement specified. If the tenant does not pay the tax, the tax liability falls on the landlord, who must take legal or other action against the tenant to collect on the tax.

The lease should specify rent increases to be applied over the duration of the lease. To avoid leasing to tenants who may not be willing to adhere to the payment terms of the lease, the property manager should invest time and resources to acquire the following information, which will help to paint a financial picture of the prospective tenant and his or her ability to pay:

- Credit report

- Dun and Bradstreet rating

- Bank statements

- Accounts receivable for existing business(es)

- History with previous landlords

Configurations

The commercial property manager should seek to engage a variety of businesses in multi-unit properties. Diversity ensures that if one business unit fails, the others may still prosper. If the video rental business cannot compete with the newly established Blockbuster two blocks away, the well-received supermarket may still flourish. The businesses should show stability, and the property should have at least one anchoring business. The anchoring business should be a well-established and known business. It is most beneficial to anchor an established business or franchise that offers a variety of products and serves as an alternative to other business. This is most often seen in shopping centers, one of the most lucrative commercial property investments. They are often anchored by supermarkets that offer a variety of products and/or well-established restaurants, such as McDonald's.

Shopping Centers

Shopping centers enjoy so much success because they are relatively easy to manage. In the retail market, shopping center tenants are reliant upon customer satisfaction and generally take responsibility for the upkeep of their business units. The tenants understand that most customers will not patronize dirty and disorganized businesses, particularly when a business that offers competitive products or services is in reach. It is common to find several shopping centers within a couple of blocks of one another. In fact, there are many instances where shopping centers sit across the street and next door to one another. The opportunities for shopping centers and other commercial properties exist in all communities, urban and rural.

Office Space

Tenants of commercial properties seek properties that meet or exceed the climate of the community in which they are located. The investor should be sure to discuss improvements with the tenant and implement agreed-upon improvements before signing the lease. Office buildings should have a similar look and feel across all the units. Office buildings are categorized in classes: A, B, and C.

- Class A — Upscale, usually high-rise office buildings, with the latest and greatest in terms of architecture, structure, services, and amenities.

- Class B — Post-World War II structures with defects from ordinary wear and tear as well as add-ons to meet modern-day standards.

- Class C — All other and older office space without adherence to modern-day building codes. They are likely to have no sprinkler system, central air-conditioning, handicap access, and so on.

Restaurants

While restaurants, particularly well-known and favored restaurants, provide good anchoring for commercial properties, they are high-risk commercial investments. The numbers and types of equipment, such as gas grills and stoves, combined with flammable and combustible inventory, such as oil, alcohol-based products, and other chemicals, create a catastrophic risk with respect to fire. Specific lease clauses that address insurance and inspections must be documented and adhered to. Compliance with local ordinances, state ordinances, and health codes should reduce some of the risk.

A well-maintained restaurant offers a valuable asset in the transfer of tenantship. A restaurant that is operational within established codes provides a good investment opportunity for the next potential tenant. A failed or relocating tenant, looking to recoup expenditures for equipment, furniture, and inventory, may also prove to be a valuable asset in the transfer of tenant-ship. In an effort to recoup losses, the departing tenant may seek and provide contacts for potential tenants of the business unit.

Farmland

Ranches and farmland are another risky commercial property investment. Farmland typically serves some specialized purpose, such as raising animal stock or some other agricultural activity. The investor who acquires farmland, which serves no specialized or distinct purpose, assumes the risk of being able to convert the land into a space that provides some useful and profitable activity. As an alternative, the investor may secure tenants who will be able to make profitable use of the land.

On the other hand, farmland, properly situated in the path of residential or commercial development growth, may offer a lucrative return on investment as development progresses.

Industrial Properties

Financing

The financing of industrial properties is similar to that of commercial property. The lender will require more capital from the investor than would be required for the purchase of a residential property. The investor is expected to provide upfront financing of between 25 and 35 percent of the value of the property.

Leasing

Industrial properties are most often used as land development. The investor, therefore, must determine the zoning ordinance that applies to the land. Zoning is the legal instrument used by governments to control and restrict the use of private land. The intent of zoning is to prevent conflict of use and promote orderly development efforts. Specifically, it is intended to maintain proper spacing between residential, commercial, and industrial properties. A responsible government, for example, would ensure that a proposed nuclear power facility is not housed across the street from the local high school. The zoning authorities, usually city or county government, hold the zoning ordinances for properties within a given jurisdiction. The ordinances specify:

- The need for the ordinance

- Classifications for the zone

- Restrictions for use

- Procedures for non-conformance

- Procedures for amendments

- Appeals processes

- Penalties for violation

A block of land could be zoned for different uses as defined by the jurisdiction's zoning map. A block could be zoned, for example, such that the neighborhood corner store, a commercial property, is situated on the same block as residential properties. Zoning is subjected to change, and rezoning may take from six months to one year and beyond. Concerns of government and community entities may serve to either hinder or help rezoning efforts. Though one block has a light commercial storefront property, the residents of the next block may object to having such a business in their block. On the other hand, neighbors in the next block may welcome the addition and convenience of a local store. The investor must stay current of changes and modifications that affect his or her chosen property location.

Configurations

The investor should consider multiple properties or an assemblage of properties to add value to acquired properties. An assemblage is a combination of individually held properties. If land is being acquired in expectation of a development effort, the investor should form an assemblage by contacting individual landowners. A single property may not offer the space required for a particular development effort; however, an assemblage of properties may be more suitable for development efforts. An established assembly of properties is often more valuable than the individual pieces of property. An assemblage requires a lot of paperwork and negotiation from each of the individual landowners. The assemblage should be formed by confidential contact with the individual landowners rather than groups of landowners. Group negotiations may lead to unnecessary competitiveness, and if too much commotion is created over land deals, landowners may raise the stakes and increase the selling price of their land.

The investor must be sure to determine who has rights to the land. Land, in real estate, is defined as the surface of the earth. The investor must determine how much of the purchased land is acquired by the purchase and how much of it can actually be used for intended purposes. Title searches should conclude whether the area immediately beneath the surface is included in the sale or being held by another person or entity. Another consideration is with height restrictions above the land. Thorough research should include restrictions set by or for airports, utility companies, satellite companies, and other entities that make use of air space. The investor should be careful to know exactly what dimensions of land, undersurface, and air space are being acquired and be sure to obtain full rights to all of them.

Doug Wansley
ProHome Rentals
Lawrenceville, GA
678-377-2567
prohomerentals.com
"Gwinnett and North Fulton Home
Rental Specialists"
info@prohomerentals.com

After a 12-year stint as a professional pop musician, I followed my wife into the real estate Industry and received my real estate license in 1978. By 1988, I'd spent the better part of a decade concentrating on new home sales, winning the Agent of the Year award that year. Almost immediately after entering the real estate arena, I began to buy investment homes. Today, I specialize in residential, single-family homes only, and I currently manage 55 rental properties.

Managing rental properties can be a challenge, and determining rental rates is of the utmost importance. To determine monthly rental rates, we look at our competition, the time of the year, and the location and the condition of the property for rent. Since we're in the market on a daily basis, we have the advantage of being able to follow the trends in pricing.

To ensure our tenants' happiness, we strive to return all phone calls and e-mails promptly and handle maintenance issues in a timely manner. We also provide quality properties, not run down, worn out homes. Still, while we strive to keep our tenants happy, sometimes there are complaints. For example, there are times when tenants will complain that we're not sympathetic when they are unable to pay their rent on time.

Ensuring tenant satisfaction is only one aspect of managing real estate. For newcomers to real estate management, I would advise you work for a reputable company that will help you and teach you. If you make a mistake, you'll likely have someone who knows how to correct it. If you are apprenticing with someone who cares about your performance and how you represent the company, you may learn enough to not make very many mistakes. Join an organization (i.e. The National Association of Residential Property

Managers; NARPM) comprised of companies and people who are in the real estate business. The NARPM is dedicated to the education and the professionalism of property managers.

You also want to study and know the landlord-tenant laws of your state, and ensure you always operate according to the law.

It's also imperative that your bookkeeping be done correctly. When you're small and just starting out, if you don't have a lot of bookkeeping experience, you may feel overwhelmed. However, it's vital that your bookkeeping be done correctly. I use Tenant Pro 6.0, Open Office (a free alternative to MS Office, written and distributed by Sun Microsystems), and a CPA checks all of our records periodically.

To minimize risk, it's important that any real estate manager incorporate his business, keep good corporate records, maintain liability and E&O insurance, and be educated about his business.

You can also maximize your rental management profits in a number of ways, including:

Charge for your time and your expertise. Know what your time is worth, and charge that. You don't have to discount your fees if you're good at what you do. There are plenty of people who are willing to pay your price if they feel they're getting their money's worth.

If a client asks you to perform duties not covered by the management agreement, charge him for your time.

Look for legitimate profit centers, such as performing "expert witness" testimony. Finally, buy office supplies and equipment when they're on sale. Join a buying club when they're not.

CHAPTER THREE

Financial, Legal & Advertising Skills of a Good Property Manager

To become a good property manager, one must have a variety of skills. A good property manager must be knowledgeable in leveraging real estate, financial management, real estate taxes, real estate laws and regulations, property insurance, market research and analysis, advertising, and property maintenance. In addition, he or she must be dedicated and have vision.

Leveraging

The banking industry is dependent upon the borrowing of money. Real estate is one of the most promising markets in which bankers achieve a return on investment for borrowed money. As such, bankers are willing to assist in the buying and selling of real estate. To secure their investment, however, bankers require the real estate investor to share in the risk of the investment. The typical investment share of real estate is 20 percent. If the lender is convinced that the investor is able to secure his or her part of the monetary investment, the banker will likely assist in completing the acquisition of real estate, using the investor's share as down payment on the property. The lender must be convinced that the money is, in fact, investment money to be used at the investor's disposal. Contributions from both the lender and investor constitute leverage to invest in real estate.

Securing a Lender

Unless the investor already has an established relationship with a lender, the investor will need to find a lender to absorb the typical 80 percent of leverage required from lenders. Lenders don't loan money based on the individual's word; the investor will need documented evidence to convince the lender that they are partaking in a viable and profitable business venture. It is recommended that investors seek a lender by starting within close proximity to the anticipated property, moving outward until they secure a willing lender. In presenting a business proposal to the lender, the investor should:

- Consult with an accountant or other outside source of financial expertise to determine the proper documentation to present. The presentation to the lender should not be a request for information, but a profitable plan of action seeking investment capital.

- Have all required documentation in order to present to the lender.

- Consult with outside sources of financial expertise about questions to anticipate so that important issues are covered when presenting the initial business proposal to the lender.

- Present a complete proposal in one setting without having to "get back" with the lender.

- Be confident and professional in the presentation; present only the proposal.

Once a commitment to financing is obtained, the investor must be sure to understand the terms of the agreement before signing off on it. Misunderstandings, particularly those regarding the terms of payment, have proven to be most profitable to the lender. In fact, the lender may end up being the property owner with a charitable contribution from the investor. In this situation, the investor is at a total loss and receives no return on the contribution.

Financial Management

Financial management is the accounting of funds received and expended in a business venture. Though it's not required, every rental property should have its own account and files. The IRS expects that investors are able to keep rental property funds and activities separate from personal funds and activities. In all rental activities that involve money, the property manager must be diligent in the receiving and issuing of receipts. The investor should establish a budget for each rental property and manage the property within that established budget. Cost overruns are common in property management; there should be allowances for overruns in the established budget.

Maintaining Files

Good financial management begins with a good system of filing records and documents. Separate files should be established for separate entities of the business. Most filings should be kept for a minimum of three to five years, dependent upon the laws and regulations in which the property is housed. Other filings, such as ownership files, should be held for the life of the ownership. Injuries to children and minors under the age of 18 should be held indefinitely. The statue of limitations for injury to minors does not begin until the minor child reaches 18 years of age. Records and files should be maintained in case a suit evolves after a minor reaches the age of maturity.

Ownership

The ownership file should include all documents related to the purchase of the rental unit. If the owner holds more than one property unit, a separate file should be established for each unit. The file should include all documents related to the following:

- Appraisals

- Purchase offers

- Contracts

- Closings

- Insurance policies

- Loans

- Inspection reports

- Pest control

- Property deeds

Income and Expense

Each rental property should have its own file for storing income and expenses of the property. The income files should contain copies of receipts, if provided, to the tenant. Income received from other sources, such as laundry rooms and vending machines, should be filed with the income for the particular property. The expense files should contain copies of all receipts for expenses. It is a good idea to photocopy receipts acquired for a particular day onto a single sheet of paper. The original receipt can then be stapled or otherwise attached to the photocopy. This creates a file with even-sized pages that can be more easily retrieved. If expenses for more than one property exist on a single receipt, the receipt should be photocopied and a copy of the expense should be included in the file of all applicable properties. The expenses associated with a particular property should be highlighted on the sheet being stored in its file.

Auto Expenses

A detailed log of vehicle mileage used in the management of properties should be filed monthly. The log should contain the date, purpose, destination, and number of miles driven.

Maintenance

Each rental property should have a file for repairs, maintenance, and capital expenditures. This filing evolves into a time history of the conditions of the rental property.

Tenants

Each property should have a file that contains documents specific to a particular tenant. Documents should include the rental application, screening results, rental agreement, disclosure forms, legal notices, and any other documents created in response to or for the tenant.

Complaints

Each property should have a file that contains documentation of complaints made by tenants, neighbors, or others. When a tenant complaint concerns a repair or maintenance issue, feedback should be requested of the tenant and filed. A time history of complaints and feedback, or the lack thereof, will prove useful in legal disputes.

Vacated Tenants

A file should be established for the collection of tenant files for tenants who vacate the property.

Insurance

Each property should have a file that contains documentation for the insurance coverage and any claims against the insurance company.

Calculating Rate of Return

The mathematical measure of progression in real estate investments is based on the rate of return of the particular property. The rate of return is calculated annually and incorporates the amount invested in the property as well as four other types of return: appreciation, cash flow, mortgage principal, and income-tax depreciation. The values of cash flow, principal, and appreciation are variable from year to year, while depreciation will remain constant so long as the investor remains in the same tax bracket. The purpose in calculating and establishing a rate of return on properties is to establish a measure that the investor may use in determining the need for restructuring his or her property investments. Restructuring includes using equity in one property to leverage the purchase of another property or exchanging one property for another under the 1031 tax-deferred exchange. The investor is in the best position to restructure properties when the rate of return is low. The investor should be able to establish the limit on rate of return that best suits his or her investment purposes.

The rate of return on rental property is highest in the first year of acquisition and decreases as the amount of leverage decreases. A realistic expected rate of return is at least 20 percent in the first year of property acquisition. This rate will decrease as the investor increases equity in the property and decreases leverage in acquiring properties. If, however, the investor chooses to use the increased equity to leverage more capital, to invest in additional properties, the rate of return can be increased to values obtained in the initial years of investment.

Investment

The amount of capital invested in a property should vary dependent upon the number of years vested in the property. In the first year of investment, the investment amount is a combination of out-of-pocket capital invested as well as the cost of any capital improvements. Typically, this should include the down payment to the lender, the closing costs, and any money spent to improve the property. Improvements include large expenditures that must be depreciated for tax purposes. The costs for ordinary maintenance and repairs are not capital improvement expenditures. Maintenance and repair costs are deductible in the tax year in which they are incurred.

For each successive year of property ownership, the investment amount is calculated by adding together the prior year's investment amount, appreciation, and mortgage principal payments. In addition, any capital improvements in the prior year are added to the current year investment amount. If the property is refinanced in the prior year, the investment amount is reduced by the refinanced amount as well as the closing costs. If, however, the refinancing was used to purchase another property, the investor has a choice of applying the closing costs of the newly acquired property either to the investment cost of the previously held property or to the investment cost of the newly financed property, but not to both.

Appreciation

Appreciation is the growth in property value that allows the property investor to establish leverage in generating capital. Appreciation also increases the resale value of acquired property. Depreciation is the decline in growth of property value. Though depreciation is a reality, property values have historically appreciated. Even in times of low inflation, property values have a tendency to remain consistent or drop only temporarily.

Cash Flow

On a monthly basis, income from a rental property should ideally exceed the amount of expenses for the property, such as the mortgage payments and repairs. Cash flow management is the skill set necessary to ensure such profits. The investor who properly leverages property should establish rents to cover the mortgage payment and other expenses of the property with enough cash left for profit or cash flow. Any disruptions to the cash flow are cause for analysis and adjustment. The investor should analyze the property's activities to ensure that the disruption is not the result of poor bookkeeping. Poor bookkeeping can be alleviated with the expertise of an accountant. However, if expenses are higher than anticipated or rent is lower than necessary, the investor must institute a plan of action and incorporate adjustments that allow for cash flow.

Mortgage Principal

The principal on mortgage payments will decrease over time, allowing the investor both to gain more equity in the property and to increase his or her overall net worth. The investor may use increased equity in the property to leverage more capital to engage in more investment opportunities. Given that the property is properly managed, maintained, and rented, time will allow for the mortgage to be paid, offering one of the biggest opportunities for cash flow. The property investor who skimps on repairs, maintenance, or capital improvements to increase cash flow during the term of the mortgage loan may find himself or herself having to reinvest the newly acquired cash flow into improving the property in order to sustain decent rent income.

Depreciation (Income Tax)

The IRS allows property owners to shield part of their income from tax by allowing for the depreciation of a rental property over 27.5 years. The IRS permits the depreciation even when the property is actually appreciating. The tax shield is a benefit offered by the government for establishing the ownership of property.

Taxes

The federal government, states, cities, and municipalities have differing methods of assessing real estate taxes. An investor must know the laws that apply to the area in which he or she holds real estate. Some cities may assess and increase taxes significantly and without bounds. Others may restrict any increase in taxes until the property is sold. Investors should know and keep track of modifications to such laws. Though an accountant is usually hired to take on the responsibility of ensuring that taxes are properly filed, the legal responsibility for taxes falls on the individual whose signature appears on the tax forms. Property owners and managers must be sure that they understand the implications of tax filings generated on their behalf.

Federal

The federal government, particularly the IRS, establishes that income from the rental of real estate is a short-term capital gain, which is taxed as ordinary income. All operating expenses from the rental activity are deductible expenses from the rental income. Deductible expenses include the costs for maintenance, repairs, payroll, management fees, advertising, mortgage interest, property taxes, damages, and depreciation. The cost of capital improvements is not a deductible expense. Capital expenses, however, can be depreciated.

Security deposits, paid by tenants for rental properties, are held as security against potential damage to the property or the non-payment of rent. As such, security deposits are an accounting liability to be repaid to the tenant when the tenant vacates the property. Taxes on rental income do not include money received as a security deposit until the tenant actually vacates the property and the deposit becomes income. If the tenant vacates the property and the property has sustained damage in an amount equal to or exceeding the amount of the security deposit and the landlord spends an amount equal to or exceeding the amount of the security deposit to repair the damage, the owner will not owe taxes on the security deposit. If, however, the amount spent to repair damage is less than the amount of the security deposit, the difference between the amount spent for repairs and amount of the security deposit is taxable. Likewise, if the tenant vacates the property without paying rent, the security deposit is applied to the unpaid rent. Any amount of the security deposit in excess of the unpaid rent is taxable. In short, when a tenant vacates a property, the property owner calculates and adds the amount of unpaid rent to the cost of repairs. If the sum of these two amounts is less than the amount of the security deposit, the property owner must pay tax on the difference between the sum and the security deposit. For example: The monthly rent on a rental unit is $500. The security deposit paid to the landlord before move-in is also $500. Upon move-out, the property manager is provided an estimate of $300 to repair damages. The amount to be returned to the tenant is calculated as $500 (deposit) minus $300 (damages), equaling $200 dollars. Rather than hire the contractor who estimated the repair of damage to be $300, the landlord completes the repair at a total cost of $150. The remaining $150 becomes taxable income for the landlord. As another example, both the monthly rent and security deposit is equal to $500. Upon move-out, the tenant fails to pay one month's rent and the landlord spends $300 to repair damages. The unpaid rent of $500 plus damages that amount to $300 total $800 that is owed to the landlord. The landlord may retain the $500 paid as a security deposit, but the security deposit is not enough to cover the $800 that is due to the landlord. The landlord is still owed $300 and is exempt from paying taxes on the $500 security deposit.

The IRS allows for the property owner to deduct an expense called depreciation. Depreciation of a rental property is allowed for 27.5 years. The allowable deduction is calculated as 1/27.5, for each year except the first and final years of property ownership; depreciation is prorated for the first and final years of ownership. Depreciation only applies to the structure, not the land beneath the structure. The investor must determine how much of his or her investment is applied to the purchase of land and how much is applied to the structure in order to calculate depreciation.

The IRS establishes different rules for the taxation of professional property managers and owners of managed property. A professional property manager is defined as one whose business is at least 50 percent real estate related and also performs at least 750 hours per year in real estate activities. Professional property managers are considered to have active participation in real estate and are allowed to deduct all real estate losses in the year in which they are incurred. The owner-manager is considered to have passive activity in real estate, and the IRS imposes limitations on the amount of passive losses that can be deducted. However, if the passive owner-manager is actively involved in the rental of real estate, they are not subjected to the passive-loss limitations. To be actively involved, the individual must oversee and approve rents, tenant selection, and capital improvements. The IRS allows passive owner-managers to deduct up to $25,000 in losses from personal income that is less than $100,000. For income above $100,000, the deduction is reduced by 50 cents for every dollar earned in excess of $100,000. Losses that cannot be applied in the year in which they were incurred can be deducted in future years of passive income. If losses cannot be applied during ownership of the rental property, losses can be applied when the property is sold to reduce the amount of capital gains tax in the year the property is sold. (Griswold, 2001)

The IRS also establishes tax-deferred exchanges for real estate property. Section 1031 of the IRS code allows property owners to defer paying capital gain taxes on the sale of property if the property is properly exchanged for other real property. The exchange must be for similar property, which implics any real property held for business, trade, or investment purposes. The exchange must be completed within a specified time frame, established by the IRS. The exchange does not limit the dollar amount, so the exchange can be for property of greater value than the property previously held by the owner. This allows an investor to increase the value of his or her assets without having to pay capital gains taxes in the process. (Griswold, 2001)

A neutral third party must be hired to facilitate the exchange. The third party, referred to as the facilitator, exchanger, or accommodator, must be hired prior to closing on any properties of the exchange. The facilitator is bound by a written agreement and holds the proceeds of the exchange, except in circumstances where the closings of the currently held property and newly acquired property are performed simultaneously. The property owner cannot withdraw capital from the sale of property during the exchange. The exchange is limited to properties located in the United States and is subject to the following rules:

- The investor has 45 days from the close of the currently held property to identify the potential new property.

- The close of the new property must occur within 180 days of the close of the currently held property.

- The price of new property must equal or exceed the price of the currently held property.

- The mortgage of the new property must equal or exceed the balance of the mortgage on the currently held property.

Additional guidelines established by the IRS allow for a reverse 1031 exchange. A reverse exchange allows for investors to first purchase the new property and then follows the established guidelines of 1031 for closing the sale property within 180 days. (Griswold, 2001) Again, the facilitator must be in place prior to the initial closing of the exchange.

State

In addition to the revenue tax that is charged on income generated from rental properties, states impose a transfer tax, which is the fee incurred to transfer property between individuals. The transfer tax is assessed as an amount per dollar value of the property. The amount is determined by the particular state and the location in which the property is housed.

Local

Government tax assessors, also known as appraisers, assess real estate taxes based on the market value of property. Assessors or appraisers usually determine market value within a jurisdiction by using at least one of three methods of valuation: sales comparison/market approach, cost approach, or income approach. The sales comparison or market approach places value on property based on the most recent sale of a property, within a specified area surrounding the property, and/or recent sales of comparable properties. The cost approach places value based on the cost to replace the property, and the income approach places value based on the potential of the property to generate income. The three approaches are often compared against one another to narrow the range of estimates for market value. The market value is then used to estimate the price that the property would sell for in the competitive housing market.

An assessment is used to determine the rate of property tax to be charged to the property owner. Taxing authorities require property assessments periodically. The higher the assessed value of the property, the higher the property taxes due. Unpaid property taxes become liens against the property, and the property may be publicly sold or auctioned by the assessing government entity in order to recoup the cost. The assessed value and resulting property tax can be challenged if the property owner feels that the amounts do not adequately represent fair values. Each jurisdiction has specific rules for appealing property assessments and property taxes. The owner must contact the assessment authority in the jurisdiction in which the property is located to learn the necessary process to follow.

In addition to property taxes, some jurisdictions impose an annual building registration fee on income-producing properties, such as rental properties. The fee is usually documented as a charge to support inspections or code enforcements, but they are typically a way for governments to generate additional revenue.

Tax Evasion

The IRS establishes penalties for tax evasion. The penalty for a mistake that results in the underpayment of taxes is 5 percent of the unpaid amount. The penalty for fraud against the IRS is

50 percent of the unpaid amount. The total amount to be paid is calculated with added interest, generated from the day the mistake or fraud took place. The burden of proof for tax evasion, mistakes, or fraud falls on the property owner. The owner must prove that he or she has tried, in good faith, to operate within established laws and regulations.

Tax Audits

The hired accountant and lawyer are best situated to assist with tax audits. These professionals can provide the necessary paperwork and procedures to follow in response to an audit. Audits may result from discrepancies in calculations or misunderstandings. Most audits involve an initial request for information or clarification of information through the mail. A proper and accurate response may be all that is necessary to bring the audit to an end. The request will specify the specific area of concern. It is advised that the response include records or other information that address the particular area of concern during the tax year indicated. Even when in-person audits are required, individuals are not required to provide records of business functions outside of those requested. Only relevant documents should be presented. Clear and direct responses with relevant records, rather than resentment, hostility, and evasiveness, may make the difference between a simple audit and an investigation into business practices. The IRS is interested in resolving matters quickly and will not extend time, resources, or manpower to auditing unless the audited party gives them reason to do so. One of the most common mistakes made during IRS audits is to present auditors with previous tax filings that are not requested, making the argument that because certain procedures were followed in previous years, without consequence, that those same procedures should be allowed in the year in question. An anomaly of the IRS is that statutes of limitation or errors made on their behalf do not bind them. By providing unnecessary information, the audited party may open the door to having the IRS assess penalties for those previous years as well as the year in question. The IRS may determine that they made a mistake in those previous years and the audited party, not the IRS, is required to pay for the mistake. The Federal Tort Claims Act gives citizens the right to sue the government for damages, but not as they apply to tax matters.

Laws and Regulations

In real estate, property management, and life in general, anything can be become a legal issue. To prevent or reduce the loss incurred to address legal issues, property managers should put forth their best effort to maintain properties within established laws and regulations. Also, property managers should respond and react to issues of concern promptly and courteously.

The property manager's primary responsibility is to ensure that a rental unit is habitable and meets the minimum standards for health and safety. All rental property is legally bound by the warranty of implied habitability. This warranty implies that tenants have the right to expect certain conditions and services in return for rental payments. In particular, the rental unit should comply with the following:

- Provide a safe and clean environment.

- Be in compliance with all applicable building codes.

- Provide safe drinking water.

- Provide adequate sanitation systems.

- Provide functioning plumbing and electrical wiring.

- Have stable floors, walls, and ceilings.

- Provide functioning and appropriate heating and cooling systems.

- Have secure doors and windows.

- Provide adequate lighting and ventilation.

- Offer proper maintenance and repairs.

In addition, the property manager should ensure that tenants are provided all applicable rules, disclosures, and rights.

Property managers must have an understanding of laws and regulations applicable to the following:

- Taxes

- Partnerships, investment groups, and contracts

- Screening procedures and the Fair Credit Reporting Act

- Fair Housing Act

- Americans with Disabilities Act

- Uniform Residential Landlord and Tenant Act

- Rent control

- Rent subsidies

- Zoning laws

- Building permits

- Insurance laws

- Health and safety threats

Details of such laws and regulations are explained in more detail later in this book.

When acquiring a previously held rental property, it is possible to acquire the debts of the pervious owners. Some states require a property buyer to obtain an IDOR for the property. An IDOR indicates that the prior owner is free of any due sales tax or revenue associated with the property. If no IDOR is obtained, the liabilities of the previous property owner are passed on to the property and the new owner becomes liable for their payment.

In real estate and property management, an attorney is necessary to assist and advise on legal issues. The attorney must be trained and knowledgeable in real estate law, contracts, and tax laws that govern the jurisdiction where the property is located. The attorney must be competent to handle tenant-landlord disputes that are too extensive to be handled in district courts. Attorney fees should be clear and document the type and extent of services to be rendered for the fee. Exceptions to service fees, which require additional fees, should be explained and documented, and the attorney should be willing to abide by the established fees. Rather than traditional fee-for-service, client-attorney relationships, property owners, and managers may consider acquiring membership in pre-paid legal services that offer legal services at a flat rate. The flat rate covers most legal expenses, though the type and extent of services may vary based on the particular law firm, type of membership, and state regulations. For a membership fee, clients are assigned attorneys from a network of lawyers and law firms as needed for the term of membership. Members must be careful to understand and obtain written documentation specifying the extent of services and any particular stipulations with regard to covered services.

Insurance

When an investor borrows money to invest in property, the lender will require the investor to insure the property for the duration of the loan. If the investor owns the property and holds no mortgage or debts against it, the investor is not required but should insure the property to protect against loss and damage.

There are many different types of insurance. Investors will have to research the various insurance companies to find a company that will tailor the coverage to meet the independent needs of the property. Investors must be sure to obtain landlord insurance coverage for rental properties as opposed to homeowner's insurance. The investor must also determine the type of insurance coverage held by hired management and acquire any additional insurance to ensure total coverage for the property. Some insurance companies abide by coinsurance laws, which dictate the minimum amount of specific coverage that should be applied to rental properties. A penalty is applied for failure to meet minimum requirements. The penalty reduces the percentage of payment for losses by an amount equal to the percentage that coverage falls short. For example: The insurance company requires that a property hold $1 million in coverage; however, only $750,000 of coverage is acquired for the property. When a claim is filed for the property, the insurance company will pay three-quarters of the loss since three-quarters of the required coverage was acquired.

Basic Insurance

Most insurance companies offer some form of the three basic types of insurance

1. Basic coverage packages protect against loss to perils, which may include the following:

   - Aircraft

   - Vehicles

   - Fire

   - Storms

   - Windstorms

   - Vandalism

   - Burglary

   - Riot

   - Civil commotion

   - Lightning

   - Smoke

   - Explosion

   - Sprinklers

   - Hail

The basic package, generally, will not protect appliances, equipment, machinery, and other contents housed in or on the property.

2. Broad-form coverage includes basic coverage in addition to protection against the following:

   – Falling objects

   – Glass breakage

   – Water damage caused by plumbing

   – Weight of ice and snow

   – Collapse of specified structures

3. Special-form coverage protects against all losses except those specifically identified and excluded in the policy.

Additional Insurance

Insurance companies also provide comprehensive coverage, which includes protection against injuries and loss suffered as a result of defective conditions on the property as well as legal costs to defend the policyholder in personal-injury lawsuits. Additional insurance or insurance with specific clauses must be obtained to cover losses from natural disasters, such as floods, earthquakes, and hurricanes, as well as the loss of the structure, its contents, or major appliances, such as air-conditioning and heating units and boiler systems. This additional insurance is usually provided with high premiums and large deductibles. Research of the property should take into consideration all aspects of the property. If the property is located in a flood-prone area, the additional expense to obtain flood insurance is small compared to the damage incurred from flooding. Likewise, if the property has an aging heating system, it may make sense to purchase additional insurance to cover losses that may result from failure of the system.

Income-producing property should be supplemented by business interruption insurance, which guarantees income in the event of loss or damage that disrupts the receipt of income from the property. Business interruption insurance should cover the amount of income that would otherwise be collected as well as the cost of other expenses incurred during the restoration of the rental property, such as the payment of rent for displaced tenants.

Insurance should include total replacement cost insurance as opposed to actual cash value (ACV) insurance. ACV insurance pays the cost of replacement, after subtracting depreciation. Building materials and other accessories of the property increase in cost over time. The older the property, the less likely it is to be replaced at ACV. Many insurance companies offer ACV replacement as the standard coverage; replacement cost coverage will likely incur an additional expense.

Investors who hold multiple properties should insure all properties under the same policy to qualify for discounted insurance premiums and better coverage, particularly if an aggregate deductible is applied. Using aggregate deductibles, the investor could insure four properties for $4 million rather than insuring each of the four properties at $1 million. Each property would then have a $4 million limit under the single policy. In addition, an aggregate deductible allows losses from all four properties to be used toward the deductible paid for claims. The investor would have to pay a one-time deductible for claims against all four properties.

Other types of insurance that will sustain the value of real estate investments include the following:

- Liability insurance protects all types of property. The

liability should cover twice the value of protected assets.

- Mortgage insurance will pay the mortgage in the event of disability. There are two types of mortgage insurance to consider: One will pay the owner and the other pays the lender.

- Title insurance protects buyers against errors or omissions in the property's title. Many lenders insist upon title insurance as part of their lending requirements.

- Fidelity insurance provides reimbursement if an employee steals collected rents.

- Workers' compensation insures workers who may be injured while working on the property.

- Umbrella insurance covers remaining costs after all other insurance options are exhausted.

- Non-owned automobile liability insurance provides coverage for employees while working on the property and using their own vehicles.

- Building ordinance insurance covers the cost of demolition and cleanup when property is partially or completely destroyed. It also covers the additional cost to meet new building code requirements when the property is rebuilt.

Agents

Insurance agents provide convenient access to insurance companies. Agents act on behalf of the insurance company to provide the necessary information to establish individuals with the parent insurance company. Insurance premiums should never be paid directly to the insurance agent; insurance premiums should be paid to the parent insurance company. Some insurance agents are deceitful enough to pocket insurance premiums paid to them in hopes that the investor will never file a claim.

Adjustors

An insurance adjuster offers the ability to assess property damage and estimate the cost of reconstruction, repair, and other conditions. The insurance adjuster is trained and qualified to work within the oddities of the insurance market to seek damages of which the investor or property manager may not be aware. Adjusters usually charge 10 percent of the amount paid by the insurance company and are, in most cases, able to get funds dispensed much faster than private individuals.

Market Research

Investors must devote the time to research and study the neighborhood in which the property of interest is located to understand the behavior and cultural oddities unique to the neighborhood. Every neighborhood has its own unique personality, and the investor must be able to define the boundaries of the neighborhood. A single block or multiple blocks may characterize a neighborhood. It is not uncommon, particularly in urban communities, to find one block that indicates a sense of pride next to another block that is dilapidated and neglected. Investors must learn to evaluate property and assess the state or potential for:

- Current and future use of the property

- Population trends of the area

- Natural disasters

- Zoning ordinances

- Traffic patterns and parking

- Soil and land erosion

- Deterioration and existing damage

- Existing and necessary utilities

- Educational and recreational opportunities

- Safety and access to police, fire, and emergency resources

- Sanitation, trash, and garbage disposal

- Access to public transportation

Advertising

Investors need to advertise rental property in order to acquire tenants to occupy the property. Advertising and public relations are integral parts of property management. Advertisement is available through a number of different mediums. The chosen media depends on the location of the property, the market of potential tenants, and the allocated advertising budget.

Newspapers

Investors of commercial, industrial, and residential property are served well by advertising in major newspapers. Most newspapers devote an entire section of the paper to real estate alone. The real estate sections of most newspapers offer advice, commercial advertisements, and other useful real estate information in addition to classified ads. Investors have the options of advertising properties in the classified ads or advertising his or her business in commercial advertisements or both. The type of ad that an investor uses is dependent upon budget allocations for advertising. Location and market demographics are also important when determining how to spend advertising budgets. In small towns with a single newspaper, advertising may reach a large population of residents. Even in big cities, newspapers are the backbone of real estate advertising.

News Releases

Realtors and investors may also make use of the local paper to promote their business efforts using news or press releases. Realtors or investors must be careful to structure releases such that they contain newsworthy content that the editor will feel justified in publishing. Newspaper editors receive many such releases and sort through them to determine the most newsworthy of the bunch.

Radio

Radio offers many formats: talk radio, news radio, and every type of music radio to include rap, rhythm and blues, country, rock, western, and more. If investors are interested in targeting a specific segment of the community, radio offers a format to reach just about every segment of the population. The disadvantage is that radio advertisement generally limits advertising to just the listening audience. It can become quite costly for an investor to spread radio advertisement across multiple radio formats.

Magazines

Magazines, like radio, are targeted to specific segments of the population. Local magazines, particularly freely distributed magazines, offer an effective method of advertising to the local population, though the circulation is not always consistent.

Television

Television advertising is probably the most costly of all advertising media yet it has the potential to reach the most prospective tenants. Television advertisement is not cost-effective for newly established or local investors. The circulation is so widespread that it will reach audiences outside of the target audience, creating a form of waste circulation. Cable television offers networks that target specific audiences. If the targeted potential tenants of the investment property match the targeted audiences of a cable network, the cable network may offer a less wasteful method of circulation. The cost, however, remains high.

The Internet

The Internet is also a viable medium for the advertisement of rental properties. The Internet, however, is not a luxury that everyone can afford, and potential tenants may not make good use of the technology in locating properties. Some people consider the wealth of information provided on the Internet to be too exhaustive to search through. The Internet is often used as a secondary source to investigate a property that is advertised elsewhere. Technology allows Realtors and investors to use the Internet to display internal and external views of available properties. Prospective tenants are able to zero-in on specific areas of the property, change the focus point of the view, as well as map the property location and surrounding community.

Signs/Signage

Signs are probably the most economical of advertisement media. Signs, strategically placed on or the near the property, are able to point prospective tenants in the direction of an available property. Signs are most commonly placed in the front yard of a property or in a side yard, if the side yard is visible to passing foot and vehicle traffic. Signs are also strategically placed at cross streets or busy intersections close to the property. The oddity about signage is that signs should limit the amount of information presented so that passing motorists are presented only the essential information necessitating further investigation of the property. Typical FOR RENT signs are 18 x 24 inches and should contain, at most, a phone number and the number of bedrooms, and at a minimum, a phone number to make contact. Some multi-unit property owners and managers are reluctant to put up signs for fear that existing tenants may get nervous and retaliate by moving or creating problems for the owner or other tenants. However, signs are the only avenue of advertisement that require a one-time expense, can be acquired cheaply, and market the property 24/7. Another increasingly popular advertising vehicle is an 800 number, which will be included on signs that possible tenants will call to hear the features of the house, apartment, or other dwelling for rent.

Rental Guides

Rental guides provide specific and detailed information about available rental properties. They offer widespread distribution in select and chosen markets. Rental guides are expected to provide the type of information that offers readers an opportunity to make a decision about further investigating a property. Listed properties should specify location, price, size, and contact information.

Location: In addition to the street address, rental guides are organized by city or county, with further division by direction (northern, southern, northeastern, and so on). Rental guides often specify major landmarks within close proximity to the property. Typical examples include "close to schools," "close to park," or "close to shopping district."

Price: Rental guides usually specify the price for rental units. This gives the potential tenant an opportunity to assess whether the advertised property is one that he or she can afford. This benefits property managers by eliminating time that would otherwise be wasted with prospective tenants who cannot afford the requested rent.

Size: Rental guides may be used to specify size, not necessarily as dimensions but as a function of usability. For example: "One bedroom and one bath" indicates a relatively small rental unit, while 900 square feet is difficult for most people to conceptualize. Other size descriptions may include "spacious," "large bath," "small den," "2-car parking" and "half-bath."

Contact Information: Rental guides should always specify contact information, with specific times to either contact the property manager or visit the property location.

Referral Systems

Establishing a referral system is most beneficial to property managers who maintain multiple properties. A referral system is a database of potential tenant leads who are referred by friends, family, associates, neighbors, and anyone with whom the property manager has contact, including existing tenants. It is commonplace to offer a referral bonus in the range of $50 to $100 for referrals that actually lead to a signed lease. The offer of a bonus creates a method of verbally promoting rental properties. A referral system, and its associated bonus, provides a good conversation piece that is not likely to bore listeners. The offer of a cash bonus also attracts attention when included in various forms of print advertisement, such as newspapers and magazines, as well as memos, mailings, receipts, business cards, and other correspondence of the business. Referral systems are a cost-effective method of advertising properties, and they have the potential to bring good results.

Tenant Location Services

Tenant location services are rather costly services offered by rental or real estate agencies. The rental agency maintains a listing of vacant rental properties. A potential tenant specifies his or her requirements for a rental unit, and the rental agency provides a listing of properties that meet the prospective tenant's requirements. The disadvantage of tenant location services is that rental agent databases are limited to those properties of participants of their service. Prospective tenants are provided a limited listing taken from the Realtor's network of paying customers. An advantage to property managers is that the rental agent is paid only when services result in a signed lease or rental agreement. The advantage to the prospective tenant is that the rental agency is able to narrow down listed properties to those of interest, and the potential tenant does not have to sort through classified ads or other advertisements to find properties that meet their requirements. Rental agents charge locator fees that may range from a half month's rent to a full month's rent. Unless a property is experiencing high vacancy rates, it may not be cost effective for the property manager to engage in this type of service, particularly when the property is rented month to month or bi-annually.

Dedication

Property management entails many risks that can be overcome by dedication. Most people who invest in real estate are interested in increasing their wealth. Providing rental properties is a proven method of establishing wealth, but there is a learning curve involved in properly acquiring and managing properties. Property management can be performed by anyone, but professional property managers must be trained and certified in either real estate or property management. The terms property owner, property manager, and landlord are often used interchangeably as they are in this book. The property owner holds deed and title to the property. Once the property is converted into a management property, the landlord or property manager is the responsible party who collect rents and perform other duties in conjunction with management of the property. When the owner takes on the role of property manager, the owner becomes a landlord. When the owner hires another party as property manager, the hired party becomes the landlord.

Property investors who devote time and capital in acquiring rental property must also dedicate time to develop the necessary skills to manage property. Even when owners outsource property-management duties, they must oversee the hired management to assess whether the management practices are in the best interest of the property. In particular, investors must determine whether established management practices are the best possible practices to be used in maintaining the property and whether collected rents are sufficient to cover expenses of the property and offer cash flow.

Investors must understand concepts and practices used in finance, law, and accounting. The required level of knowledge is such that some new investors seek classroom training. Community colleges and other community entities offer real estate training. Realtors also offer training by professionals with real-world experience in real estate. For those investors who prefer to learn at their own pace, a number of sources of information can be obtained from the Internet. Also, reference materials, such as brochures, pamphlets, and handouts, can be acquired from Realtors, bankers, and other community entities.

Landlords must have the people skills necessary to deal with differing personalities. Personalities of tenants and contractors can be both varied and volatile. Landlords must adopt a business attitude that is honest, fair, and firm, without appearing angry or mean. Landlords must possess the ability to emotionally remove themselves from the job and establish business relationships as separate and distinct from friendships. Landlords need to be visible and accessible. They should establish a schedule of visits to the property to let the tenants know that they are concerned about the upkeep of the property. The visits can also be used as an opportunity to inspect the property and inquire about tenant concerns. Tenants should be provided methods of communicating problems to the landlord that result in a response. Whether through phone communication, e-mail, or face-to-face response, tenants should feel that issues are not ignored. Tenants should also be aware that a response will be initiated for complaints by or about the tenant.

Vision

Vision is a skill that investors must acquire before investing in real estate. Investors must be able to envision a neighborhood or community as it might exist in the future. The current state of some properties, such as dilapidated and vacant properties, is the result of conditions of the past. Investors who are able to envision the future may invest in land purchases and fixer-uppers with the vision of appreciation and market changes. Investors who engage in research and analysis are better able to envision property as it might exist in the event of demographic, industrial, or economic change. Low-cost land and property in forgotten neighborhoods are often the areas slated by governments for renewal. Investors who are willing to risk investment dollars in expectation of redevelopment and renewal usually make a substantial profit in the long-term.

Greg A. Fedro, MPM
Director of Operations
Recar & Associates, Realtors
8400 N. Mopac Expressway, #200
Austin, TX 78759
(512) 345-9886 Office
(512) 345-2302 Fax
E-mail: greg.fedro@recar-realtors.com
www.recar-realtors.com

Greg A. Fedro, MPM is the Director of Operations for Recar & Associates in Austin, Texas. As a NARPM member since 1996, Greg served on the NARPM Austin Area Chapter Board from 1997-2001. He was the NARPM National Certification Chair 2001-2003 and is currently serving on the NARPM Board of Directors. Greg enjoys folk music, boating, and is a certified Hatha yoga instructor.

I began managing apartments when I was in college. Today, I'm the Director of Operations for Recar & Associates in Austin, Texas, and I manage 400 single-family units, which is a full-time job and then some.

A major part of the job is setting rental properties which is, fortunately, rather simple. We have a very good MLS system in our market that is also used for rental inventory. We can easily determine what's available of comparable type/size. More importantly, we can also see what actually has been renting, so we don't waste a lot of time guessing what it takes to move a unit.

Of course, one of our goals is to keep our tenants happy. We give new tenants a lot of information when they move in, and we have an orientation for all new tenants. At the orientation, each new tenant is given a complete Tenant Handbook. We also keep them updated with periodic newsletters and reminders.

Furthermore, we make follow-up calls after maintenance is completed to make sure that the tenants are happy with the service and that the problem has been remedied.

Renting houses comes with more areas of responsibility for tenants, and some don't make the transition from apartment living to maintaining a home well. Security deposit deductions will always be an issue. Tenants don't see their own dirt and always feel that they left the place nicer than when they moved in. One of my biggest problems when I first started real estate was getting the residents to take me seriously. Try to evict someone when you have dimples! It's not so easy.

To minimize your management risks, put everything in writing. Have written procedures and ongoing training. Continue to educate yourself with every opportunity to make sure you know when the laws change. Have great management agreements and leases. In Texas, our legislators listen to us and give us a great tool to work with.

Alternately, you want to maximize your profits, and there are numerous strategies to accomplish that goal. First, unbundle your services. Train your clients not to assume that the monthly management fee includes anything and everything you do.

You also want to be clear on fees when the client signs on with you. No one likes surprises and it's harder to change terms later.

Finally, make sure you charge for administrative time. The more time you spend, the more you should be paid.

Finances are also extremely important. We have a corporate CPA who oversees our business accounts and is available when we have questions, particularly from owners. We prepare an end-of-year 1099 and summary statement in-house, using Promas accounting software. However, all of our owners handle their own tax payment and filing.

For those just starting out in residential property management, keep your sense of humor! Don't take everything personally. Care about your tenants, but don't take ownership of their dramas. Have a life outside of work.

If you're trying to decide if a career in property management is for you, consider going to work for larger, established apartment companies. The training programs can be the best, and I would say that advancement potential is faster in larger companies. Before you accept a job, make sure the employer has written procedures and systems. During your interview ask them how they handle new tenants.

Finally, if you do go into property management, remember what it feels like to be a renter. Treat tenants with the same compassion you would want. Don't become a power wielding landlord stereotype. There are a lot of bad landlords, so the good ones stand out easily.

4

Acquiring Management Property

Investors have two options with respect to selecting management properties: 1) They may choose to continue the management of existing properties as is, or 2) they may renovate, rehabilitate, or develop existing properties for rental and management. Investors need to establish ownership of the properties before they become responsible for managing them. Ownership is established with the purchase of management properties. Gaining ownership introduces a unique skill set of its own. Investors usually need to secure finances to purchase management property. Once financing is secured, investors should inspect the property to ensure that it offers the type of space that fits into the investment plan. Investors must collaborate with the appropriate real estate agent, attorney, accountant, and financial advisor trained in real estate laws, regulations, processes, and contracts. Once all parties sign a contract or promissory note, the purchase begins, and it continues until all terms of the contract have been satisfied. Most investment plans also include the eventual sale of rental properties. Management practices, particularly good management practices, play a vital role in the marketing of properties for resale.

Financing and Loans

Financing involves the borrowing of money to establish ownership of management property. Not all property acquisitions require financing. Some investors are independently wealthy and provide their own funds for the purchase of property. Most investors, however, require some type of financing to purchase properties. Lenders that provide financing will require the investor to contribute a down payment to the purchase. The required down payment is dependent upon a number of factors, but generally ranges between 5 and 20 percent of the purchase price of the property. Some purchases require less and some require more.

No Money Down

Some property purchases are purported to require no money down. No money down usually signifies that the borrower was able to secure the down payment by converting funds from available lines of credit and bank loans to cash. The down payment is, in effect, borrowed money rather than cash savings. When the borrower is able to extend his or her line of credit to cover 100 percent of the down payment needed to purchase property, it is referred to as a nothing-down transaction. The term "nothing" is a bit misleading since the borrowed money has to be repaid. Also, the borrower increases his or her debt ratio, a factor used by lending institutions in qualifying applicants for financing. The borrower should be sure that the converted line of credit does not allow for a debt ratio beyond that which is required to secure financing for the purchase of the property.

Mortgage Loans

Though there are many types of loans available to finance the purchase of rental property, mortgages can be grouped into three broad categories: 1) government-backed loans, 2) conventional loans, and 3) portfolio loans. Government-backed loans include Federal Housing Authority (FHA) and Veterans Affairs (VA) loans. Loan financing differs for owner-occupants and investors. Investor loans will almost always require higher closing costs, interest rates, and down payments because investments are considered to be more risky than homeownership.

Government-Backed Loans

Government-backed loans offer very low or no down payment to be applied toward the purchase of property. Instead, costly mortgage insurance premiums and/or funding fees are charged to the borrower. Government-backed loans are primarily provided to owner-occupants. However, the FHA does provide for investor loans with higher down payments than are required for homeowners.

Conventional Loans

Conventional loans can be either conforming or non-conforming loans. Conforming conventional loans strictly follow or conform to guidelines established by Fannie Mae. Non-conforming conventional loans are more flexible, allowing the lender to bend the guidelines established by Fannie Mae. Non-conforming loans allow the borrower to have higher qualifying ratios than are necessary for conforming loans. Conventional loans require minimum down payments in the range of 3 to 5 percent for owner-occupants and 10 to 20 percent for investors. Conventional loans offer the best fixed interest rates, but costly mortgage insurance premiums are standard unless or until the borrower gains at least 20 percent equity in the property. Conventional lenders originate loans with the intent of selling the loan to other companies, causing the borrower to make payment to more than one company during the life of the loan. In order to be salable, conventional loans need to follow Fannie Mae guidelines exactly. The strict guidelines, however, make the loans unachievable for small investors with limited cash flow.

The secondary loan market is established to allow large institutional investors to buy mortgages that originate elsewhere. To protect their interest in buying mortgages, investors seek loans that conform to Fannie Mae guidelines, which ensures that the loans are standardized with low default rates. Local mortgage lenders may sell mortgages that they originate so that they may originate more mortgages in their local market. Local mortgage lenders profit from loan origination fees, not the interest payments made on the loan. The investor that secures the resold loan profits from the interest payments.

Conforming loans can be originated anywhere in the United States and sold immediately in the secondary market. Likewise, non-conforming loans can be sold in the secondary market, but not immediately. Non-conforming loan originators may have to hold their loans for a period of one to two years to ensure that the borrower is able to stay current on loan payments. Non-conforming conventional lenders are willing to hold loans until they can be sold in the secondary market. Many investors are willing to buy these loans after they have been held and proved profitable. Borrowers should secure the services of a mortgage broker who works with various investors and is knowledgeable about these types of loans.

Portfolio Loans

Portfolio loans do not follow Fannie Mae guidelines. Lenders are allowed to establish and break their own rules to accommodate borrowers who present a good credit risk. Unlike conventional lenders, portfolio lenders rarely sell their mortgages to other companies. Portfolio lenders keep most or all of the loans that they originate in their own investment portfolio of loans. They also service their own loans and have the flexibility to incorporate common sense in the evaluation of applicants. Portfolio loans are best suited for small investors and other borrowers who cannot meet the strict loan requirements established by Fannie Mae. Portfolio lenders are flexible in qualifying borrowers and may tailor loans to meet individual needs. Portfolio loans are provided to individuals who are self-employed, on limited income, and in other unique circumstances. Portfolio lenders usually do not have established limits but implement specialized and particular processes to minimize their risks to financing.

Owner-Occupant Qualifying Ratios

Conventional lenders use qualifying ratios established by Fannie Mae to determine how much to lend to a borrower. Lenders have two ratios: 1) front-end and 2) back-end ratios. A front-end ratio is also called a housing ratio, which is used to determine the maximum payment that an individual is able to pay. A back-end ratio determines the limit on monthly debt obligations. Portfolio lenders also use front-end and back-end qualifying ratios, but they establish their own limits, at their own discretion. Conventional front-end ratios are computed by multiplying the borrower's gross monthly income by the Fannie Mae established ratio of 28 percent. The resulting value represents the maximum monthly mortgage amount that the borrower is determined to be capable of paying. The front-end ratio represents a maximum mortgage payment, which is inclusive of principal, interest, insurance, taxes, second mortgages, or homeowner association dues. The conventional back-end ratio is computed by multiplying the borrower's gross monthly income by the Fannie Mae established ratio of 36 percent. The resulting value represents the maximum monthly debt that the borrower is determined to be capable of paying. The back-end ratio represents a maximum of all long-term monthly debt obligations inclusive of the calculated front-end mortgage payment, car loans, lease obligations, alimony, child support, student loans, credit card payments, and other loan payments. The lender compares the front-end calculation against the back-end calculation and qualifies the borrower with a loan approval in an amount equal to the lesser of the two calculated ratios. Qualifying ratios are a necessary first step in qualifying borrowers for a loan, but being qualified does not mean the loan will be approved. Other requirements, such as the borrower's credit rating, must meet approval.

Investor Qualifying Ratios

Lenders use different factors to calculate qualifying ratios for investors of rental property. The lender will include the anticipated rental income as part of the investor's gross income, but the lender may not give the investor credit for the full amount of anticipated rents. Conventional lenders may discount the anticipated rent by 75 percent, making an allowance of 25 percent for the cost of maintenance, advertising, and other expenses of the rental property. If the mortgage payment on the investment property exceeds the discounted rent calculated by the lender, the difference between the anticipated rent and the discounted rent is included as a debt against the back-end ratio. Portfolio lenders usually do not discount anticipated rent on investment properties. In fact, any positive difference between the anticipated rent and the mortgage payment is added to income to help investors qualify. However, portfolio lenders consider all investment properties in the investor's portfolio before determining qualifying ratios. If the investor acquires a loan for the purchase of a new investment property, the lender may provide the investor with a low-documentation loan. "Low documentation" implies that no tax filings supplement the loan application and the lender is allowed to discount the rent on current properties by 25 percent. If, on the other hand, the investor supplements the loan application with tax filings, the investor may engage a full-documentation loan. Using a full-documentation loan, lenders will discount rent by the actual amounts indicated on tax filings. If the resulting value is positive, it helps the investor to qualify. If the resulting value is negative, the value is subtracted as debt against the back-end ratio calculation.

Even though conventional mortgages are more attractive loans and attainable for a first investment property, the conventional lender's method of discounting rental income for each held property would decrease the investor's back-end ratio to the point of being disqualified. Unless the investor has very high income or minimal debts, the discount applied to additional investment properties will eventually reduce the back-end ratio to a value too small to qualify for conventional loans. The investor will need to switch to portfolio lenders that offer higher ratios and also do not discount income from newly acquired rental properties.

Mortgage Rates

Investors may engage in either fixed-term or adjustable interest rates. Fixed-term interest rates are generally higher than adjustable interest rates because the interest rate on fixed-term loans cannot be changed. To compensate for the risk of losing money should interest rates increase, fixed-term loans are offered at a higher rate so that the lender is able to obtain higher interest ahead of time. Adjustable rates ensure the lender of being able to raise mortgage interest should interest rates increase. The borrower is required to make larger payments on the mortgage should interest rates increase. The borrower is encouraged to prepay an adjustable-rate mortgage to decrease the principal amount of the loan. The lower the principal, the less impact an increase in interest rates will have on the payment amount.

Adjustable-rate mortgages are acquired with a teaser rate. Teaser rates are abnormally low interest rates that will be adjusted upward during the term of the loan. Adjustable-rate mortgages also have a fully indexed rate, which is calculated as the interest that would be paid if the mortgage had been held past the teaser rate. The fully indexed rate cannot be determined for the future, but it can be calculated and determined for the present. A fully indexed rate is calculated as the current index plus margin. Margin represents the lender's gross profit margin, with no deductions for expenses. Margins are established when the teaser rate has expired and remain constant throughout the life of the loan unless specified otherwise in the deed of trust.

Index is calculated based on other entities in the banking industry. Conventional lenders use the rate of interest paid on treasury bills. Portfolio lenders are likely to use the Cost of Funds Index (COFI). The COFI is calculated by adding the interest rates paid on Certificates of Deposit (CDs) to the average monthly interest rate paid on all savings and checking accounts in the 11th District of the federal banking system. Individual lenders may have similar or different index values.

Most adjustable-rate mortgages have two rate caps: 1) a lifetime cap and 2) an annual interest or payment cap. An annual interest cap limits the amount by which lenders can increase the interest rate during an adjustment. Adjustments may be made annually or semi-annually. Some lenders will use a payment cap rather than an interest cap. A payment cap limits the amount by which the lender may raise principal and interest payments. The limit is calculated as a percentage of the mortgage payment. The borrower must be careful to understand the language of caps. Some caps limit the amount of interest paid while others limit the payment amount and not the interest rate. The latter are referred to as negative amortization loans.

When rate cap limits do not provide the lender with enough capital to cover increased interest rates, the lender may add the additional cost to the borrower's loan balance. Using negative amortization loans, the lender cannot increase the borrower's payment above the limit established by the rate cap. Instead, the lender increases the borrower's loan payment by applying the amount to the loan balance as unpaid interest. The lender is, in fact, making an additional loan to the borrower without consent from the borrower. The borrower's effort to pay down the principal by prepaying the monthly mortgage amount is cancelled out by the amount added as unpaid interest. If interest rates continue to rise, particularly when the amount applied to unpaid interest is greater than the amount being applied to the loan principal, the loan balance could actually increase and extend the mortgage beyond its amortization period. A property investor may increase rents on rental property and make additional payments to cover the unpaid interest to maintain the loan's amortization period or seek a lender willing to swallow the increased cost. Most portfolio lenders offer negative amortization loans while conventional lenders may swallow the increased cost.

A lifetime cap limits the amount of interest that can be charged for the life of the loan. Even when rate cap limits do not provide the lender with enough capital to cover increased interest rates, the lender may not add the additional cost to the borrower's loan balance. A lifetime cap prohibits lenders from applying unpaid interest, above the cap interest, to the balance of either conventional or portfolio loans, whether or not the loan is a negative amortization loan.

100% Loans

Loans in which the lender provides 100 percent of the financing necessary to purchase property are called 100% loans. These loans are best suited for individuals who assist others, such as a minor, in financing the acquisition of property without having to co-sign for the loan or risk their credit rating. Instead of the borrower applying an amount to the down payment, the borrower is expected to have a sponsor that is capable of investing up to 20 percent of the purchase price in CDs to be held by the lender as collateral against the property, along with the property itself. The sponsor remains the owner of the certificates, receives any interest earned on the certificates, and is not required to co-sign the loan. If the borrower defaults on the loan and the lender forecloses, the sponsor may have to forfeit his or her interest in the collateral, but the sponsor's credit rating is not affected. The sponsor is still able to borrow money and qualify for loans because the sponsor is not a co-signer of the mortgage. The CDs become part of the sponsor's estate in the event of death and handled accordingly.

The sponsor is not required to pledge the full 20 percent toward the purchase. If the borrower is able to make a down payment, the sponsor is only required to secure the remaining amount that accounts for 20 percent of the purchase price. When the borrower gains 20 percent equity in the property, the CDs are released as collateral.

Limited-Income Loans

Limited-income loans are established to assist low-income individuals in obtaining financing. "Low income" is defined according to geographical location and includes accounting of income for each individual that resides in a household. The loans may be used for the purchase or refinancing of property. The lender's closing cost may be as low as $500, though other parties to the closing, such as the title company, may impose additional costs. These loans are extended to low-income individuals at fixed interest rates and are only available to owner-occupants, not investors.

Investor Loans

Investor loans require documentation of the investor's income and debts. The investor is usually required to qualify to handle his or her personal mortgage payments as well as other monthly debts. Rental properties must be capable of producing a cash flow once anticipated expenses are deducted from anticipated rents. Investors will require a down payment in the 20 to 25 percent range. Some conventional lenders may offer investors non-conforming conventional loans with down payments as low as 10 percent. Portfolio lenders, on the other hand, use more obtainable front-end and back-end ratios to qualified investors. The portfolio lender's down payment of 20 to 25 percent should be sufficient to produce a cash flow, pay for maintenance, and secure a profit. If portfolio loan rates remain low and prepayment assists in paying down the loan balance, cash flow is expected.

Convertible Loans

Convertible loans are adjustable-rate mortgage loans that are converted into fixed-rate mortgages. The conversion can be accomplished during the second through sixth year of financing, without requiring the borrower to re-qualify. The fixed interest is usually higher than that offered by conventional lenders, but the closing costs are likely to be less for an adjustable-rate mortgage than a fixed-rate portfolio loan. Convertible loans are best suited for individuals who qualify for adjustable-rate loans but not fixed-rate loans. They are only available to owner-occupants.

Lines of Credit

Lines of credit include home equity loans and credit card loans. Home equity loans are only available to owner-occupants. The loan is actually a second mortgage, secured by the homeowner's equity in his or her property. A home equity loan may be obtained at 100 percent of the value of the home, sometimes more. This type of loan offers flexibility that allows the homeowner to engage in the loan by simply writing a check. The borrower is cautioned to research the terms and conditions for securing funds for a particular home equity loan. Some lenders will accept this type of check as a down payment on rental property, others will not. To avoid this issue, the homeowner interested in using a home equity loan for a down payment to acquire property should deposit the secured funds into his or her bank account so that it represents cash savings. Home equity loans offer the advantage of having lower interest rates than other lines of credit, but the terms of payment are usually longer.

Bank Loans

Local banks also provide lines of credit that may be converted into cash. Banks may extend lines of credit to homeowners, secured by their homes, or they may extend lines of credit to investors based on their credit ratings, with no collateral. The bank will establish limits on the amount of credit extended. Banks usually offer a minimum amount and increase the amount based on the borrower's history of payment. Local banks may also provide financing for the purchase and/ or improvement of rental property. Local banks offer the advantage of requiring less documentation than conventional mortgage companies.

Conventional Mortgages Versus Lines of Credit

Conventional mortgages are established for the purpose of financing the purchase of real estate and investment properties. Conventional mortgages offer competitive rates under a variety of terms and conditions. The interest rates used for conventional mortgages differ from those used in extending lines of credit and bank loans. Interest on bank loans and lines of credit are based on the prime lending rate. Interest on mortgages is based on a spread or margin in the value of treasury notes. Investors with good credit are more likely to secure better rates with conventional mortgages than with bank loans or lines of credit. Some conventional mortgages may finance as much as 90 percent of the sale price of investment properties, leaving the investor responsible for securing a down payment of only 10 percent of the purchase price. Mortgage companies are also more inquisitive than other lenders. They may require cancelled checks and other forms of proof to substantiate the source of funds held by the borrower, particularly funds deposited in the previous two years. The borrower who converts a line of credit to cash and deposits the amount into his or her bank account is cautioned against trying to pass off the recently acquired cash deposit as a savings amount. The mortgage lender's request and research of documentation will identify any attempts to defraud the company. Many mortgage companies impart strict rules regarding the money used as down payment. The borrower is required to have acquired the money on his or her own, and the mortgage company may disqualify a borrower if the mortgage company ascertains that the money used for down payment is borrowed from friends or family. Conventional mortgages usually carry a 30-year amortization period, which distributes monthly payment amounts over 30 years. The more years used for amortization, the lower the monthly payment amount to be paid to the lender. Conventional mortgages offer the disadvantage of requiring lots of documentation and numerous loan fees. Banks, on the other hand, may amortize payments over 15 or 20 years, sometimes less. Banks may also offer interest-only loans where the monthly payment is required to pay only the amortized interest. This type of loan is useful to investors interested in acquiring property for a short period of time and then flipping or selling the property. Interest-only loans reduce the amount of expenses paid for the property during this type of short ownership.

Options

An option agreement allows for the purchase of property at a predetermined price, much like the process used by investors in the stock market. Options are bound by time and have a date on which they expire. Options give investors a legal interest in properties, during the option period, with the option to sell the property without ever having to take title to it. Options require an investor to pay a nonrefundable premium for the option. The property owner may also require that the investor pay carrying costs for the property, such as taxes and insurance, during the option period. During the option period, the investor may choose to purchase the property or the investor may allow the option to expire without any additional costs. Options offer investors a great opportunity to take ownership of property that has yet to be developed. Should the development effort indicate an opportunity to profit, the investor may take ownership during the option period. If, however, the development effort indicates a potential for loss, the investor has the option to allow the lease to expire or sell the property to another buyer during the option period. The smart investor usually finds another buyer willing to pay a price in excess of the amount that he or she is locked into paying. A disadvantage of using options for the purchase of undeveloped property is that the tax liability may increase greatly once the property is developed, as the investor is required to assume the tax liability as owner of the property.

Lease Options

Lease options are similar to options in that the investor is offered a window of opportunity to lock into a predetermined price for the property. The difference is that lease options allow the investor to control the business aspects of the leased rental property. The investor may sublease the rental property or resell the property without ever having to take title to the property. A lease option requires the establishment of a loan against the property. The lease option agreement specifies an amount of income from the property to be applied to the purchase of the property and, thus, the loan held against the property. Prior to the expiration of the lease agreement, the investor may purchase the property and pay off the loan held against the property. The investor also has the option to resell the property, which transfers title from the original seller to the new buyer, not the investor. If the investor chooses to allow the lease option to expire, the investor forfeits the premium deposited to engage in the lease option and the original seller retains monthly lease payments that would have been applied toward the purchase of the property.

Owner Financing

A property owner may choose to finance the sale of his or her own property. If an owner holds no debts against the property, he or she may offer as much as 100 percent financing. Most owners, however, will specify an amount to be applied as down payment. If the owner holds a debt against the property, the owner may choose to carry back a second mortgage at a percentage of the purchase price, which allows the buyer an opportunity to purchase the property with a smaller down payment. If the buyer engages in a loan or mortgage to purchase the property, the buyer must understand the lender's position on secondary financing, such as that required for the second mortgage. Owners who finance their own properties do not usually impose the same strict rules used by lenders to qualified borrowers. Owners may not be so concerned about where the buyer gets the funds; only that the buyer is able to make timely payments. Owners are not likely to impose the loan fees traditionally required of lenders, such as fees for the loan application, underwriting, and origination. Owners do not engage in methods of assessing points and require no formal loan approval processes.

Owners may offer a wrap-around mortgage that allows them to retain title to the property and continue to make payments to the original lender, if a mortgage is held against the property. Wrap-around mortgages allow the buyer to make payments to the owner and the owner to make payments to the lender.

The owner retains any difference in the amount that is paid to the owner and the monthly payment paid to the lender. If the owner, for example, has held a mortgage for 10 years with a monthly mortgage amortized over 30 years, and the buyer agrees to pay monthly mortgage payments to the owner for 30 years, the owner's mortgage will be paid off 10 years prior to the buyer paying off his or her mortgage to the owner. Considering that the buyer is paying more to the owner than the owner is required to pay to the lender, the owner profits by the difference in payments every month for the next 20 years and then profits the totality of the buyer's payment for the remaining 10 years. The owner must be careful to understand his or her mortgage agreement with the lender to ensure that a documented due-on-sale clause does not exist to prevent wrap-around mortgages.

Though the most common forms of owner financing involve second mortgages, the terms of financing do not have to be dependent upon the payment of debt. Owner financing may involve agreements to share in the equity of a property. Equity agreements allow the owner to maintain partial ownership of the property. The agreement, for example, may specify methods of sharing profits from income of the property or sharing the capital gain from the sale of the property.

Loan Documentation

Loans, real estate loans in particular, require a lot of documentation. One of the characteristics of some of the larger mortgage companies is that they seem to require excess documentation. Small and localized lenders tend to require less documentation, though they may be more selective in choosing borrowers. Some of the required documentation required by lenders includes the following:

- Loan application forms

- Credit references

- Bank statements that verify the existence of cash required for down payment and reserves

- Purchase agreements and addenda

- Other related agreements

- Proof of ownership for personal assets

- Property tax bill

- Income tax filings for the past two years

- Third-party reports, such as appraisals, inspection reports, and surveys

Required documentation unique to rental properties includes the following:

- Insurance binders for rental property

- Current lease agreements

- Historical operating statements

- Income statements and balance sheets

- Business income tax filings for the past two years

- Property tax bills for the business

Loan Terms

The term of a loan is often confused with the loan's amortization period. The term or life of a loan specifies the period in which the loan must be paid or renewed. The amortization period is used to calculate the monthly payments that will be required for the loan. A short-term loan can have a long-term amortization period of 15 or 30 years. In some situations, it is beneficial to have the term of the loan equal to the amortization period of the loan. In other situations, it is not. The investor must determine how long he or she wishes to hold the property. When the buyer purchases property, with cash flow as the basis, and market conditions indicate that the best time to sell the property at a profit is within the next few years, the investor may want to consider a short-term loan. Short-term loans offer lower rates and mean fewer expenses for the property during ownership.

Loan Fees

The financing of properties is subject to expenses other than the interest incurred on the loan. The financing of rental property requires that the investor understand the terms of the loan as well as fees and penalties that may be assessed against the loan. Financing incurs loan fees, which may include any number of fees assessed by the lender such as application fees, origination fees, underwriting fees, broker fees, or points. Both lenders and mortgage brokers are required to disclose all reasonable and customary loan fees in compliance with the Truth in Lending Act. However, the investor must investigate the cost and consequences of such fees before committing to a sale contract because some fees and charges are not disclosed until the property closing.

Lenders may assess a loan application fee for applying for a loan. The fee is advertised to cover the cost of processing loan applications. Loan application fees have proven effective in deterring potential applicants from applying when the applicant believes that he or she may not be able to qualify for the loan. Application fees vary by lender and may cost as much as $500. Some lenders have been known to negotiate the application fee while others assess a nonrefundable fee. Some lenders may waive the fee for applicants with excellent and proven credit histories, if asked to do so.

Some lenders require applicants to pay an underwriting fee. The underwriting fee, like the loan application fee, is advertised to cover the costs of processing an application, as well as underwriting the loan.

Lenders may charge loan origination fees, advertised to cover the cost of engaging in the loan process, once a loan is approved. Engaging in the loan process includes drafting and processing the necessary legal documents as well as properly recording funding used in the loan. Loan origination fees are usually equivalent to 1 percent of the loan amount. Lenders may waive the origination fee or roll the cost into the loan's interest rate. The roll-over method usually increases the interest rate by 0.25 percent.

Lenders may charge a prepayment penalty for paying off the loan before the expiration of terms. Prepayment penalties are most often applied to commercial loans as opposed to residential loans. The penalty may be structured in any number of ways to include decreasing fees as the term of the loan is reached. Many lenders offer financing that does not include prepayment penalties.

Mortgage Brokers

A mortgage broker, real estate broker, and lender are separate and distinct parties in the sale of property. Mortgage brokers assist the borrower in obtaining financing from the lender.

Lenders offer mortgage brokers additional compensation when they are able to sell loans at higher interest rates than the base rates established by the lender. When a mortgage broker is involved in the property acquisition process, the mortgage broker may not know the lender's complete schedule of fees. Though the mortgage broker should research all applicable loan fees, the mortgage broker falls in compliance with the Truth in Lending Act by disclosing only those fees that he or she is aware of, particularly when the broker is collaborating with a newly established lender or with a lender that he or she is not acquainted. A mortgage broker is similar yet distinct from a real estate broker. Both types of brokers receive compensation only upon achieving a sale, and their compensation is calculated on a percentage basis. The difference is that real estate brokers sell property and are paid commission while mortgage brokers sell loans and are paid points. Mortgage brokers generally charge between 1 and 2 percent of the loan amount, but it could also be more or less dependant upon other factors that influence the fee paid to mortgage brokers. Mortgage brokers may factor in the size of the loan, the borrower's credit worthiness, and/or the lender's willingness to offer back-end fees.

Points

Points are paid to mortgage brokers upfront of the financing, and they are used to assist the borrower in lowering the interest rate being applied to a loan. One point is equal to 1 percent of the loan amount. For every point paid by the borrower, the interest rate may be lowered from one-eighth to one-fourth of a percent. The exact amount by which interest rates are lowered is a dynamic value that may change with market fluctuations. A quoted value may change by the hour, day, or week, depending on market conditions. There are circumstances in which it makes sense for the borrower to pay down the interest rate by paying points up front. The borrower must be able to calculate the break-even point, which is the number of months of ownership required before paying points provides a cost benefit.

Pre-Purchase

Inspection

An inspection should precede the purchase of any commercial or residential property. The investor may inspect the property on his or her own or obtain the assistance of a qualified housing or building inspector. An inspector is certified by the state and participates in the buying and selling of property at a cost. The inspector is trained to assess the property for defects and may offer expertise that the investor may not have acquired. The initial cost of having a trained and certified inspector will save on the cost of making unexpected repairs for undetected defects. The bottom of a structure is the foundation upon which the rest of the property is built. The inspection should start with the bottom of the property and work to the top. The basement or bottom floor should receive a visual inspection for possible damage and defects. Water damage is the most obvious type of damage that is found in visual inspections. Other signs of damage and defects include the following:

- Bulging walls

- Crumbling or cracking mortar

- Water marks

- Patched surfaces

- Water leakage or seepage

- Dampness

- Mildew/mold

- Odors

The inspection should include a check of the fuse box, its wiring, and the area in the immediate vicinity of the fuse box. Signs of sparks and fires from past electrical problems can be spotted with a visual inspection.

The inspection should include an examination of the rest of the house for warped, cracked, and patched structures. Careful thought, experience, and common sense should be used to assess the possible cause of such defects and also the cost of eliminating the damage. The under-roofing, for example, will reveal signs of damage, particularly water damage to the roof. Water damage to the rooftop may trickle down to all parts of the structure; the investor must make a determination as to whether water stains are the result of current damage that needs to be addressed or past damage that has been repaired.

The configuration of plumbing and heating units should also be inspected. Residential housing should contain either a gas or an electric water heater. A typical electrical water heater for a single-family residence should hold at least 60 gallons of water. A typical gas water heater should hold a minimum of 30 to 40 gallons of water. Particular attention should be paid to multiple-dwelling units. Are the gas and electric appliances configured so that individual units may be billed for their individual use of resources? Likewise, is the water system configured so that individual units are billed for their use of the water supply? If these units are not properly configured, the investor must consider the cost of implementing such systems. A decision must be made as to whether it is more cost effective to modify or completely overhaul existing systems. As an alternative, the investor must be prepared for complications that arise when shared utilities are included in the monthly rent or lease amounts.

> **TIP:** When looking into acquiring a property, the potential investor should always make it a habit to speak with the neighbors of the potential property. These chats could lead to very helpful information as they often know about problems that have plagued the property that the seller might be slow to share.

Water Damage

Signs of water damage may be the result of flooding, leaking pipes, or equipment. Flood histories can be obtained from neighbors and others familiar with the neighborhood or community. Equipment, such as heating systems and hot water heaters, should be inspected for corrosion and other signs of leaking or malfunctioning parts. The property manager must determine if the damage is the result of current problems or past problems that have been resolved. Piping, such as old galvanized piping, may be the cause of damage. Copper should be used for hot-water lines while copper or plastic is sufficient to handle cold-water transport. Insulated piping is the most suitable type of piping, so long as the insulation is not being used to hide faulty piping.

Structural Damage

The inspection should include an examination of wood structures that support and form the foundation of the property. Signs of pest and rodent infestation that may cause damage are usually visible. The inspector must be able to distinguish termites from ants. Neither is good for the property, but termites are particularly troubling since they eat away at structures. Rats and mice are disease-bearing rodents that create health consequences. Droppings left in corners and other inconspicuous places indicate their presence. The inspector must examine joists and beams that support the property for cracks, splits, or missing boards. A determination must be made as to whether the existing joists and beams are capable of holding the load.

Health Threats

Radon

Radon is a naturally occurring radioactive gas that is present in the earth's soil and rock content. Radon is formed as a byproduct of the natural decay of radium. Radon may be found in any structure that sits on the earth, but it is more likely to be present in tightly sealed and insulated properties with limited airflow and poor ventilation. Levels of radon may not remain consistent within a structure. The levels may vary daily or seasonally. In most instances, the radon captured in building structures is not significant enough to pose a health risk. On the other hand, radon has no odor or taste; it may be unknowingly present in structures at lethal levels that are known to cause lung cancer.

The only method of detecting radon is to conduct radon testing. Radon tests are relatively inexpensive and easy to implement. The federal government does not establish any regulations or requirements for the testing of radon or for the disclosure of radon in the sale or rent of properties. However, some state governments have established rules and regulations regarding radon, its detection, and removal. Property owners should check with the appropriate state authority governing the location of their rental properties for specific requirements. As a precaution, property owners may want to check for the presence of radon in rental units.

There are two forms of radon testing:

1. The short-term test requires that a detector device be left in the property for 2 to 90 days to measure radon levels.

2. The long-term test requires that a detector device be left in the property for 90 or more days.

Property owners may seek the services of professionals who are trained and certified by the EPA or state authority. As an alternative, property owners can invest in more cost-effective home kits. The property owner should be careful to acquire a radon-detecting home kit that is approved by the EPA or state authority. The home kit requires that a radon detection device be placed inside of a structure for a predetermined length of time. The device is then sent to a laboratory for testing and the results are provided to the tester. If the test results indicate the presence of radon, other areas of the structure should also be tested. While low levels of radon may be detected in one area of a structure, higher levels of radon may be existent in other areas of the structure. The removal of radon is the responsibility of the owner and should include the installation of blowers, fans, and ducts to direct radon out of the structure. Tenants should be made aware of the presence of detected radon and made aware of all efforts put in place to remove it.

Asbestos

Asbestos is a fiber material traditionally used in a variety of products to add tensile strength, provide insulation, and provide fire resistance. Asbestos-based materials were used in products such as ceiling panels, roofing materials, carpet padding, insulation, vinyl flooring, spackling compounds, and furnaces. Asbestos fibers are generally bound with other

106

materials so that the fibers are not free to escape from products. However, many asbestos-based products are friable. As such, they crumble into small particles or fibers when disturbed. As long as asbestos-based products are not disturbed, such as with punctures, tears, sawing, scraping, and sanding, the fibers do not present a threat to human health.

Although there is no known or established safe level of exposure to asbestos, exposure to small amounts of asbestos fibers is not thought to pose a health risk. Exposure to high levels of asbestos fibers over long periods of time has proven to be dangerous, with symptoms of cancerous diseases appearing 20 to 30 years after such exposure. When asbestos fibers are released from disturbed products, they are inhaled in the lungs and may remain there for years. Scientific research has concluded that exposure to large doses of asbestos fiber leads to cancer, particularly lung cancer, mesothelioma, and asbestosis. Smokers are thought to be even more susceptible to lung cancer and asbestosis. Asbestosis is a scarring of the lungs by fibrous tissue; mesothelioma is a cancer of the abdominal cavity and chest lining. The federal government does not establish any regulations or requirements for investigating asbestos, removing asbestos, or disclosure of asbestos in the sale or rent of properties. However, some state governments have established rules and regulations regarding asbestos and its detection, repair, and removal. Property owners should check with the state authority governing the location of their rental properties for specific requirements.

In 1981, asbestos was banned from use in most products. Most asbestos-based products, manufactured before 1981, did not indicate that they contained asbestos, and many of those pre-1981 products are still in use today. The Occupational Safety and Health Administration (OSHA) established regulation to presume all buildings constructed prior to 1981 contain asbestos-based products unless they have been tested and verified to be free of the hazard.

There are many types of asbestos fibers, and only a specially designed microscope is able to positively detect the presence of asbestos. The best methods for treating asbestos-based products is to seek the advice of an environmental professional. In general, property owners should leave suspect materials alone if they appear to be in good condition. If suspected asbestos-based materials appear to be soft and crumbling, the material must be completely covered to prevent the release of asbestos fibers or completely removed. If materials appear to have been damaged or disturbed but not aged or otherwise softened to the point of crumbling, they should be repaired or removed. Repairing asbestos-based materials involves encapsulating or coating the material to seal its contents. Asbestos removal is a complex, expensive, and hazardous process that should be left to a licensed contractor. Property owners who have acquired properties built before 1981 should be careful to have suspected and damaged materials examined by a professional before attempting any restoration or renovation projects. Untrained workers may disturb asbestos-based materials in the process of trying to remove, sand, saw, or scrape them. This creates a hazardous environment for the workers and other occupants of the structure if toxic asbestos fibers are released in the process.

Lead Paint
Most states have federal disclosure requirements with regard to lead paint. Prior to 1978, lead-based paints were commonly used for painting interior and exterior surfaces of structures. Scientific research has since concluded that lead paint can be poisonous and hazardous, particularly to growing children. Lead paint has been shown to be responsible for learning

disabilities, behavioral problems, seizures, and death. When cracking or peeling disturbs lead paint or the paint ages to form a chalky substance, it can be toxic. In 1978, lead was banned as a component of paint.

Lead-based paint is neither easy to detect nor remove. A visual inspection of painted surfaces will not indicate the presence of lead paint. A special lead test is the only method to determine whether paint contains lead. Lead paint is also difficult to remove. The process of scraping and sanding painted surfaces to remove lead paint requires meticulous processes that generate substantial amounts of lead-based dust. As such, removing the paint is expensive, requiring expert services to control the toxic dust. The most common and effective method of dealing with lead paint is to manage painted surfaces to prevent cracking and peeling. Applying non-lead paint on top of smooth surfaces known or suspected to be lead paint is an effective method of managing the surface. Windows treated with lead-based paint are best removed from property, particularly when children occupy the property. The opening and closing of windows treated with lead paint will ultimately lead to disturbance and exposure to the paint. Children are most likely to ingest any freed lead-based particles. Children are also more likely to pick and prick holes in wall surfaces, exposing lead-based particles and dust.

The federal Residential Lead-Based Paint Hazard Reduction Act, established in 1992, requires owners of dwellings built before 1978 to notify tenants that the property may contain lead-based paint. The EPA provides a lead-based paint disclosure form, which provides the appropriate format for disclosure, as shown in Form 1. Owners must be sure to have the tenant sign and date the form and to keep a copy for their records.

- If a tenant held lease prior to this date, the tenant should have been notified of the new regulation and provided a disclosure statement prior to receipt of the first rent check collected after this date.

- Rental property owners that have newly acquired and occupied units must ensure that signed and dated disclosure forms exist for tenants in suspect properties. If disclosure forms are not readily available, the owners of newly acquired and occupied units should immediately provide the forms to tenants for signatures.

For all other tenants, the disclosure statement must be provided at the time of acceptance of the rental unit and prior to signing the lease or rental agreement.

Dwellings built before 1978 that have been inspected and certified as free of lead are exempt from the federal regulation. Other types of rental properties may also be exempt from the regulation, as long as they are not used to house children under six years of age. Exempt properties include:

- Properties that provide housing for the elderly.

- Properties that provide housing for individuals with disabilities.

- Some university housing units.

- Studio or efficiency housing units.

If a property owner believes that his or her property qualifies as an exempt property, he or she should seek documented verification from the appropriate state authority.

Disclosure of Information on Lead-Based Paint and/or Lead-Based Paint Hazards

Lead Warning Statement

Housing built before 1978 may contain lead-based paint. Lead from paint, paint chips, and dust can pose health hazards if not managed properly. Lead exposure is especially harmful to young children and pregnant women. Before renting pre-1978 housing, lessors must disclose the presence of known lead-based paint and/or lead-based paint hazards in the dwelling. Lessees must also receive a federally approved pamphlet on lead poisoning prevention.

Lessor's Disclosure

(a) Presence of lead-based paint and/or lead-based paint hazards (check (i) or (u) below):

    (i) _____ Known lead-based paint and/or lead-based paint hazards are present in the housing (explain).

    _____

    _____

    (u) _____ Lessor has no knowledge of lead-based paint and/or lead-based paint hazards in the housing.

(b) Records and reports available to the lessor (check (i) or (u) below):

    (i) _____ Lessor has provided the lessee with all available records and reports pertaining to lead-based paint and/or lead-based paint hazards in the housing (list documents below).

    _____

    _____

    (u) _____ Lessor has no reports or records pertaining to lead-based paint and/or lead-based paint hazards in the housing.

Lessor's Acknowledgement (initial)

(c) _____ Lessee has received copies of all information listed above.

(d) _____ Lessee has received the pamphlet *Protect Your Family from Lead in Your Home.*

Agent's Acknowledgement (initial)

(e) _____ Agent has informed the lessor of the lessor's obligations under 42 USC 4992d and is aware of his/her responsibility to ensure compliance.

Certification of Accuracy

The following parties have reviewed the information above and certify, to the best of their knowledge, that the information they have provided is true and accurate.

Lessor	Date	Lessor	Date
Lessee	Date	Lessee	Date
Agent	Date	Agent	Date

Form 1: EPA Lead-Based Paint Disclosure Form (Griswold, p.132)

Federal regulation also requires that property owners provide tenants with a lead paint information pamphlet to educate them about the dangers of lead-based paint. Owners may use the pamphlet published by the EPA entitled *"Protect Your Family from Lead in Your Home"* at **www.epa.gov/lead/leadpdfe.pdf** or other pamphlets approved by the EPA. The EPA also publishes a handbook for use by property managers at **www.epa.gov/lead /interiorfinal2.pdf**.

Federal laws do not require that property owners remove lead-based paint, only to disclose to existing and potential occupants that the potential for danger exists. The law does require owners to provide tenants with copies of all existing reports or other documentation that specifies the presence or hazard of lead-based paint. Some states extend the act, specifically requiring owners to manage surfaces treated with lead paint and also requiring owners to provide testing for lead in painted surfaces, particularly heavily contacted or moving surfaces that have the most potential for cracking and peeling, such as windows, window sills, doors, railings, banisters, and trim.

The penalties for noncompliance include heavy fines imposed against the owner and/or property manager. Complaints of possible exposure to lead-based paint, from current and former tenants, may lead to investigation by the EPA as well as the Housing and Urban Development (HUD) agency. If investigators are not satisfied that tenants have been presented the required disclosure form and associated pamphlet, a notice of noncompliance will be sent to the landlord. In addition, the following fines and penalties may be imposed:

- A civil penalty of up to $11,000 per violation.

- A criminal penalty of up to $11,000 per violation.

- An order of restitution of up to three times the actual damage to each affected victim.

Electromagnetic Fields

Electromagnetic fields (EMFs) are an environmental hazard whose present danger and potential danger are not fully understood. EMFs are forces that result from the generation of electricity. One of the premises studied suggests that the EMFs may be the cause of cancer, particularly childhood leukemia. Though science is able to detect the presence of EMFs, there is no conclusive evidence that the EMFs cause cancer. EMFs may be released from power lines, transformers, electrical wirings, and appliances. EMFs are also present in the human body. If a tenant believes EMFs are having an effect, he or she has no recourse but to move. The property manager has a responsibility to inform the tenant on the current state of EMFs, but the property manager has no authority to insist that power lines and transmitters be relocated. The property manager must judge the validity of the tenant complaint and make a decision as to whether to release the tenant from his or her lease or rental obligations.

Trash Removal

Trash-removal methods must be understood as they vary by state, county, and community. In some jurisdictions, trash removal is included as part of government services. In other jurisdictions, trash removal is provided at cost. Some cities offer recycling programs in which recyclable waste is removed free while all other trash is removed at cost. Those tenants who practice recycling have a decreased supply of trash, and thus, a reduced cost for trash removal.

Purchase

The purchase of management property may include the purchase of vacant properties or functioning residential, commercial, or industrial properties. The investor is expected to have performed all research and analysis to be able to determine the use and rent for a particular property in order to place limits on the purchase amount. The acquisition of previously held rental properties, particularly multiple-unit properties, should include a rent roll, which specifies the amount and duration of rent for each unit for some specified length of time. Before investing dollars into the purchase of real estate, the investor must understand who should be engaged in the process and the role those parties play in the acquisition of property. Real estate agents, attorneys, accountants, and financial advisors play a role in the purchase of management property, but each has its own separate and distinct functions.

The Real Estate Agent

Only a broker is licensed to buy and sell properties. A real estate agent is a salesperson who does the legwork on behalf of the broker. Brokers obtain and share property information, which is listed and available through the agent's multiple-listing service (MLS) books. These books offer the advantage of reducing the time and expense necessary to research potential properties. An investor should allow the agent to do the initial screening of properties to narrow down the numerous offerings that fit his or her discussed needs and requirements. Real estate agents warehouse property information provided by community groups and leaders. They are also a resource of information about goods, services, and home maintenance providers in the community, such as plumbers, roofers, suppliers of home and garden equipment, and insurance agents.

114

When seeking a real estate agent to assist in the acquisition or sale of property, the investor should seek a dedicated agent who offers an exclusive buyer arrangement. The dedicated agent may have more concern and interest in satisfying the investor's requirements than a large prestigious agency that would probably do well with or without a particular investor's business. Most large agencies assign agents on a rotating basis and take no consideration for a client's particular needs. The investor should:

- Talk with many agents before making a commitment to assess the differences in what the various agents have to offer.

- Choose an agent with whom he or she is comfortable.

- Choose an agent who understands the needs and requirements of the business.

- Choose an agent familiar with the potential property or community of interest.

- Be honest about finances, remain loyal to the agent, and expect loyalty in return.

Services provided by real estate agents should be paid for as they are used. Brokers and real estate agents are hired to act on behalf of sellers and receive fees from the sale of the property. Real estate agents offer products and services to the buyer that may save the buyer valuable time in acquiring real estate. An investor should only pay for such services when they are needed.

The Attorney

In real estate purchases, the role of the attorney is to assist and advise in the closing of real estate transactions. The attorney must be:

- Trained in real estate law and contracts.

- Competent to read and interpret laws and regulations to develop contracts or interpret contracts on behalf of the investor.

- Knowledgeable of both the real estate and the tax laws that govern the jurisdiction where the property is housed.

- Trusted to handle partnership agreements and other legally binding documents that form the foundation of property investment groups.

The attorney is the overseer of all other parties in the business. If the accountant, for example, makes a mistake that results in a legal dispute, the attorney's expertise will be needed to defend the action in a court of law. The attorney should act as a partner and be accessible when an investor is seeking his or her services. The attorney or law firm that is overwhelmed with cases or does not exercise good time-management may not be the lawyer to pursue. An investor must investigate and evaluate the particular attorney who will handle his or her affairs, not the employing law firm. The investor should ask for references, specific to the particular lawyer, not the entirety of the law firm. Contact with previous clients of the attorney will provide insight into the attorney's response times, fees, and dedication to seeing cases through to their close.

Attorney fees should be established and documented before

bringing the attorney onboard. The attorney should clarify the type and extent of services to be rendered for a fee. Exceptions to service fees, which require additional fees, should be explained and documented to the investor's understanding. The investor should feel comfortable that the attorney is honest and willing to abide by established fees. An investor's inquiry into fees charged for service should not violate the attorney's time or cause the attorney to become defensive.

In all purchase transactions, the investor should allow time to get the attorney's approval or disapproval before closing deals. A transaction that is so rushed that it does not allow for the attorney to review and evaluate may be a transaction that the investor is better off not pursuing. The attorney is trained to seek out ambiguities and omissions in the legal jargon of real estate contracts.

Investors may consider acquiring membership in one of the many pre-paid legal service companies. Pre-paid legal services are actually organizations with a network of lawyers, law firms, and clients. Clients are assigned attorneys from the network of lawyers and law firms as needed. For a membership fee, usually collected monthly, an investor may acquire legal services for the term of his or her membership. Rather than the traditional fee-for-service client-attorney relationship, pre-paid legal services offer legal services at a flat rate. The flat rate covers most legal expenses without incurring additional charges. However, the type and extent of services may vary based on the particular law firm, type of membership, and state regulations. Members must be careful to understand and obtain written documentation specifying the extent of services and any stipulations with regard to covered and uncovered services. Some basic considerations for selecting prepaid legal services include:

- The length of membership commitment. Some companies may offer month-to-month memberships while others may require a commitment for one year or some other specified time frame.

- Whether the organization networks with attorneys experienced in real estate laws.

- The organization's policy for clients who are dissatisfied with services. Investors may find it more cost effective to limit services to less complicated legal issues.

- The organization's policy for changing the appointed legal firm. Investors should feel confident that the organization offers a good fit and that personnel are responsible to meet the needs of their particular situations.

- Whether the network of attorneys is in good standing with local bar associations and the Better Business Bureau (BBB).

The Accountant

An accountant is an employee of a business who is responsible for using business records of income and disbursements to analyze recorded actions. The accountant must be able to interpret such analysis to the understanding of the employer. An accountant differs from a bookkeeper in that the bookkeeper tabulates income as it is received and expenses as they are paid. Bookkeeping is simply a tallying of values for completed events. A landlord generally performs the bookkeeping of rental properties. An accountant ensures that expenses are properly allocated to necessities of the business and ensures that taxes are properly filed, with assets properly depreciated. An accountant needs to have access to data provided by the bookkeeper in order to properly evaluate the necessity of expenses and the sufficiency of income in supporting the business. As such, an accountant needs to have knowledge of real estate accounting, real estate transactions, and real estate law. The accountant has the responsibility to understand real estate laws and regulations that govern the jurisdiction in which the property is located and be able to translate, to the landlord, the effects that changing regulations have on current and future business operations. A good accountant will evaluate and analyze the following activities:

- Tax preparation

- Bookkeeping and recordkeeping processes

- Business and personal insurance coverage

- Financial loan statements

- Estate and retirement plans

The accountant must be able to produce a number of financial forms that financially describe the business or specific aspects of the business. Four primary forms are of particular interest and need to be understood by property owners and managers:

1. **Income statement**
   The income statement is also referred to as a profit and loss statement. This statement should be made available on at least a quarterly basis. The values in this statement should reflect revenue and expenses as provided to the accountant by the bookkeeper.

2. **Balance sheet**

   The balance sheet indicates currently held assets and liabilities of the business and should also be made available on at least a quarterly basis. The balance sheet provides a financial snapshot of the business at a specified time.

3. **Cash flow analysis**

   A cash flow analysis compares the revenues generated by the business against revenue dispensed by the business to determine if and how much profit is generated by the business.

4. **Asset ratio**

   The asset ratio compares current assets that could be liquidated against liabilities that can be eliminated within a one-year time frame.

The accountant should be able to provide sound judgment as well as good credit and investment advice. A good accountant is objective, listens to ideas, and offers the pros and cons of those ideas. The accountant should not dictate, but advise, even when the advice is in conflict with the hopes and expectations of the employer. The property management accountant's responsibilities are to analyze the financial aspects of the company, which requires cooperation on behalf of the owner and property manager, and to provide accurate data that detail the following:

- Earnings

- State and federal tax payments and the dates paid

- Tax records for at least the past five years

- Closing or escrow documents for newly acquired or sold properties

- Cost of any property improvements

- Securities sold, along with costs, proceeds, and the dates of purchase or sale

- Itemized expenses, such as loan interest, maintenance expenses, and contributions to charitable organizations

- A listing of income, expenses, and losses that are of question or not understood

Because the accountant must be as competent as a lawyer with regard to real estate and tax laws, it may seem logical to have the business attorney handle the business accounting. There are lawyers who are competent accountants and vice versa. However, it is best to have an accountant who is a separate individual from the attorney, though it is always good if the two parties are able to work together. As part of his or her professional business function, a good accountant will provide necessary documentation on at least a quarterly basis and check with the business periodically to ensure that agreed-upon business practices are being followed and that necessary documents are being filed and submitted with necessary parties. This would be an additional challenge for most law firms, and the challenge, most likely, would be evidenced in the fee charged to perform such services. Furthermore, when an accountant makes an accounting mistake, the lawyer is likely to catch the mistake in the process of performing his or her duties. When the lawyer and accountant are one and the same, it is more likely that mistakes will go undetected. Having separate and distinct individuals to perform legal and accounting functions provides the business with a built-in system of checks and balances. In the complex world of real estate, two heads are better than one.

The chosen accountant should be a human being, not a technological innovation. Many of the software packages, advertised as virtual accountants, cannot perform the functions required of an accountant. Software programs are developed months or years before they are released. They are most often provided for universal use and must incorporate laws and regulations specific to each country, state, city, and other municipality within each of these subdivisions. It is an awesome task to interpret and program software to be so efficient. Eventually, software companies will incorporate changes in laws and regulations and provide users with updates to their software packages. However, good accounting is dependent upon analysis, forecasting, and planning. A good accountant needs to be aware of changes in real estate laws and taxes as they are being implemented, and it is best that the accountant is aware of potential changes that are in the planning stages for jurisdictions. No computer software can incorporate this type of real estate "intelligence."

Technology, however, has provided for computers and computer software to simplify bookkeeping functions that were traditionally handled by paper, pencil, and ledgers. Computer software is available to perform all types of bookkeeping functions, and the various programs require various levels of expertise. The chosen software program should match the skill level of the individual chosen to handle bookkeeping functions. When property managers or bookkeepers are new to computer software or indecisive about which program to purchase, a good rule of thumb is to choose the program that other business partners and colleagues are using. If problems arise, there is someone readily available to assist with resolving problems.

Again, two heads are better than one. Also, it is much simpler to exchange information between like and compatible software programs. One of the most overlooked aspects of computer programs is the licensing of the software. If the business needs to have multiple versions of a bookkeeping program or other software stored on multiple computers, the buyer must be sure to check that licensing permits more than one installation of the program. Some perceivably low-cost software solutions are supported by expensive licensing schemes. Buyers must be sure to check the licensing requirements before investing in a software package.

The Financial Advisor

A financial advisor is an employee of a business with the responsibility of advising on banking and financial issues. A financial advisor is separate and distinct from a banker or lender. The lender is responsible for lending money or leveraging financing so that the bank receives its expected return on the investment. The lender's primary interest in the purchase of management property is in determining whether the borrower fits the profile of a good risk. Some lenders do offer and advertise financial advisement services, but those services are often limited to investments in stocks, bonds, retirement accounts, and mutual funds. Property owners and property managers need to seek financial advice as it relates to real estate. References and credentials should be requested and investigated before selecting a financial advisor.

A good financial advisor will extend advice beyond financing and leveraging to buy and sell residential, commercial, or industrial real estate. A good financial advisor will provide advice on other types of investment opportunities and investments in the stocks and bonds of companies either directly or indirectly involved in the acquisition, use and sale of land, and structures. Other types of companies that may offer opportunities for investment include:

- Builders

- Developers

- Building suppliers

- Mortgage insurers

- Bankers

- Insurance companies

- Railroads

- Farming

- Forestry

- Mining

- Oil development

- Gas development

- Real estate investment trust funds

- Real estate partnerships

A financial advisor may also offer advice for investments outside of the real estate industry. Other outside investment considerations include:

- Government-issued and government-backed securities

- Privately held securities

- Publicly held securities

- Mutual funds

- Trusts

Though a good financial advisor is able to advise on financial and banking issues, property owners and property managers should seek to network with other professionals in the real estate industry. Other experts and professionals outside of paid accountants, attorneys, and financial advisors may offer different opinions based on lessons learned and firsthand knowledge acquired. They may offer insight into issues specific to the area in which the real estate property or investment company is located. Outside professionals may also be retained as consultants or sought as mentors if it is economically feasible.

The Contract

The contract agreement for the sale or acquisition of rental property is more complex than the contract for buying retail merchandise. Even so, the contract serves the same purpose: to establish an agreement between the buyer and seller. The contract for the sale of property is only valid when specific elements are clearly defined, as follows:

- The contact must specify the offer made by the buyer to the seller. The offer specifies the amount to be paid and the terms of the payment. The buyer has the option of either accepting the offer as is, rejecting the offer, or making a counteroffer.

- Both parties must indicate an acceptance to the finalized

125

terms of the contract agreement by including their signatures in the appropriate places.

- The contract must specify that signatures reflect those of individuals with legal competence. A minor child or mentally challenged adult cannot sign a contact; a legally authorized representative may sign on their behalf.

- The contract must specify the consideration paid or exchanged for the property. Consideration can be money, land, or other thing of value being exchanged for the property.

- The contract must specify the legal purpose or legitimate use of the property. A property cannot be sold for the purpose of performing an illegal activity or running an illegal business.

- The terms and conditions of the contract must be specified as written documentation. The contract cannot be supplemented, legally, by verbal contracts and handshake deals.

- The description of the property must be specified as a legal property description, specifying the address, relative location, and any attached items.

More specific basic requirements include:

- An agreement of parties specifies that the contract and the contract addenda embody the totality of the agreement and no other agreements will have an effect on the contract.

- The date of possession indicates the specific date that

the new owner will take possession of the property. Normally, the date of possession occurs after the transfer of deed and payment to the seller. The date of possession is negotiable as specified, typically in an owner's use and occupancy clause. This type of clause is subject to holdback; money to be paid once certain events have occurred. When the seller cannot guarantee a date of possession, the new owner may provide the seller with a window of opportunity to vacate the property. The clause allows the new owner to charge a daily fee to the seller for each day of occupancy within the window.

- The terms of financing indicate the terms of the mortgage used to acquire the property, if financed. The terms include the amount financed, interest rate applied, amortization schedule, and balloon period, if applicable. If the property is paid for in cash, the cash payment will be noted. Also, if seller financing is being used, the terms of that financing are specified.

- A consult-your-attorney section is used to advise both parties to the contract to seek the advice and expertise of an attorney before signing and indicating an acceptance of the contract. This section specifies that real estate agents are not to give legal advice or act as a substitute for a professional attorney.

- An attorney-approval clause provides time for the buyer's attorney to review the contract.

- The attorney's fee stipulates that legal and court costs are to be paid by the party that prevails in any legal action involving the contract.

- An inspection-period clause specifies a window of

opportunity for the buyer to have the property inspected before making a final commitment. Buyers may perform their own inspections or hire the services of a professional inspector. The professional inspector will perform a thorough analysis of the property's conditions and document his findings. Further negotiations may be initiated based on the information provided by the property inspector. When financing is used for the purchase of property, the lender may require any defects reported by the inspector to be corrected before committing to the financing of the property. The seller is required to make repairs based on the inspection unless both parties agree to do otherwise. In some instances, the buyer is refunded the cost of making such repairs.

- The closing date specifies the date on which the buyer makes payment and the seller transfers deed to the property. The closing date is the day of transfer of ownership.

- An earnest money consideration is required as a deposit on the property. Earnest money is paid to the seller as acceptance and commitment to the contract offer. Earnest money does not necessarily have to be in the form of currency. It may be anything of value that both parties agree on. The seller may require the totality of earnest money upon acceptance of the contract or the seller may allow for payments of earnest money during the elapsed time between acceptance of the contract and closing of the sale.

- A title policy is necessary to ensure that no outstanding liens or other debts are held against the property. A title company performs the title search and issues the title policy as specified in the contract. Should the title company find outstanding debts against the property, the debts will have to be resolved before closing on the property. If the debts are not resolved at closing, the buyer assumes the debt. When no debts are found, the title policy protects the buyer against any debts that may arise after closing.

• The broker's fee is specified when a broker is used in the buying and selling process.

• A special provisions section is used to outline anything that falls outside of the standard provisions of the contract. A commonly used provision states that the agreement is contingent upon the sale of the buyer's house. This provision is tricky because it allows the buyer to opt out of the agreement for any number of reasons under the auspices that the buyer could not find a buyer for his or her house.

• Settlement charges are unique to the state and jurisdiction in which the property is located. Some charges that are to the benefit of the buyer and typically paid by the buyer, include the appraisal fee, points, mortgage recording fees, and deed preparation fees. Settlement charges requiring payment by the buyer in one jurisdiction may be required to be paid by the seller in another. Unless otherwise specified, the seller is required to pay the transfer tax on the sale of property.

• Prorations indicate costs and expenses of the property that are prorated as of the date of transfer of ownership. Typical costs that are prorated include the property taxes, maintenance fees, association fees, rental income, and other income of the property. Costs are prorated on a daily basis. The amount of expense or income is determined by dividing the expense amount by the number of days of the year to achieve a daily amount. The buyer is required to pay expenses for each day in the year that has elapsed since the transfer or closing date. Likewise, the buyer is the recipient of all income received for the remaining days of the year.

- Casualty loss specifies that the seller is responsible for casualty losses that may occur before the actual transfer of ownership or closing. The seller is required to make repairs, necessitated by a casualty loss, before the closing date or some other mutually agreed-upon date. If repairs are not timely and to the satisfaction of the buyer, the buyer may break the contract and also receive a refund of the earnest money vested in the sale of the property.

- Dispute resolution may be provisioned through the services of an impartial third party as an alternative to the costly and extended time necessary to resolve disputes using the legal system.

- The escrow account is established to deposit the buyer's earnest money. An escrow agent, usually the title company, is required to secure earnest money on behalf of both parties. In the case of a dispute or break of contract, both parties must agree and sign to have the escrow agent release the money from escrow to the non-default party. If either party believes that the other is not entitled to the escrowed money, the party may refuse to sign for the escrow agent's release of the money. Under such circumstances, the disputing parties must resolve the issue either through arbitration or through the legal system.

- The federal tax requirement stipulates the collection of taxes by the federal government for a sale as specified by real estate and other applicable laws.

- A third-party financing addendum specifies that the buyer make reasonable efforts to obtain financing. The addendum outlines efforts to gain approval in greater detail than the contract itself. The addendum specifies terms and conditions required to secure conditional loans, VA loans, and Federal Housing Administration (FHA) loans.

- A loan assumption addendum specifies the conditions of assuming the preexisting loan of the seller. The addendum allows the seller to investigate the buyer's creditworthiness for assuming the loan. Most lenders include a due-on-sale clause that prevents the assumption of an existing loan. However, loan assumptions are possible and they may offer a cost-effective method of financing at a lower cost. Loan assumptions require review and approval by the lender. Upon approval, the lender may charge a loan origination fee, just as they would for a new loan, or the lender may adjust the interest rate of the assumed loan. Under these circumstances, the buyer may find it just as easy to secure a new loan.

Breaking the Broker's Contract

Breaking a contract to purchase real estate is a legitimate action when put into place at the appropriate time. It may have dire consequences for the buyer or seller who decides to terminate after appropriate windows of opportunity have closed. The contract should stipulate the seller's recourse in the case that the buyer breaks the contract. The stipulation may require that the buyer forfeit any money paid as earnest money in binding the contract agreement.

When a buyer engages in a contract to purchase real estate, windows of opportunity exist in which the buyer could consider breaking the contract. The buyer's windows of opportunity include:

- The attorney-approval period—The attorney may object to elements of the contract.

- The inspection period—The inspector's report may indicate structural or other deficiencies of the property that were not anticipated when engaging in the contract.

- When environmental audits indicate hazardous conditions that must be corrected in line with regulatory statutes greatly increasing the cost of developing the property.

- When a mortgage contingency is included and the buyer cannot obtain the specified financing.

If the buyer has no objection to any of the above, it is assumed that the buyer intends to move forward with satisfying the contractual obligations of the sale. If, however, the buyer does object to moving forward with the contract, the contract may be broken, but a seller's recourse may specify that the buyer forfeit any earnest money paid to the seller.

The seller of real estate is legally bound to the terms of a contract and carries a greater burden when he or she decides to break the contract. The seller may be court ordered to follow through on the contract or pay damages to the buyer. The seller is considered to have entered into a contract in good faith, but the buyer is entitled to earnest money paid and may also be entitled to collect interest on the amount.

Breaking the Seller's Contract

A seller-financing addendum is added to the sale contract when the seller is financing the sale of his or her own property. The addendum allows the seller to investigate the creditworthiness of the buyer and outlines the terms and conditions of the promissory note that will bind the sale of the property. A promissory note may provide for either a single balloon payment, payments amortized over some specified period of time, or interest-only payments. Interest-only payments convert to interest-plus-principal payments at some predetermined time, as defined and agreed upon by both parties to the contract. The promissory note must be complemented by a deed of trust, which specifies that the property be used as security for the outstanding debt owed to the seller for the property. A trustee, who is responsible to hold the property in trust for the parties of the sale, holds the deed of trust. The deed of trust may specify requirements for reselling a seller-financed property. The seller may allow the buyer to sell the property without the buyer's consent or the seller may require consent before a resale of the property.

The seller is recommended to make use of established practices used by lenders and mortgage companies. The seller may grant or deny an assumption of the loan by another buyer. It is recommended that the seller add a due-on-sale clause that requires that the total of the sale price be paid in full before a resale of the property. This will effectively eliminate any right to loan assumptions. The seller may also include a provision that requires the buyer to pay taxes and insurance of the property into an escrow account. If this provision is not established, the seller must establish a method of determining whether the buyer is making such payments and ensure that they do not become delinquent. As with mortgage companies, the seller may prevent the borrower from paying taxes outside of an escrow account unless the borrower has established less than 80 percent loan-to-value (LTV) ratio, which is equivalent to having invested at least 20 percent of the property's value in the property.

Jon A. Marchant
Marchant Chapman Realtors
780 Sir Francis Drake Blvd.
San Anselmo, CA 94960
415-451-1474
415-456-8393 Fax
jon@marchantchapman.com

I started in real estate by working in my parents' and grandparents' real estate business, and I eventually took over the rentals my family owned. From there, I developed a management division of the company. Today, I manage approximately 300 units in 175 residential properties. I sell a few of my managed properties each year, and I run a sales office with ten agents and the management.

My main goal as a residential property manager is to respond to service requests quickly and effectively. Most of the calls we get relate to appliance and plumbing problems, a few leaky roofs, obnoxious neighbors, and the odd floor here and there. By the end of the day after the tenant's call, he should either have the problem solved or have an appointment for the vendor to take care of it.

I also set property rents which I determine from my general knowledge of the market combined with research of the competition, which I do by reading classified ads and by browsing through the ads on craiglist.com.

As a residential manager, I must ensure I minimize my risks. For example, I use competent repair people I trust. In addition, to maximize profits, I raise rents with the market and don't allow management rates to get too low. Most owners aren't price shopping managers: they want quality.

Of course, another important aspect of property management is managing finances. We pay taxes on most of our rental properties. We start planning a month before they are due, in case we need money from the owner. Toward the end of the month, my bookkeeper goes to the tax collector with the bills and a check, and she receives a receipt for each property.

We use Yardi Property Management Software, and

don't utilize a CPA except for an occasional spot check to keep the staff honest. The CPA also prepares our corporate taxes.

When I first started in real estate, I took over a lot of neglected properties with below-market rents. Of course, plenty of people gave me advice when I was new to the field, but I ignored it. I'm still learning that letting tenants get behind on their rent is no favor to them. It almost never gets better, and it just makes their debts bigger.

The best advice I can give newcomers is: Don't let a few demanding owners take over your life and your business unless they are big enough clients that you can't live without them. About ten years ago, I fired approximately five percent of my owners. Afterward, I discovered I had at least 30 percent more time to do other things. If the owners take too much time or energy, I explain that the arrangement isn't working for me and ask them to take their business elsewhere. Don't be afraid to trade a few bucks a month for greater peace of mind.

You also don't want to let tenants get behind on the rent. It only makes it harder and more expensive in the long run. Even the best tenants can go bad, and it's no kindles to send them off with a huge money judgment hanging over them.

Finally, watch out who controls the books and signs the checks. If an owner's account runs out of money, be clear that no bills will be paid until you get your money.

5

CHAPTER FIVE

Property Maintenance

A good property manager will retain maintenance workers who will be available before problems occur. The best plan for maintenance involves making prompt repairs to maintain the entire property and promptly maintaining and repairing individual units to keep them safe and habitable for tenants. Tenants will expect a response to emergency situations as well as small repairs. Property managers should establish policies for dealing with a variety of maintenance situations to include the following:

Emergency Maintenance

Emergency requests for maintenance may occur at any time, day or night. Emergency situations require immediate response from the landlord or repairperson. Property managers must determine if the situation warrants an immediate response and from whom. The objective is to minimize the endangerment to occupants in and near the property as well as damage to the property or nearby properties. Tenants should be provided with procedures or processes to follow in emergency situations before move-in. Tenants should be made aware of shut-off locations for utilities, processes necessary to shut them off, and situations that may warrant shutting them off. Without this information, the landlord may find himself or herself having to get up in the middle of the night to shut off a water valve or, even worse, paying a plumber to perform emergency services that could have been eliminated by shutting off a leaking valve.

Preventive Maintenance

Preventive maintenance requires routine inspections of rental units to locate potential sources of repair or replacement. Preventive-maintenance programs will extend the operating life of the property and its units by addressing minor problems before they escalate into major problems.

- Service contracts for major appliances and equipment, which include routine maintenance, provide cost-effective preventive maintenance. The cost savings for service contracts are realized in the increased life of appliances and equipment as well as savings on the repair or service of covered units.

- In areas of the country where temperatures fall below freezing, property managers should require that tenants maintain a minimum temperature inside of the rental unit to prevent the freezing of water pipes that may burst and create major damage.

Corrective Maintenance

Corrective maintenance is the necessary maintenance required when things break or fail. Tenants are aware of the fact that things break. Tenants also expect responsible preventive maintenance to reduce the number and frequency of such situations. Tenants will appreciate a timely response from the property manager.

Custodial Maintenance

Custodial maintenance involves maintaining the curb appeal of the property and its grounds. When the tenant is not responsible for lawn maintenance, for example, the property manager is expected to perform routine grass cuttings and shrub trimming without the tenant having to request such services. Every tenant wants to approach a property that is presentable, with clean painted surfaces, free of holes and graffiti. Trash and garbage are, in most cases, the responsibility of the individual tenant. When excessive garbage is dumped on the property, the tenant expects the property manager to put some type of controls in place to prevent it.

Cosmetic Maintenance

Cosmetic maintenance involves improving and upgrading the interior of rental units. Some local jurisdictions may require cosmetic maintenance, but, housing laws in general, do not require it. Cosmetic maintenance, such as painting surfaces or updating equipment, may improve tenant retention, reduce vacancies, and increase the return on investment.

Building Relationships

Developing a relationship with a handyman, plumbing company, electrician, etc., is a key to great maintenance care of the property. Once you have built these relationships, should an emergency arise, the property manager will have confidence that the emergency call will be answered, even in the middle of the night or a holiday. The property manager will also be more confident about the quality of the work done if it is someone with whom they have spent time building a good working relationship. Another option is realizing that many property management companies have their own maintenance companies. These companies will often do work for other property managers. Since they work for a property management company, they will have the expertise with rental property a manager may not find with other contractors.

Wendy Frenzel

e-PRO A Vantage Properties
200 South Wilcox Street #172
Castle Rock, CO 80104
Phone: 303-621-9262
Fax: 303-539-9820
AVP@AVantageProperties.com
http://avantageproperties.com

My background is actually in teaching. When we moved to Colorado, I taught computers to preschoolers. However, I would often go to the property manager of our community to ask why she did this or why she did that. I think she got tired of my questions because she asked me to come work for her in a new position, within the community, of Community Liaison. When the community was sold, my job was eliminated, so I went to work in the residential screening industry. A client asked me to come work for him, which led me to managing single family homes.

I currently specialize in residential management, focusing my energy on it full-time, and I manage 50 Door single family homes. With HOA management, we have 450 Doors. To determine the monthly rental rates, I take two factors into consideration – what the owners want and what the market will bear.

Most of our homes are newer (less than five years old), so we have very few complaints. The biggest complaint is renters who want to purchase the home they are currently renting. To keep our tenants satisfied, we send out monthly statements to let them know what's going on; they can visit our website to contact us, and we have a live person answering phones 24 hours a day, seven days a week.

When I first started, one of the biggest issues I quickly faced was in Colorado there is no set management agreement or leasing agreement, so a lot has to come from what I know or what others will share. Since I belonged to the National Association of Residential Property Managers (NARPM), however, there really isn't anything that I missed informational wise. If someone isn't a part of this group, I would highly recommend finding a chapter as members are willing to share.

CLASSIFIED CASE STUDIES
directly from the experts

To minimize risk, it's critical to document, document,

document. E-mail whenever possible so there is a record. Alternately, to maximize my rental management profits, I've found the keys to success are having a portable office, working smarter and not harder with systems in place, and hiring specialists to help when needed.

The owners handle taxes on their rental properties; however, I use Promas software for the accounting and tracking, and Outlook, Word, and PDF programs that allow for items to be PDF fileable for management agreements.

For those interested in managing rental properties, ask questions of others in the business. Be ready to be on call 24 hours a day, seven days a week. Look for new technology that will help you to work smarter, not harder.

6

CHAPTER SIX

Renting Management Property

The best time to rent management property is during the months of June and July, followed by the months of May and August. April and September are the third best months, while the month of December is the worst month. (Thomas, S. 2005) Prospective tenants will want to see the property before making a decision to rent. Most tenants will call in response to an advertisement to verify that the conditions are as specified in ads and also to inquire about things that are not specified. The property manager has several options with respect to the inquiry phone call before actually showing the property.

The property manager could use this opportunity to speak with the prospective tenant, pre-screen, and offer an opportunity to view the property. The exchange of information during the phone conversation should eliminate prospective tenants who discover that they cannot meet the conditions specified, such as the unit being out of their price range or utility costs not included in the rent. This exchange of information will also allow the property manager to assess the qualifications of the prospective tenant. A qualified tenant should:

- Meet the requirements for income and employment.

- Have a satisfactory credit rating.

- Be able to pay the security deposit and first month's rent in advance.

- Have an acceptable rental history.

- Vacate current living accommodations legally.

- Be satisfied with the type and size of the unit.

- Be satisfied with the limit on number of occupants.

- Be satisfied with guidelines established for pets, smoking, and so on.

In the process of obtaining information with regard to these qualifications, both the property manager and tenant will be better able to assess whether the unit meets the tenant's need before scheduling a showing of the property.

The property manager could also make use of technology, with the use of voice mail or the Internet, to provide callers with information, instructions, and times for future communication. Voice mail and the Internet provide methods of describing the same features and benefits of the property to all prospective tenants. If interested, prospective tenants may leave messages and contact information for the property manager. The Internet offers the additional convenience of being able to visually display properties to allow prospects to assess whether the property meets their needs. Even with the technological advances in describing properties, most prospective tenants prefer to speak to someone before venturing out to inspect a property. To keep prospective tenants interested, the property manager must be available at times specified in voice mail messages or posted on the Internet. If a prospect provides contact information, the property manager should be sure to reply, as the potential tenant may not attempt to make a second contact. Once the contact is made, an appointment can be made to show the property.

If the property manager intends to hold an open house, the initial contact may be used to provide callers with time, location, and directions to an open house for the property. Many property managers attempt to conserve time by eliminating an initial phone conversation and requiring all interested tenants to view the property in some specified time interval during an open house. An open house offers the property manager the advantage of being able to host minimal showings at his or her convenience. The disadvantage is that many prospective tenants are not receptive to being forced to see properties that they know little about. In addition, the property manager may find that the open house attracts only a few or no participants or that the participants are not qualified to rent the property. Open houses are best reserved for pre-qualified tenants.

Showing

Phone contacts should allow prospective tenants to determine the fit of the property beyond that which could be determined by advertisement. If the property manager is successful in answering inquiries about the specifics of the property and the prospective tenant feels that the property presents a good fit, the next step is for the prospective tenant to tour the property for a visual inspection or showing.

Different methods apply to showing occupied properties as opposed to showing unoccupied properties. The law requires property managers to provide tenants of occupied properties with an advanced notice of intent to show the property. Most states give the property manager the right to enter and show occupied properties if a 30-day notice to vacate the property has been issued by either party or when the occupants are nearing the end of their lease. In some states, tenants are able to waive the right to be notified, but the landlord must be sure to have the signed waiver in hand when entering the premise for a showing. The law, however, does not require the tenant to clean the property or otherwise assist the property manager in impressing potential tenants. Different states may have differing requirements; as such, the property manager should be sure to check the requirements that apply to that particular property. If the tenant is leaving on bad terms or being evicted, it may be best to wait until the tenants have vacated the property before showing it. Likewise, it may be best to wait for tenants who have not cared for their units and/or furnishings to vacate the property before showing it. Tenants in these circumstances are not likely to assist the property manager in impressing the new tenants.

Unassisted Showings

Property managers may hold unassisted showings, where a prospective tenant is given either a key to the property or combination to a lockbox that contains a key to the property. This allows the prospective tenant to tour the property on his or her own. This type of showing is commonplace for large apartment complexes where turnover rates are high. After a pre-screening process, the management company provides the prospective tenant with keys to vacant properties and waits for the prospective tenant to make a final decision about the fit of the property before moving further in the rental process. Unassisted showings present some risks to the property since the prospective tenant is usually allowed unsupervised access to the property. Property managers should engage in this type of showing after securing a rental application and other sources of personal information from the prospective tenant, such as a driver's license and vehicle tag number. Should any damage or destruction occur during the unsupervised tour, the property manager has the necessary information to pursue civil or criminal charges for damages. Another option is to request a cash deposit or other collateral as an incentive to have the prospective tenant return the key. This type of showing offers the additional benefit of bringing the prospective tenant within proximity of the property, allowing an opportunity to make a visual inspection of the exterior and its surroundings before actually touring the interior of the property. If a prospective tenant is not satisfied with the exterior curb appeal, he or she is not likely to bother with securing the keys and will seek housing elsewhere. The property manager need not spend any more time on the potential tenant.

Open-House Showings

Open houses are a method of showing rental properties that generates interest from a variety of prospects, ranging from the curious to the qualified. Open houses are most beneficial when they are held to invite a large number of pre-qualified and interested prospective tenants. Rather than having to show the property for individual prospects, the property manager benefits by only having to show the property during the open-house period. Open houses are commonplace for newly established housing developments where a single or couple of units represent the housing development.

Individual Showings

Once a prospective tenant has committed to touring the

property, the property manager may offer an individual showing. The property manager should follow up with the prospect by making a final phone call on the day of the showing to verify that the prospect is actually planning to show up. This offers the advantage of making the prospect feel confident that the property manager is interested in securing him or her as a tenant. Property showings have a tendency to be delayed due to traffic congestion, confusing directions, or other circumstances. Property managers may have to schedule multiple showings within a day's time, and prospects may be trying to fit the showing within their busy schedules. The final phone call may make a difference in determining whether either party waits beyond the scheduled time frame to complete the showing. The showing should be a guided tour where the prospect is not wandering aimlessly throughout the property. The property manager should know the property and point the prospect in the direction of the important features of the unit, particularly those specified in advertisements and those specifically questioned previously by the prospective tenant. The property manager should provide a tour of the property in its entirety. This includes any exterior accommodations such as outdoor pools, garages, and storage.

TIP: Property managers should be cautious of meeting the prospect in secluded or vacant lots as they are strangers to them. Unfortunately, we are not guaranteed safety with people and a few options for rectifying what could be a potentially dangerous situation are: don't meet after dark; bring a friend, colleague, or family member along; be sure someone knows where you will be, the time of the meeting, and who the meeting is with. Another good idea may be to speak with other property managers about how they handle these types of showings and come up with the best strategy for you.

Renting and Leasing

Completing the Application

A completed rental application should be a collection of all information necessary to screen and select a qualified tenant. To safeguard against claims of discrimination, the property manager should provide an application to each prospective tenant who makes a request. An application should be provided for and completed by each applicant of legal age, 18 and over. The application should indicate the number of occupants and include the following information about each adult occupant:

- Work history

- Source of income

- Rental history

- Credit information

- References

The property manager should make it clear to the tenant that submission of the application does not mean acceptance to rent the property. The application should include permission to perform the necessary screening of personal information provided in the application. To guard against having to process applications from tenants who have no real intent to rent the property, the property manager should request and include an application fee to subsidize the cost of processing the application.

Screening

The information provided in the rental application should be comprehensive enough to perform a thorough screening of the potential tenant. Though screening will not guarantee a good tenant; it will increase the odds of getting a good and stable tenant. Property managers should develop and document a systematic screening process that is applicable to all prospects and adheres to all applicable laws, particularly laws regarding discrimination. Though the law does not require it, prospective tenants should be provided with a rental policy that outlines the screening criteria. That way, each tenant knows that he or she is subjected to the same rules and criteria.

The screening process can be time consuming, requiring contact with a variety of individuals. Some individuals may be receptive to inquiries, others not. Still others may not be willing to provide information over the phone and will respond only to written requests. Property managers should be prepared to issue written requests for information. To expedite the process, it is a good idea to include a self-addressed stamped envelope along with the request.

The Internet offers automated methods of quickly retrieving information that was traditionally acquired through verbal and written communication. There is a wealth of companies offering complete screening services, with results provided within hours or days, depending on the request. Credit reports, tenant histories, and criminal background checks are available within seconds over the Internet. The information, however, is only as accurate as the data-entry procedures and databases that support them. Online screening services offer to objectively evaluate applications and make decisions about accepting and declining tenants. Most services use a point system to rank applicants against minimum requirements, thereby developing their own definitions of financial stability, risks, and other devised factors. There are no laws governing these services.

The property manager should check with the appropriate state agency to ensure that the practices used by these companies not do violate laws with respect to discrimination. Screening processes involve verifying the following information about prospects:

- **Identification**
  The property manager should meet each prospective tenant and photocopy his or her driver's license or other acceptable forms of photo ID. If the information on the photo ID does not match the information provided on the rental application, the property manager should request and document any responses to the discrepancy. This type of discrepancy may be the result of a prospect moving before needing to renew the photo ID or it may indicate a problem tenant. Verification of other information contained in the application should be used to authenticate the identity of prospects.

- **References**
  Prospective tenants are most likely to provide references who will speak favorably of them. Property managers should make an attempt to contact the listed individuals; they may find that the listed references do not exist. On the other hand, the references may offer insight into the prospective tenant and assist in building a character profile.

- **Work history and income**
  Property managers should request the most recent pay stubs of all adult prospects. This information should be verified with the employer's human resource department. If a prospect indicates a weekly or monthly salary amount, the property manager must verify that

the presented salary is achievable for every month of the tenancy. If part-time, temporary, or seasonal salaries are provided, the property manager has to ascertain whether the salary is sufficient to meet rent requirements for the term of the lease. If the prospect's income is in some form other than salary, the property manager may request copies of income tax forms from previous years. The past two years is usually sufficient to determine if the prospect is able to meet rent requirements. Property managers are cautioned against prospective tenants who are able to put up cash for initial deposits but have no work history, as the prospect may be involved in illegal activities.

- **Credit history**
  An applicant's credit history is available through credit reports provided by the three established credit-reporting agencies: Experian, Equifax, and TransUnion. The credit report will indicate previous names and aliases, addresses, credit card standings, loan standings, bankruptcies, and other judgments. Credit reports can be obtained for as little as $15, with membership to a credit-reporting agency. Memberships require monthly fees, and they may not be cost effective to property managers unless they are responsible for multiple units and request one or more reports per month. Without membership, credit reports may range from $30 to $50. This fee is often incorporated in the rental application fee required of prospective tenants.

- **Rental history**
  Property managers should contact current and previous landlords to inquire about prospects. The information provided by previous landlords can be helpful, but

landlords are not exempt from dishonesty. If the landlord is upset that the tenant chose to vacate his or her property, he or she may give negative responses in an effort to keep the tenant from moving. On the other hand, the landlord could be trying to get rid of a problem tenant and offer positive responses in an effort to expedite the process. Property managers should consider and evaluate both sides of a situation. Some prospects may approach the property manager with letters of reference from previous landlords. A responsible property manager will engage in the necessary research to ensure that the documentation is valid and provided by a credible source.

• **Criminal history**
Most states do not require property managers to perform criminal background checks of tenants. Even with technological advances that provide immediate access to criminal records, states traditionally have not held accurate or up-to-date records and many only track felony records, not misdemeanors. Every county within every state offers a database search of criminal records in the range of $10 to $25 per county. However, only half of the states offer a statewide database search. When available, a statewide search ranges in cost between $5 and $11 per state. These searches may not offer a cost-effective method of screening applicants. A thorough screening would require a separate search for each state for each applicant. Many property managers effectively deal with this challenge by requesting rental applicants to indicate whether they have been convicted of felony or misdemeanor charges. If the applicant provides a positive response, criminal background checks can be performed, based on the information provided. Whatever

process the property manager chooses to engage in, it should be documented and systematically presented to all potential applicants.

Making the Decision

Property managers must choose among many potential applicants and comply with fair housing laws. Fair housing laws are established to protect renters against discrimination. In particular, the laws are designed to address two specific areas: 1) discriminatory treatment of protected classes and 2) familial status discrimination based on disparate impact. Protected classes include those categories of individuals who traditionally have faced discrimination based on the following:

- Race

- Color

- Religion

- National origin

- Sex

- Family status

- Physical handicap

- Mental handicap

Familial status applies to families with children. Prior to the 1980s, many rental property owners were allowed to categorize rental properties as "adults only" to limit or eliminate tenants with children. Other property owners used occupancy standards to avoid renting to families with

154

children. In some areas of the country, complaints for familial status discrimination have outnumbered complaints based on discrimination against all combined protected classes. Federal and state fair housing laws have since required most rental properties owners to rent to families with children. Only rental property owners who meet specific requirements established by HUD may offer "seniors only" rental property. A property must be documented and designated as exempt from renting to families with children.

The Fair Housing Act is included as Title VIII of the Civil Rights Act of 1968. The Fair Housing Act prohibits discrimination in the selling, financing, and renting of property to members of a protected class. The laws apply to the selling, financing, and renting of both structures and raw land.

The leasing and renting of property is considered to be a form of extending credit to individuals. As such, property managers and landlords must adhere to guidelines established by the 1976 Equal Credit Opportunity Act. This act prohibits the denial of such credit to the protected class as well as discrimination based on age or because an individual receives public assistance.

Because landlords and property managers make use of credit reports in qualifying prospective tenants, guidelines established by the Fair Credit Reporting Act must be adhered to. The Fair Credit Reporting Act establishes that only regulated agencies be entrusted to report on consumer credit, provide data to reporting agencies, and make use of consumer reports. Property managers and landlords who make use of software and computer programs for the screening, acceptance, or denial of applicants must ensure that the vendors of such services are able to meet the disclosure requirements of the Fair Credit Reporting Act. When it is determined that a prospective tenant is required to pay higher rental fees because of information contained in credit reports, the property manager must be sure to have secured the services of a software vendor that is able to provide the tenant with a detailed notice of denial. The methods used in denying tenants must meet the requirements of the Fair Credit Reporting Act.

Landlords and property managers are also required to comply with the guidelines established by the Americans with Disabilities Act. This act prohibits discrimination against both mentally and physically challenged individuals in both employment and housing. The act requires property managers to make rental properties accessible to disabled individuals when changes or modifications to achieve accessibility are practical and achievable.

To establish standards for landlords and tenants, each state has adopted some form of the Uniform Residential Landlord and Tenant Act. This act establishes that landlords cannot:

- Draft a clause eliminating tenant's rights under the act.

- Impose punishment, to include raising the rent, in retaliation for the tenant filing a claim against the landlord to a governing body.

- Enter into an unfair lease. Courts may refrain from enforcing leases or parts of leases that are found to be unfair.

This act also establishes that landlords can:

- Inspect the property along with the tenant, and both parties should sign a drafted inventory of the property within five days of rental.

- Deduct the cost of damages, repairs, and unpaid rent from the security deposit.

- Enter into a lease or rental agreement with an unsigned lease or agreement if either the landlord accepts payment or the tenant makes payment.

- Be held responsible for not maintaining a safe and habitable property.

- Enter into the property for reasonable repairs, maintenance, or showings with suitable prior notice.

- Seek the termination of leases for tenants who operate an unapproved business on the property.

- Seek compensation for damages, repairs, and legal action related to violations of unapproved businesses.

- Seek payment for rent when a tenant abandons the property.

- Be held liable for refusing to make reasonable repairs. The tenant may provide notice of termination and recover prepaid rent, the security deposit, damages, and legal fees.

- Be held liable for renting uninhabitable space. The tenant may provide notice of termination or deduct a portion of the rent as compensation for the loss of use.

There are many other state and local laws that apply to real estate, rental property, and rental property management. The list of applicable laws is too extensive and too complex to list here. This is why it is so important for managers and landlords to hire competent attorneys and accountants who keep the property-management business in compliance with applicable laws. When approving a chosen applicant, the property manager should contact the prospect, complete a walk-through of the unit, sign all necessary documents, and collect all required deposits before the lease is secured. Other potential tenants should not be rejected until all of the above have been completed and a move-in date is established.

Fair housing laws allow property managers to deny prospective tenants when they are incapable of meeting screening criteria. The screening criteria, however, must be fair and applicable to all prospective tenants. Violations of fair housing laws have produced court settlements in excess of $100,000. When a prospect's application is denied, the denial should be documented in writing and held by the property manager for at least three years. The letter of denial or letter of nonacceptance should indicate the reason for denial as well as the process to follow if the prospective tenant is in dispute of the information. A sample letter of nonacceptance is provided in Form 2.

Reason for Nonacceptance

From: _____

Date: _____

Dear:_____

Your request for tenancy has been denied for the reason(s) indicated below:

____Application incomplete   ____Unable to verify employment

____Insufficient credit references   ____Temporary or irregular employment

____Unable to verify credit references   ____Length of employment

____No credit file   ____Insufficient income

____Insufficient credit line   ____Unable to verify income

____Delinquent credit obligations   ____Bankruptcy

____Profit and loss account(s)   ____Previous eviction(s)

____Excessive obligations   ____Garnishment, foreclosure, or repossession

____We don't offer rentals on the terms   ____Too short a period of residence
       you have requested

                                      ____Because of negative information received
____Other   from third party listed below

Disclosure of Use of Information Obtained from Outside Source
(If you were turned down because of information provided by a third party, that party or agency is listed below.)

Information was obtained from: _____

                                     _____

                                     _____

Under the Fair Credit Reporting Act, you have the right to make a written request, within 60 days of receipt of this notice, for disclosure of the nature of the adverse information. The Federal Equal Credit Opportunity Act prohibits creditors from discriminating against credit applicants on the basis of race, color, religion, national origin, sex, marital status, age (provided the applicant has the capacity to enter into a binding contract), because all or part of the applicant's income derives from any public assistance program, or because the applicant has in good faith exercised any right under the Consumer Credit Protection Act. The federal agency that administers compliance with this law concerning creditors is the Federal Trade Commission, Equal Credit Opportunity, Washington, DC 20580.

Form 2: Letter of Nonacceptance (Taylor, p. 37)

Collecting Deposits

Some states have laws and regulations regarding the amount of deposits that may be collected for a rental property. The property manager should be sure to establish deposits that comply with applicable state laws. All states allow property managers to collect a security deposit, which is typically equal to one month's rent. The security deposit is money held by the landlord to cover losses due to unpaid rent or damage to the rental unit. Security deposits are refundable to the tenant upon vacating the property so long as the rent is paid and the property is not damaged. As such, the security deposit is a psychological tool used to ensure that the tenant pays the rent and maintains the property in a reasonable manner. The security deposit is different from the first month's rent that is typically charged to new tenants. A common lease deposit includes an amount equal to one month's rent for the security deposit, one month's rent paid in advance, and an additional half month's rent if the tenant has a pet. Some landlords, particularly those dealing with more high-risk tenants, may require both the first month's rent and last month's rent before move-in. The advantage is that the landlord has greater leverage with respect to losses. The disadvantage is that the landlord takes a loss if the rent increases during the tenant's tenure. Courts will likely take the position that the last month's rent is paid in full, even if the amount that was paid and documented as a deposit is less than the current rent. Some states allow landlords to collect nonrefundable deposits from new tenants to cover the cost of cleaning when a tenant vacates a property. This type of deposit may be counterproductive since the tenant cannot expect to recover the fee upon vacating the property, giving the tenant no incentive to maintain the property.

Deposits should be collected prior to the move-in date and distribution of keys. The landlord should request payment in the form of a cashier's check or money order. Cash is also an acceptable form of deposit, but the rental agreement should caution against any future cash payments. It is not uncommon for landlords who collect cash payments to become crime victims, particularly with door-to-door collections in multiple-unit properties. Personal checks also present a risk since personal checks can be drawn upon insufficient funds. Whatever form of payment is accepted, the tenant should be given a receipt.

Reviewing the Lease or Rental Agreement

The landlord must explain the lease or rental agreement and all of its clauses and addendums to the new tenant before the actual signing of the agreement. The landlord cannot assume that the tenant is aware of his or her practices because the tenant rented a similar unit or the tenant previously rented a property from the landlord. It is good policy to have the tenant initial clauses to indicate that they have read and understood them. Some important elements of an agreement that require explanation and understanding include:

- Environmental disclosure forms

- The installation of and safe operation of smoke detectors and other safety equipment

- Care and limitations for pets and animals

- Rent payments, non-sufficient fund charges, and late fees

- Cost and policies regarding lost and stolen keys as well

as lock changes

- Rules regarding utilities and their turn-on or cut-off

- Rules for the use of laundry facilities

- Rules for garbage and trash disposal

- Use of designated storage facilities

- Limits for occupants in the unit and all attached spaces, such as decks, pools, and yards

- Rules regarding disturbances and complaints

- Ordinary maintenance required of the tenant

- Excessive maintenance requests

- Property damage

- Lease terminations

- Move-out

- Security deposit

- Renter's insurance

Non-Rent Revenue

Though rent payments account for the majority of revenue collected from rental properties, the skilled property investor or manager may institute other means of generating revenue. By controlling and offering such amenities as laundry facilities, vending machines, parking, storage, and Internet access, the residential property investor or manager may generate substantial amounts of non-rent revenue. These types of amenities are also convenient for tenants and may attract and retain good tenants. The type and extent of non-rent revenue that may be generated is dependent upon the type of property being rented and the needs of the tenants. Non-rent amenities and services may be charged separate from rent or bundled together with the rent. The exclusion of such expenses from the rent payment gives the tenant an opportunity to engage such services on an as-needed basis and lowers the perceived cost of rent. Market conditions should be used in determining the method of charging for such services and amenities. Landlords may also offer tenant lease options that allow tenants to engage in rent-to-own agreements at an additional cost over that charged for a standard lease or rental agreement. The additional fee necessary to engage a tenant in lease options provides additional revenue for the landlord that increases cash flow.

Laundry Facilities

Laundry facilities offer a good opportunity for the landlord to generate non-rent revenue. Paid laundry facilities may be very effective and convenient for tenants of apartments or multiple family units. It is recommended that one washer and dryer be available for every eight to ten rental units. One of the biggest issues with paid laundry facilities is location. Tenants need to feel safe and secure while engaging such services. Also, when the facilities are not located in well-lit areas of the same or adjacent building, tenants are likely to opt for public laundry facilities instead. Property owners and managers may maintain their own laundry facilities or they may contract the service to an outside contractor. When the landlord is responsible for maintaining the laundry facility, he or she must bear the expense of purchasing and maintaining the equipment. Equipment maintenance could be very costly and time consuming for the landlord. As an alternative, the landlord may hire the services of a laundry contractor who installs, services, and collects revenue from the machines, or the landlord may lease equipment with a service contract and collect revenue on his or her own. The landlord must be sure to engage the services of licensed and bonded contractors to care for and properly maintain the equipment. When the equipment does not function, no revenue can be collected. When a garage, basement area, or other part of the rental property is converted into a laundry room, proper permits must be obtained from the local government before establishing the facility. Landlords may also increase rent revenue by charging higher rent for single-family rental homes that include a washer and dryer; however, he or she must ensure that the tenants are also able to pay the associated water and sewer bills.

The establishment of laundry facilities requires planning and research. The property manager may make use of coin-operated machinery or coinless machines that may be accessed with the use of smart cards. Coin-operated machines, traditionally used in laundry facilities, require the use and responsibility for cash by the tenants and facility operators. As such, coin-operated facilities are a source of crime that includes the robbery of tenants, laundry room personnel, and the machines themselves. Smart cards are a technological innovation that resembles a credit card. Smart cards have an embedded microchip that stores electronic information. The technology offers safety and security by not requiring tenants and personnel to engage in cash transactions or cash processing. The card is inserted into a card reader attached to a machine and the reader interprets information stored in the card's microchip. A personal identification number (PIN) must be entered before the machines will function. Smart cards offer better security than can be provided with lock-and-key systems, but smart-card systems are dependent upon tenants to be responsible for allowing, limiting, and denying access. Smart cards may be used to store a variety of information; as such, the same card could be used to gain access to the laundry facility as well as operate machines inside of the facility, inclusive of the washers, dryers, and vending machines. The disadvantage of smart-card systems is that functionality is dependant upon the real-time operation and functioning of a computer system. When the computer system fails, access to facilities and machines also fails.

Vending Machines

Vending machines offer additional revenue for property owners and managers when placed in safe and secure locations. The installation of vending machines must be properly researched and planned. Coin-operated vending machines are often the target of vandalism and petty crimes. Smart-card technology allows for the non-cash use of vending machines. To be effective, vending machines must be properly maintained and filled. Many instances of vandalism result from money lost to the machines. Property owners and managers may maintain their own vending machines or they may contract the services to an outside vendor. When the landlord is responsible for maintaining his or her own machines, he or she must bear the expense of purchasing and maintaining the machines, which could be very costly and time consuming. As an alternative, the landlord may engage the services of vendors that install, service, and collect revenue from the machines. The landlord may also lease equipment with a service contract and collect revenue on his or her own. The landlord must be sure to engage the services of a licensed and bonded contractor to care for and properly maintain the machines because no revenue can be collected when the machines are not functional.

Parking

Providing tenants with reserved parking can offer additional and lucrative non-rent revenues. In cities, particularly downtown areas, free parking can be limited or nonexistent. The property manager should offer parking as an additional expense to rent payments. In many such congested areas, tenants may not have vehicles and be dependent upon public or other transportation methods. Including parking fees with the rent may turn away many good prospects because they would be charged for a service for which they have no use. The landlord must be sure to make parking rules and regulations clear to tenants before signing the lease or rental agreement. Tenants should understand that towing and fines are to be used to enforce violations of the parking rules. Proper signage should also be put in place, in accordance with local laws, and tenants should be provided parking stickers or permits to identify their vehicles as legitimate.

Storage

Providing tenants with additional storage outside of that which can be safely held in their rental units generates additional non-rent revenue. Tenants should be instructed to keep their rental units within established building, health, and safety codes. These codes prohibit the storage of excessive amounts of personal belongings that block movement and access as well as exceed weight restrictions of the property. Tenants have a tendency to use balconies, yards, and basements as their personal storage units rather than living quarters. Besides violating building and safety codes, excessive storage diminishes the curb appeal of rental properties. Property owners and managers may make use of tenant's excessive storage requirements by offering paid storage facilities to secure their personal belongings. Property owners are cautioned against offering poorly constructed structures as storage facilities. The property owner or manager becomes liable for damage to items placed in storage by the tenant. An ideal storage facility should be:

- Accessible from ground level.

- Constructed of solid materials so that contents are not visible to the public or damaged by leakage or seepage.

- Weatherproof and shielded from wind, rain, snow, and other adverse weather conditions.

- Free of rodents and other infestations.

- Locked with heavy-duty or controlled locking mechanisms.

- At least 5 x 5 square feet in diameter.

- At least 6 feet in height.

Internet Access

Property owners and managers are encouraged to wire rental properties for Internet access. The demand for Internet access makes it as commonplace as phone, gas, and electric utilities. Internet service providers (ISPs) are readily available to provide high-speed Internet access through cable modems, satellite, digital subscriber lines (DSL), or fixed wireless access. Property owners and managers should research the various access methods to determine the type and extent of service that is most cost effective for the location of a particular rental property. Some ISPs are willing to assist with the installation of service and allow the property owner or manager to share in the generated revenue.

Tenant Lease Options

Tenant lease options allow the rental property lease or rent agreement to be supplemented with a separate contract that gives the tenant an option to purchase the property. The property owner agrees to sell the property during a specified time frame, for a mutually agreed-upon price. The tenant pays a monthly rent amount in addition to an option fee to be applied to the down payment of the sale property. The monthly option fee is nonrefundable to the tenant should he or she decide not to engage in the sale of the property.

Other Revenue-Generating Opportunities

Opportunities exist to engage in the management and renting of commercial and industrial properties, such as hotels, motels, and parking garages. The knowledge and expertise must extend beyond that required of residential property ownership and management to an understanding of business processes. The investor or property manager must have the skill set necessary to promote, maintain, and enhance business functions. Any business presents an opportunity for a property manager to generate income, but a good property manager will engage in market research specific to a particular business function before engaging in the acquisition and management of the business property. When acquiring a business as management property, the investor must assess whether the property:

- Is accessible by all potential customers, including handicapped and otherwise challenged individuals.

- Is accommodated by sufficient parking.

- Can accommodate delivery vehicles.

- Adequately accommodates the business purpose.

- Will be affected by current trends in demographics.

- Can continue to sustain competition.

- Requires a skilled staff or a few employees.

The most common forms of business property investments include shopping centers, retail stores, restaurants, office buildings, hotels, motels, movie theaters, and industrial properties.

- Shopping centers are expensive both to build and maintain, but may be acquired in various sizes to accommodate different populations; the smallest of which include neighborhood shopping centers. They are generally expected to accommodate a small population of 2,500 to 40,000. Community shopping centers are medium-sized shopping centers that are expected to accommodate upward of 150,000 customers. Regional shopping centers, the largest of shopping centers, are established to accommodate enormous populations by offering many stores that both anchor and compete with one another. Neighborhood shopping centers are designed to accommodate the local community and are sometimes established as shopping strips rather than enclosed, mall-like environments. However, the local neighborhood shopping-strip design has proven effective when constructed in the path of larger community and regional shopping centers. Customers are better able to manage their shopping needs without the long and often tiring experience of mall shopping.

- Office space offers the benefit of serving small and

large businesses. The property manager must be able to effectively evaluate and forecast the market potential of such a business venture. Many large office complexes are overbuilt, generating an abundance of empty spaces or spaces offered at low and below-market rent. Office complexes are also heavily dependent upon demographics. Downsizing, takeovers, and realignments may force companies to relocate. The property manager may have to resort to offering concessions, such as offering to pay certain expenses of the business, temporary rent reductions, or periods of free rent, in order to maintain a tenant base. Stable renters of office space are typically medical businesses. Medical office space, located in proximity to hospitals, offers stability since hospitals are not likely to relocate. In fact, hospitals are more prone to expansion than downsizing and relocation.

- Hotels and motels are expensive to build and maintain. When a major chain is engaged in the rent or lease of hotel and motel space, the responsibility to manage the individual units falls on the motel or hotel entity. The property manager must engage in many on-site functions to properly manage the activities of the business and perform the continual maintenance that is required.

- Service stations that are properly situated with the flow of traffic offer another great opportunity for investment. The property must be easily accessible for traffic and may need to be modified to account for any changes that are implemented for traffic flows.

- Restaurants are low profit margin, but they may serve different purposes, dependent upon market and demographic changes. As with most business, leasing with a brand company offers the most opportunity for success, particularly in a highly competitive area.

- Movie theaters are dependent upon the movie industry to supply the business with quality material that audiences are willing to view. The trend toward larger multiplex theaters that offer a variety of movie choices is continuing to grow. Small, single theaters are still in existence, but they must offer discounts in order to attract viewers.

- Investment groups that are able to envision the future of investments usually acquire industrial properties. Industrial properties are acquired to serve specialized functions, and the investor must engage in research to evaluate the potential of the property to sustain growth and development. Most industrial developments involve large acreages of raw land. Dependent upon the ultimate purpose, an industrial property may also need to be in proximity of interstates, railroads, aircraft, and/or watercraft. The property must also be accessible or made to be accessible from local streets and roadways.

K. Kemper
K. Kemper Real Estate
Phoenix, Arizona

Managing rental properties is a part-time endeavor for me, from which I've learned a lot. To begin, no complaints from tenants are ever typical. The best way I've found to deal with tenants is to simply leave them alone and to keep the property maintained. I do this, in part, by requiring the maintenance staff to complete their work in a timely manner.

Furthermore, to ensure quality tenants, I've found it's important to do background checks, and to get a payroll deduction for the rent. If you don't get a payroll deduction for a tenant's rent, collect the rent yourself, and don't keep the tenants who are consistently slow in paying their rent. When I first started as a property manager, my biggest problems were those tenants who simply didn't pay their rent and those maintenance people who collected the rent and shouldn't have.

For those just starting out, the best advise I can give is to keep the rental properties close to you; use payroll deduction for collecting rent; and require maintenance to complete work in a timely manner.

CHAPTER SEVEN

Establishing Good Relationships

Investors

When participating in property management as part of an investment group, the group will consist of at least two individuals who, collectively, pool their individual resources to reach a goal. The establishment of an investment group should include equal responsibility, authority, and liability. It doesn't necessarily mean that the partners are equally vested financially, though they could be.

The group must consist of a leader who is able to act on behalf of the group. The leader must be able to balance the pros and cons of the business entity and offer solutions that best suit the needs of the group. The leader must be prepared to deal with issues when one or more investors strongly disagree and be able to negotiate the best of all possible solutions.

When Investors Form a Partnership

Any group of two or more individuals can form an investment group or partnership. In fact, it would be a rather simple process for two or more individuals to purchase and lease or rent a piece of real estate. Complications arise when incidents occur on or with the property that result in dispute or one of the partners no longer wants or needs to be included in the partnership.

Establishing Rules and Guidelines

The rules and guidelines of the partnership should be developed, documented, and agreed upon by all parties. Partners should get to know one another prior to establishing the partnership to determine whether the differing personalities can be managed to reach the goals and objectives of the group. Time and expenses used to resolve disputes, particularly legal disputes, create a loss for the group.

Establishing Legal Representation

Different partners may come to the table with legal representation. The group must collectively decide on the legal representative that will act on behalf of and for the good of the group. The agreed-upon representative becomes part of the partnership. The attorney will provide knowledge and expertise in contract law, and as such, provides one of the most valuable resources needed by the group. Each individual in the group must feel confident that this individual is able to act on behalf of the entire group and engage the group in contracts and other legalities that are clearly understood by each party in the group.

Types of Partnerships

The group must determine the type of partnership that is to be formed, then establish and document the rights, responsibilities, and limits of each partner. Ownership of property prior to, during, and in the event of dissolution should be defined before establishing the partnership. As a general rule, property acquired by and for the partnership is the property of the partnership, not of an individual partner. Complications arise when bookkeeping indicates a history of money transference between the partnership and individual accounts. Ownership is further complicated when there are inconsistencies in the tax filings of the partnership and its individual partners.

There are four primary types of partnerships that establish general definitions for the limits of liability for the partnership and each of its partners. The regulations and definitions are more accurately specified by the state in which the partnership is formed and operating. The general forms of partnership are as follows:

Unincorporated Partnerships

Unincorporated partnerships are the simplest form of partnerships. These partnerships are commonly formed among close friends or family members. Some states do not require any type of documentation to establish such partnerships, others do. You must check the laws governing the state and jurisdiction in which you intend to do business. It is important to understand the particular state's interpretation of the terms "partner" and "partnership," particularly as these terms are used in lawsuits. In some states, a partnership can be sued, but the individual partners cannot. In other states, the individual partners can be sued. While unincorporated partnerships are the most simple to establish, they become complicated when one of the partners leaves the partnership, either willfully or by circumstance, such as death or disability. Though the partnership has dissolved, established procedures must be followed in order to keep the business going. These procedures should be documented, recorded, and stored for safekeeping by all partners as well as any representative legal authority.

Limited Partnerships

Limited partnerships are more formal than unincorporated partnerships because they must be established and documented with the state. Limited partnerships include two types of partners: general and limited. General partners handle the day-to-day activities of the business and are liable for the debts of the company. Limited partners are passive. They simply offer financial investment, advice, and counsel. They assume no liability for the debts of the business though they are entitled to the benefits of tax deductions, ownership, and profits. This type of partnership offers benefits to the limited partner as reward for the financial investment. This is the longest standing form of partnership.

Limited Liability Limited Partnerships

Some states provide for the establishment of limited liability limited partnerships (LLLPs). This type of partnership is similar to the limited partnership with the exception that the liability of the general partners includes some limitations. The company must be established and designated as an LLLP with the state.

Limited Liability Partnerships

Limited liability partnerships are established for limited liability corporations (LLCs). The U.S. Internal Revenue Service established statue for LLCs in 1988. An LLC, generally, is understood by all statutes to place the legal liabilities and obligations associated with the corporation on the corporation. The partners, most of whom are usually limited partners, have no involvement in the day-to-day activities of the corporation. The general partners are responsible for managing and running the corporation. They have both a moral and legal obligation to report investments, progress, and problems to the limited partners. In a good partnership, the general partners seek and accept input from the limited partners. The composition of the LLC is such that a single individual can incorporate himself or herself as an LLC and limit liabilities to his or her business, not his or her personal assets.

Limited liability partnerships must be established and documented with the state. Though each state has specific rules, each LLC must be designated and documented as an LLC. The LLC must have a documented name, business address, and registered agent. It is important to understand the particular state's interpretation of an LLC. Some states consider an LLC that is managed by its partners to be different from an LLC managed by an outsider on behalf of the partners. Also, some states prohibit any of the partners from being designated as the resident agent for the corporation. The individual state's regulation would be the best source of information for such rules as well as regulations regarding the transfer, modification, and dissolution of partnerships.

Property Managers

Property owners with a small number of rental properties may be able to manage properties on their own with the help of a few contractors. Property owners with many rental properties or property managers who don't care to take on the management responsibilities may hire professional property management services.

On-Site Property Managers

Some states require owners of rental properties to hire and maintain on-site property managers if the owner leases a minimum number of units at a single location. In New York

City, for example, if the owner rents a property with nine or more units, the property must have an on-site property manager. State laws do not require that the hired on-site manager be a professional licensed in real estate or property management. The owner must be willing, however, to train or provide training opportunities through the Institute of Real Estate Management for on-site managers.

On-site managers have a responsibility to manage the day-to-day activities of the property, ensure that the property is maintained, and coordinate the maintenance of rental units. On-site managers are expected to market vacant units, solve tenant conflicts, and handle emergency situations. An on-site property manager needs to have good people skills and be able to exercise honesty, integrity, and perseverance in performing his or her duties. Besides incurring an additional expense, quality on-site managers are difficult to find and hard to retain. The property owner should consider offering rewards and other types of financial incentives in an effort to retain good on-site property management. The on-site property manager may be rewarded for producing results, such as the efficient control of expenses, low turnover rates, maintaining curb appeal, and timely maintenance. All of these things maximize income from the property, which benefits both the property manager and the owner.

Rental Agents as the Property Manager

Rental agents are a knowledgeable resource for property-management endeavors, but they operate on commission and the property owner must trust that the rental agent will be fair in securing tenants for vacant properties. A rental agent's commission may range from one-half to a full month's rent for securing a lease. Paying this commission can be more cost effective than having a property remain vacant over time, particularly when the property remains vacant longer than anticipated. The investor must ensure that the rental agent is clear on the specifics of the property and specifies amenities that the rental agent is allowed to promote. Otherwise, the rental agent has leverage to misrepresent property on behalf of the owner. The rental agent's job is to secure the lease or rental agreement, bearing no responsibility for broken, disputed, or terminated leases. The rental agent, for example, may present the property during the summer months as having gas heat. The tenant may sign the lease or rental agreement based on that assumption and when winter arrives, discovers that he or she has to pay for a supply of oil to heat the property. This could create legal and other costly disputes, in which only the rental agent wins. The tenant wants out of the lease and the investor is stuck with either paying the heating costs, losing the tenant that was acquired at cost or fighting a legal battle.

Professional Property Managers

A property manager is responsible for collecting rent from tenants and maintaining the property on behalf of the property owner. The property manager also has a responsibility to communicate progress to the owner. A method of communication should be defined in the contract between the owner and the property manager. The property owner must:

- Insist that the accounting of funds for his or her particular property be provided as its own separate account. Property managers that commingle funds for multiple properties are more likely to incur shortages and misuse funds.

- Insist that the property manager keep him or her

informed of all necessary repairs and provide an opportunity to discuss and agree upon the dollar amount to be used, before starting the job.

- Specify an amount of funds to be used in emergency situations in which repairs are made without the owner's approval.

- Establish a date, usually monthly, for which the property manager will document all activities that have occurred since the last documentation of activities.

- Establish which fees are collected for the owner and which fees are to be secured by the property manager. Some property managers retain amounts collected for screening, late charges, and other administrative services.

- Define the extent of screening and whether it includes drug testing, credit checks, and reference checks with legitimate sources.

- Investigate the property manager's license and history of violations.

- Request proof of insurance with the following minimum limits:

  - $500,000 Errors and Omission

  - $2,000,000 General Liability

  - $1,000,000 Fidelity bond per employee

Contractors/Suppliers

Property managers will hire a variety of personnel to assist in the management of property. Property managers are responsible for explaining the nature of jobs for its employees as well as how the job should be performed. A property manager assigns job functions, pays taxes, and maintains insurance for its employees. When the property manager acquires the services of an independent contractor, the contractor is responsible for his or her own business functions. A contractor to the property manager:

- Holds a business or contractor's license

- Holds its own insurance coverage

- Makes contract for its services

- Advertises and publicizes its own work for hire

- Assumes liability for its work

- Assigns its own personnel

- Engages in an area of specialization

- Makes use of its own tools, machinery, equipment, and personnel

- Pays taxes and makes its own deductions

- Maintains its own hours of operation

A wealth of independent contractors is available to fulfill the necessary service needs of property management. A property manager should research potential contractors and suppliers to ensure that they are sound enough to afford the necessary tools and equipment to complete a job and offer contracts that are not assignable to lesser skilled teams. Friends, family, and the property manager's network of associates are the best source of information about qualified workers. The contractor should be able to provide original, time-dated, and stamped copies of permits for performing work. Providing a permit does not guarantee that the contractor will build or construct according to code. A good contractor, however, understands that his or her business reputation is on the line and will try to adhere, as closely as possible, to established codes.

When a contractor provides excellent work, the contractor should be retained for services so long as the work remains excellent. However, contractors who provide excellent work for small projects may not have the personnel, equipment, tools, or skills to take on large projects. When the property is in need of major repairs or maintenance, the property manager should seek and consider multiple bids for the work. The property manager must carefully and thoroughly evaluate bids received from contractors and make a decision as to the contractor's potential to provide the necessary services. Property managers should refrain from selecting contractors based on the lowest bid. The low bidder may not be able to provide the quality of service or complete the job within the necessary time frame. The experienced property manager will be able to ascertain the number of man-hours required to complete a project and determine when the bidder does not have the necessary manpower to complete the job. This is especially important with time-sensitive work. A contractor who has proven expertise in roof repair, for example, charges a relatively low price to repair a leaking roof, but does not have the necessary manpower to resurface the leaking roof within one day. The water damage that occurs over additional days may be more costly than if the property manager had chosen a more expensive contractor who was able to complete the job in one day. Often, the low bidder will request payments in advance and delay or not complete the project. The property manager could end up spending much more than the anticipated cost savings in trying to recover losses from the company or even worse, the dissolved company. In addition, the property manager must pay someone else to complete the job.

The property manager should always have a written contract with contractors and suppliers and make minimal upfront deposits for services and products. Once a property manager establishes that a contractor or subcontractor is able to provide the types of services that are needed, the property manager should engage in contracts that allow incremental payments as services are performed. If the property manager establishes a practice of paying upfront for services, the property manager will find himself or herself spending lots of time and effort in trying to compensate for the excuses that will follow. A day's pay for a day's work will help to ensure that scheduled services are completed in a timely fashion.

Because of the timing and urgency in property management, workers will always try to maximize profits. The property manager should expect a reasonable number of cost overruns. Besides, there will be instances where a job will take more time than anticipated or cost more money than expected. This type of cost overrun should be figured into the budget for the property, calculated as a predetermined percentage of maintenance costs. To reduce such overruns, however, the property manager has a responsibility to monitor the work, progress, and expenditures of hired contractors.

Nancy Cabral
Day-Lum Rentals & Management
2 Kamehameha Avenue
Hilo, Hawaii 96720-2830
Phone: (808) 935-4152
Fax (808) 961-2459
ncabral@daylum.com

Twenty-nine years ago, I applied for a job as a resident manager. I didn't get the job, so I took a class to get my Real Estate license then answered an ad in the local newspaper for a job as a property manager. I got the job.

When I began my career as a property manager, I didn't know anything, and no one really trained me. Everything was a problem in the beginning. I didn't know very much about building repairs or maintenance, or legal standing of owners, etc. I trusted people and didn't expect them to lie about their housing needs, financial composition, housing standards, etc. It has taken many years for me to be able to more realistically assess the needs and abilities of both tenants and owners.

Today, my company and I provide residential management for individual homes, condominiums, apartment buildings, Association of Management of Condominiums and Subdivisions, and Commercial Leasing and Management. We currently manage 543 residential units, 42 commercial units, 13 Condominium Associations, and nine Subdivision Associations.

We work hard to keep in touch with what the market rent is for each of our various rental units. We keep copies of all the weekly classified ads for rental units in our market area. We discuss weekly, in our rental meeting, what is still available and what it will take to get it rented. We communicate with the owners of the rental units to advise them of the suggested market rent. We increase and/or decrease them to keep the properties occupied at the best possible rate.

Once qualified tenants are placed in our properties, the primary complaints we receive refer to building maintenance issues. We have the units cleaned and in good repair when tenants move in. However, normal wear and tear and general maintenance is the owner's, not the tenant's, responsibility in

Hawaii. In our multifamily complexes, we receive complaints about neighbors.

Our goal is to ensure our tenants' satisfaction. To do this, we screen tenants, and we attempt to have the properties meet the tenant's expectations. We have an in-depth rental agreement and lease signing procedure that details the rights and responsibilities of the tenant, the landlord, and the owner. Furthermore, we make ourselves available to the tenants and ensure we take care of their concerns as quickly as possible.

To minimize our risk as a company, we have written policies and standards, and we review these policies and standards at staff meetings and with customers, if they request a copy. We follow our own policies and procedures with our customers while being as polite and considerate as possible.

Of course, we also do all that we can to maximize our profits. For example, I work really hard, and I expect the same from my employees. I also respected my employees and their abilities, and I'm not afraid to let "non-working" employees go when they don't work out.

Our company will pay the state excise use tax for our individual rental owners and the County Property Tax for the individual properties. However, we don't pay their income taxes.

We also have a CPA complete our company tax returns, and we pay for consultations with the CPA when specific information is needed by our residential and association clients. For our in-house accounting needs, we use Yardi software.

If you're new to the industry or are considering a career in property management, you want to work with someone who is a good property manager. Read all you can about property management, general building maintenance, recordkeeping, and computers, so you can learn from others' mistakes instead of making those same mistakes yourself. You also want to read everything you can on property management and obtain the necessary forms, policies, and procedures from a professional company or training organization.

Lastly, learn all of the jobs in the office. You're not going to do all of those jobs, but knowing them means you'll know if an employee isn't doing something right. It also means you must be willing to let that employee go, if necessary.

8

CHAPTER EIGHT

Tenants

The property manager must be able both to provide tenants with a lease in compliance with established laws and regulations governing the property and to ensure that tenants understand the lease. The property manager should review all rules and policies with the tenant and complete an inspection of the property along with the tenant. One of the biggest risks in property management is a vacant property, for every time that a rental unit becomes vacant, the owner incurs the expense of advertising and cleaning the unit to make it attractive for the next tenant. At the same time, the rental unit is not able to generate income. Vacant properties create a loss in profits and, at the same time, cause expenses to increase. To reduce the risk of vacant properties, the property manager should be careful to seek qualified tenants who show the potential to pay rent and maintain tenure. The property manager is responsible for dealing with the following:

- **Screening tenants**
  The property manager should be thorough and complete in the screening of applicants for tenancy. The identity of each and every occupant of the rental unit should

be verified. Credit and background checks should be performed for each adult occupant. The property manager should check all supplied references as well as histories of work, income, rent, and criminal behavior. The screening process should be systematic, applicable to all applicants, in compliance with all fair housing laws, and void of any discriminatory practices.

- **Walk-throughs and inspections**
  Property managers are encouraged to provide walk-through inspections of a rental property and the particular rental unit, prior to the tenant moving in. A checklist of conditions should be used to document the conditions of the unit before the tenant moves in and the same checklist should also be used for inspection after the tenant moves out. The checklist may be either a formal or an informal document, such as a computer-generated form or a handwritten form, depending upon the property manager's style. The tenant and property manager should go through each item on the checklist and indicate its condition as well as the tenant's satisfaction with the item. Items of concern should be noted with specifics about the condition. Conditions noted as new, excellent condition, scratched, and broken are fine; however, terms that are more detailed should be used if possible. For instance, the phrase "broken handle" versus the term "broken" indicates that just that the handle of the refrigerator needs repair, not the entire refrigerator unit.

- **Lease and rental agreements**
  In general, a lease or rental agreement is an agreement for the property manager to provide a safe and habitable living space in return for the tenant providing rent

payment at a fair market value. The lease or rental agreement should comply with all applicable housing laws and provide the tenant with all rules, regulations, methods of compliance, disclosures, addendums, clauses, and payment information associated with the rental property. The agreement should protect both parties: the tenant and the property manager. The property manager should review and explain each clause of the agreement as well as require signatures and initials, where appropriate, before allowing a tenant to take possession of a rental unit.

Lease Options

Rental property leasing can be supplemented with a separate contract that gives the tenant an option to purchase the property. This option is referred to as a lease option. The property owner agrees to sell the property during a limited and specified time, for a mutually agreed-upon price. The tenant pays a monthly rent amount in addition to an option fee. The option fee is to be applied to the down payment for the purchase of the property and is nonrefundable to the tenant. Lease options offer the property owner the benefit of receiving additional cash flow as well as retaining the tax benefits of homeownership during the option period. At the predetermined and specified time, the tenant is expected to purchase the property at the mutually agreed-upon price. Accumulated option fees are to be applied to the down payment, as agreed. Because the tenant is contemplating purchase of the property, the tenant is expected to provide exceptional maintenance of the property. The tenant, however, is not bound to the option and may opt out of the lease option contract. Unfortunately, the tenant forfeits all money invested in purchasing the property.

Property owners usually establish the selling price of the property above the existing market value to allow for appreciation. If the tenant agrees to the selling price within one or two years, the owner receives fair market value of the property. Property owners are cautioned against engaging in long-term lease options if it is conceivable that the property value will actually appreciate over time. For longer lease options, the property owner may want to insert a clause that increases the selling price to an amount equal to average price increase for homes in the surrounding area. An attorney should be used to establish a lease option contract that protects the owner and tenant. Some lenders may consider lease options as a form of sale of the property. As such, the lender may exercise a due-on-sale clause for the property that:

- Causes the owner to lose tax benefits.

- Creates cause for a reassessment of property taxes.

- Makes the owner liable for failure to comply with seller disclosure laws.

Property owners should have an attorney properly construct the terms of the lease option. A properly drafted lease option allows the property manager to resort to the terms of the standard lease if the tenant opts out of the lease option. The owner is then free to evict the tenant for nonpayment of rent or negotiate a new lease option agreement. The tenant is likely to request a refund of the amount paid as the option fee, but the terms of the lease option contract should spell out that the option fee is nonrefundable. If, however, the lease option is found to be unethical and in violation of any real estate laws, courts may prevent the owner from evicting tenants for nonpayment of rent. One of the biggest disadvantages of lease options is that the tenant knows well in advance whether he or she is able to live up to the terms of a lease option. A disgruntled tenant may become a threat, knowing that he or she has no recourse for the reimbursement of paid option fees. Tenants may retaliate by causing damage and destruction, such as with fires, flooding, or other major structural damage.

Furnished Rentals

Property managers have the option of offering furnished and partially furnished rental properties. These types of rental units are designed to address a specific market area and offer a good return on investment when properly placed within particular market conditions. When furnished or partially furnished rental properties are placed in the vicinity of employers that frequently relocate employees in the area or near places of business, such as training institutions that accommodate students on a regular basis, the property manager may generate significant rents for the property. The government and businesses allocate per diem amounts for their employees who relocate on long-term and short-term basis. The property manager should research these per diem amounts and evaluate the potential to profit from the established rates. In many instances, these employees are willing to pay additional out-of-pocket expenses for housing in more personable, home-like environments rather than endure extended stays in motels and hotels. The property manager's research should indicate the potential to draw such tenants and the frequency with which this type of arrangement can be engaged.

- **Securing deposits**
  Prior to the tenant taking possession of a rental unit, the property manager should secure the initial deposits required and documented in the lease or rental

agreement. Deposits usually include, at a minimum, the first month's rent in advance and a security deposit. The security deposit is often confused with payment for the last month's rent. A security deposit does not serve as rent payment and is secured as a liability to property management with the understanding that it is to be refunded to the tenant upon the tenant vacating the property. Security deposits may also be interest-bearing amounts with interest to be paid to the tenant upon move-out or to the property owner upon change of management companies. The leasing agreement should specify whether the security deposit generates interest.

- **Lease renewals**
  Lease renewals are not automatic; however, when the property manager provides no instruction for lease renewal, current leases are extended for month-to-month tenancy. A new lease is implicated when a tenant provides payment and the property manager accepts payment. Unless the property is being rented under rent control, the law places no limits on the amount that can be charged when renewing a lease. The property manager may negotiate with occupant-tenants to renew a current lease at the same length and amount or negotiate for a change in length and amount. However, a good property manager understands that raising rents may lead to vacancies, turnover charges, and a loss in rent until a new tenant is secured.

- **Complaints and concerns**
  The property manager should be efficient in responding to tenant complaints, but problems should not be addressed only in response to complaints. The property manager should make regularly scheduled visits to

assess the condition of the property, even if there are no reported problems. This gives the property manager an opportunity to assess the type of work needed to maintain the property as well as the type of equipment necessary to complete the job. Many of the independent contractors used by property managers have advertisements on their vehicles and equipment. The property manager must inform tenants that they are not to make contact with hired maintenance workers. Tenants may decide that they will get more timely service by contacting the maintenance contractor directly rather than waiting for the property manager to respond to a request. All tenant complaints should be addressed through the property manager so that requests as well as responses to requests can be properly recorded and filed in the records for the property and tenant.

Occupancy

The property manager should establish guidelines for occupancy that are fair and applicable to all tenants. The number of occupants in a rental unit has a direct effect on the wear and tear of the property. Property managers may minimize the wear and tear by adhering closely to minimum standards. The Department of Housing and Urban Development (HUD) establishes that occupancy rates of rental units may be limited to two individuals per bedroom. However, state and local regulations may set other restrictions. Health and safety boards as well as building codes may also affect occupancy standards. Standards for maximum occupancy may allow for as many as seven individuals per one-bedroom rental unit. California institutes a 2+1 occupancy standard that permits two individuals per bedroom, plus one additional individual per rental unit. Under the 2+1 occupancy standard, three individuals may occupy a one-bedroom rental unit and seven individuals may occupy a three-bedroom rental unit.

Rent

The collection of rent, in full and on time, is the most important element of rental property management. Rent-collection procedures should be documented in the lease or rental agreement and then explained to the tenant prior to signing an agreement. To reiterate the necessity of timely rental payments, the property manager may send new tenants an informational letter, which outlines the rent-collection policy, soon after tenants take possession of rental units. A tenant information letter could be drafted following the format shown in Form 3.

Tenant Information Letter

Tenant Name(s) _____

Rental Unit Address _____

Dear: _____

We are very pleased that you have selected our property to be your home. We hope that you enjoy living here and would like to share some additional information that will explain what you can expect from us and what we will be asking from you:

1. Owner/Manager:

2. Rent Collection:

3. Notice to End Tenancy:

4. Security Deposits:

5. New or Departing Roommates:

6. Maintenance and Repair Requests:

7. Lockout Procedure/Lost keys:

8. Renters Insurance:

9. Guest Occupancy Policy:

10. Annual Safety Inspection:

11. Utility shut-off locations:

12. Trash collection or recycling programs:

13. Parking:

Please let us know if you have any questions.

Sincerely,

_____   _____
Owner/Manager   Date

I have read and received a copy of this Move-in Letter.

_____   _____
Tenant   Date

_____   _____
Tenant   Date

Form 3: Tenant Information Letter (Griswold, p.189)

Due Date

The tenant should be instructed to pay the rent in full on or before the due date. In many states, the due date for rent is the first day of the month unless specified otherwise in the lease or rental agreement. Some property managers institute a common method of collecting rent on the day of the month on which the tenant moved in. Other property managers, particularly those responsible for multiple rental units, may collect rent from all tenants on the same day of the month, usually the first day of the month. These property managers may prorate rent for tenants who move in on dates other than the day for which they collect rent.

Grace Period

Some states require property managers to offer a grace period for rent payments, which gives tenants additional time to pay rent before the rent amount incurs a late charge. However, rent payments are legally delinquent even if paid in full during the grace period. As such, collection and eviction processes can be initiated during the grace period. Property managers should point this out to tenants before signing a lease or rental agreement. The property manager may demand payment during the grace period and specify a deadline for payment. Agreements may be worded such that the property manager has the right to refuse payment after the expiration of a legal demand notice and evict the tenant. The property manager is cautioned to be diligent in exercising the legal right to evict tenants because of late payment. These methods are best reserved for problem tenants. Some tenants will be consistently late in making rent payments but manage to pay the rent and all associated late fees every month. Other tenants may experience some financial difficulty for only a period of time and then get back on track for rest of their tenancy. The property manager should weigh the loss due to late rents against the loss associated with a vacant unit that needs to be filled. Even if the property manager has another tenant on standby, there is no guarantee that the new tenant will be any more prompt than the vacating tenant, particularly if tardiness is the only issue with the current tenant.

Late Fees

Some states impose limits on the amount that can be charged as a late fee. Late-paying tenants should be sent a warning, which clearly states that the lateness is in violation of the lease agreement. Late fees may be assessed as either a flat fee, a percentage of the monthly rent, or a daily fee. Property managers have typically assessed flat fees in the range of $20 to $40 and percentage-wise fees between 4 and 8 percent of the monthly rent. Daily fees are a method used to make late fees fairer, and they offer an incentive for tenants to pay promptly. Daily fees prevent a tenant who is two days late, for example, from paying the same cost as tenants who are, say, ten days late. Daily late fees should be set with a cap equal to the typical rates charged for flat or percentage-wise fees. Courts have been known to waive late fees that are considered excessive. Some property managers have also instituted early rent payment discounts, which reduce rent paid before a specified date. However, courts have ruled that this method of discounting rent is the same as implementing a late fee, and the higher the discount, the more likely the court is to charge that the late fee is excessive. This type of practice could lead to civil charges and penalties. Late fees should be assessed uniformly for all tenants. Also, waiving late fees for some tenants and not others may lead to claims of discrimination.

Payment Methods

Unless specified otherwise in the lease or rental agreement, many states require rent to be collected on the premises of a property. Most property managers, however, provide and stipulate several ways of collecting rent in the lease or rental agreement. Mailing rent payments is the most common form of making payment. The property manager must be sure to include language that stipulates whether payment is made on the day it is received or the day in which it is postmarked. Acceptable forms of payment usually include personal checks, cashier's checks, and money orders. Other property management companies allow walk-in payments and electronic transfers. Often, walk-in tenants are prepared to deliver cash payments. Some property managers will not accept cash payments, and the denial of cash must be specified in the lease or rent agreement. Cash is a legal tender and can only be refused if it is clearly documented in a rental or lease agreement and signed by the tenant. An electronic transfer is a relatively new payment option, established only by companies with the technology to accept them. Money orders, cashier's checks, and electronic transfers are the most reliable and preferred forms of tender; checks can easily be written against accounts with insufficient funds. Property managers should impose a returned-check charge that is reasonable to cover the loss incurred for returned checks. Some states allow property managers to charge interest and penalties on returned checks. When tenants pay rent with a bad check, the property manager may demand replacement payment with the use of a money order, cashier's check, or electronic payment, if specified in the lease agreement. Good accounting practices require the documentation of transactions, and the property manager should provide receipts for all rent received, particularly cash payments.

Roommates

When a rental unit has multiple tenants, payments may be received from multiple parties at different times, unless the lease or rental agreement specifies otherwise. The property manager should insist on a single payment and allow the roommates to sort out their own differences rather than allow the tenants to impose their differences on the property management. When separate payments are allowed, the lease or rental agreement should clearly spell out the terms of payment and the responsibility for each tenant named on the lease. Most important, each tenant needs to understand that he or she is jointly responsible for the rent. If the property manager is not successful in securing payment from a delinquent tenant, the other tenants have a responsibility to pay.

Partial Payments

The rent or lease agreement should clearly disallow partial rent payments. In some states, if a partial payment is received and accepted, the payment voids any prior notices for nonpayment. If a tenant makes a partial payment in response to a demand notice and the property manager accepts and deposits the payment into his or her account, the property manager can only assess lateness from the date the partial payment was accepted. If the property manager allows partial payments by one tenant, the manager must allow partial payments by all tenants. Otherwise, the property manager is engaging in discriminatory practices.

Rent Increases

Raising the tenant's rent is one of the more difficult processes to put into place. Unless the property is under state or local rent control, the law does not limit the amount of rent increases. The law specifies that rent increases can only be imposed upon lease renewal and tenants must be provided a 30-day legal notice prior to the rent increase. Raising the rent always raises the concern over whether a tenant will vacate the property or stay. It is best to raise rents slightly and with frequency, rather than implement huge rent increases at once. Rent increases without improvements to the property or individual units will almost always lead to negative reactions from tenants. Relatively small improvements may make the difference between driving a tenant out and giving the tenant an incentive to stay. Improvements, such as painting, new plumbing, or new carpeting, may be more cost effective than having to fill a vacated unit. When the rent increase is less than competitive market pricing, the property manager should give more notice than is required by law. This gives the tenant an opportunity to adjust to the increase and also to compare new rental rates with market conditions. If, on the other hand, rental prices are outside of the market pricing, advance notice of any length, may not prevent tenants from packing up and moving elsewhere. Property managers are cautioned against increasing rents in retaliation of complaints to government agencies or increasing rents for select individuals. These practices may be considered discriminatory and illegal. The property manager should have a documented policy for rent increases that is instituted fairly and equitably for all tenants.

Rent Control

Some states have established rent-control laws, which limit the amount of rent that can be charged for a rental unit and the amount by which the rent can be raised. The responsible property manager should be sure to determine if a rental unit is located within a jurisdiction under rent control. The property manager must understand and operate within the rules established for the particular jurisdiction.

Subsidized Housing

The government establishes that affordable housing is a housing unit where the rent and utility costs do not exceed 30 percent of a household's income. To make housing affordable, low-income families are often provided rent subsidies to offset the cost of rent and utilities. Most states have local agencies and organizations that subsidize rental payments on a temporary basis. The federal government also provides rent subsidy programs. Traditional public-housing programs provide housing units for low-income residents, which are concentrated in government owned-and-operated high-rise buildings, multiple apartment complexes, or townhouse developments. This type of housing has earned the title "the projects," indicating a large government project. Section 8a of the federal HUD program, commonly referred to as Section 8, is a program established in 1974 to assist low-income, elderly, and disabled citizens in acquiring a wider range of safe and sanitary housing. Section 8 establishes that the government provide subsidized rental payments for privately owned properties, inclusive of condominiums, apartments, single-family homes, duplexes, mobile homes, and townhouses of the tenant's choice. The Section 8 rental subsidy program has more than three million participants, and it does not require tenants to be concentrated in the same neighborhood.

State and Local Rental Subsidy

Local housing agencies, charities, and religious groups assist low-income and needy residents by providing them with a variety of services, including food, clothing, and financial assistance. As part of the financial-assistance package, many organizations offer to subsidize rent payments for tenants of rental properties. Often, the subsidy for rental payments is limited to the security deposit or a few months of tenancy. The property owner or manager must be sure to understand and inquire about the extent of this type of subsidy when screening and selecting tenants. When determining a prospective tenant's ability to meet the financial requirements of tenancy, the income of the tenant must be sufficient to meet the rent and utility costs once temporary assistance is exhausted.

Section 8 Rental Subsidy

HUD establishes Fair Market Rents for more than three thousand local public housing authorities (PHA) throughout the nation. The PHA is responsible for administering Section 8 subsidies, surveying local rental housing markets, and establishing median rents and utilities based on the number of bedrooms in a rental unit. PHA-established rent and utility allowances may not exceed Fair Market Rents established by HUD. HUD must certify properties for acceptance of subsidies under Section 8. Owners of certified Section 8 rental properties may charge rent amounts up to the limits established by the PHA, but no higher than rents charged to neighboring individuals who are not subsidized by Section 8.

Tenants qualify for rental subsidy under Section 8 if their household incomes are less than 50 percent of the median income for the area in which they live. Subsidies are provided for five-year periods, after which they can be renewed for another five-year period. Tenants may choose rental properties with rents higher than those established by the PHA and pay the difference in price. They may also choose rental properties with rents less than those established by the PHA and keep the difference for themselves. In areas of the country where PHA established rents are lower than reasonable rental rates in the area, the PHA is allowed to adjust the rental allowance to an amount 10 percent higher than the HUD Fair Market Rents. There are advantages and disadvantages of renting properties under the Section 8 program.

Property owners and managers wishing to rent properties under Section 8 must be willing to maintain rental rates within the amounts established by the local PHA where the property is located. In some areas of the country, the established rates are neither competitive nor reasonable. As such, many rental property owners refuse to participate in the Section 8 program.

The Section 8 program requires additional paperwork that is not required for private rentals. The local PHA will prepare the documentation needed for property owners to participate in the program, though it may be a slow process. Under Section 8, property owners must engage in leases with a minimum of one-year tenancy. The lease must be secured by either a standardized HUD-approved lease agreement or the owner's lease agreement with a HUD addendum. Section 8 also requires the property owner to sign a Housing Assistance Payments (HAP) contract. This contract authorizes the property owner or manager to receive payment on behalf of the Section 8 tenant. The payment may be directly deposited into a bank account, documented and authorized by the HAP contract.

The local PHA is responsible for the inspection of certified properties to ensure that the properties meet HUD Minimum Housing Quality Standards. Property owners are required to make repairs to bring the unit up to standard before certification of the unit takes place. Inspections are performed prior to tenancy, upon lease renewal, and upon the request of the tenant, if the tenant indicates that the rental unit is unacceptable. HUD standards for housing occupancy are extended to Section 8, requiring a single bedroom to accommodate every two occupants of the rental unit.

The initial occupancy of Section 8 rental properties may be delayed by the certification process, time to complete necessary paperwork, and time necessary to meet inspection requirements. Once properties are certified for Section 8 rental subsidies, vacancies are minimal. Local PHA maintains lengthy waiting lists of potential tenants. In fact, the local PHA will refer eligible tenants to participating property owners or managers. The PHA also provides contact information for current and previous landlords of its referrals. The property manager is then responsible for implementing its own screening and selection process.

Allowances for rent may vary depending on whether the owner or tenant is responsible for paying utilities. Property owners are cautioned against paying the utilities for Section 8 properties because the utility allowance provided by HUD is usually insufficient to cover actual utility charges and the tenants are more likely to waste utility services since there is no incentive to conserve. Property owners should be sure to provide lease agreements with language that specifies the tenant as the responsible party to pay for utilities.

Section 8 rent allowances include security deposits that may be collected in amounts equal to the maximum allowed by state and local laws. Rent allowances are paid in a timely manner by the government each month and the rent is adjusted annually. Because the government pays the majority of the rent, tenants are usually able to pay the relatively small amount that is required of them. In situations where the tenant is not able to pay his or her share of the rent, the tenant may be evicted and disqualified for Section 8 rent allowance. The property owner or manager must contact the local PHA before any eviction procedures are put into place. Some local PHAs have formal procedures that must be adhered to. The property owner or manager must implement the process required of the PHA that oversees the particular property. As with other unassisted tenants, the property owner or manager may apply amounts collected as a security deposit to unpaid rent and/or damages when a tenant vacates the rental property.

Types of Tenants

Most property managers would like to retain long-term tenants who pay their rent on time. Despite their best efforts to screen and verify tenants, property managers have no real way of knowing how long a tenant will stay. There are two particular tenant situations that may help the property manager in deciding the duration of stay. The tenant who is planning homeownership in the near future will probably be a short-term tenant. The property manager who is skilled in questioning prospective tenants will know if the tenant is planning such an event. These short-term tenants will likely have excellent credit ratings and a need to keep their ratings high. The problem is that they will eventually move forward in their desires and leave the property manager in the position of having to find a new tenant. The other tenant situation to consider is the tenant with questionable credit. These tenants are good candidates as long-term tenants because they are not qualified to move into homeownership, but they present a calculated risk. Some tenants who fall into this category may be the worst tenants ever while others make excellent tenants. As long-term tenants, they offer less time and energy in the management of rental units, particularly when a home environment is a priority. They are likely to renew the lease for as long as they are able and allowed to stay.

Pet Owners

Every property owner or manager must make a decision about allowing tenants who are also pet owners. By accepting pet owners, the property manager broadens the base of prospective tenants; however, pets are very likely to cause some property damage. The objective of the property manager is to reduce the amount of damage. A proper screening of tenants will indicate that a tenant is a pet owner and also the extent of the prospect's relationship with the animal. Some pet owners, particularly pet owners who care about their home environment, tend to train their animals. When the property manager is skilled in finding good tenants, those good tenants are likely to fall into this category of pet owners. Unless the prospect has just recently acquired his or her pet, they will have some idea of the habits and characteristics of their animal. It is advised that property owners acquire some general characteristics of the animal to assist in making the decision to rent.

- Pets that are middle aged, relative to the life expectancy of their particular breed, are the best choice. Young animals are not likely to be trained and older animals may become incontinent.

- Spayed and neutered animals are less likely to mark their territories and females have no capability to reproduce.

- Some people are too attached to their animals and allow them to do as they please, including property destruction.

Smokers

Smoking has become a big issue in property management as it has in just about every aspect of living. The problem that property managers have with smokers is that the odor is absorbed by materials, such as carpet and drapes, and it stains structures, such as the walls and ceilings. Some property managers advertise that smoking is not allowed in their rental units. Disallowing smokers has the effect of decreasing the base of prospective tenants. Generally, tenants who smoke will look elsewhere once this condition is specified. Most smokers, particularly renters who smoke, feel that they are paying and should be able to engage in the legal activities of choice, including smoking. Other smokers will agree to smoke outside of the rental unit, but that is a hard commitment for smokers to keep, particularly during periods of cold and inclement weather. Making nonsmoking clear in the initial contact with prospective tenants could save valuable time for both the property manager and tenant.

Property managers have to deal with a variety of people, with various personalities and characteristics. Five distinctive types can be used to characterize tenants (Weiss, C.C.I.M. and Baldwin, 2003):

1. **Watchdogs**

   Watchdog tenants are probably the best type of tenant as far as the property owner is concerned. They tend to make the property manager aware of every little problem and expect immediate attention. They generally enjoy a clean and safe environment and are likely to provide excellent upkeep of the property. Watchdogs are most problematic for the property manager who has to spend phone time with the tenant for each complaint. A good property manager will find solutions that meet the needs of these tenants. Poor property managers, who allow small problems to escalate into major renovations, will do their best to avoid this type of tenant.

2. **Complainers**

Unlike the watchdog tenant, the consistently complaining tenant seeks some type of satisfaction from the mere act of complaining. The property manager must be diligent in setting rules and time limits for listening to complaints. The establishment of a Web-based complaint system may eliminate the phone time required to deal with this type of tenant. The property manager should make it a point to visit this type of tenant on a regular basis to inspect the property and take pictures, whether or not they are responding to a complaint. When the complainer does not receive the attention that he or she feels they have earned, they are likely to create problems. Problems may stem from belligerent and threatening language to damage and destruction.

3. **Helpless**

The helpless tenant cannot seem to manage the simplest of tasks and abuses his or her right to consume the property manager's time. Screwing a loose hinge on a door, for example, is cause for this type of tenant to initiate a complaint. A helpless tenant may fear that the door will fall off, cause injury, and then threaten legal action in the event that it does. In some instances, the property manager may be able to walk these types of tenants through a satisfactory solution to their problem. This is a very time-consuming approach. The property manager can avoid some of the headache and wasted time by specifying the responsibilities of tenants in the lease or rental agreement. They may also include clauses that include charges for excessive service calls and an itemized listing of the fees for requests, such as lost keys, jammed windows, and light bulb changes. Though annoying, these tenants may not do much to create damage if their problems are addressed in some fashion.

4. **Slow Paying**

   The slow-paying tenants are the tenants who can never seem to pay on time but do eventually pay. There are many slow-paying tenants who are consistently late with payment. The lease or rental agreement should specify late payment fees. Slow-paying tenants are often grateful to have such a clause in their lease or agreement and take advantage of it. Others may resort to helpless or complainer methods in an attempt to justify the late payment. If they become desperate, they may create damage or destruction to support their complaints.

5. **Refuse to Pay**

   Tenants who refuse to pay are the most problematic of all tenants. The property manager will spend considerable time serving notices and visiting the courthouse or attorney's office to file notices. Refuse-to-pay tenants usually have some experience or access to some subject matter expertise in delaying evictions. The property manager must be diligent in consistently serving notices as soon as established time limits have expired. These tenants are more likely to damage and destroy property when eviction is inevitable.

Part of the property manager's duties is to do everything possible to protect the property. This is particularly important when the tenant is a risk of damage and destruction. After tenants complain and services are performed, the property manager should request and document feedback from the tenant. The property manager should offer methods of communication that get immediate attention or results. A 24-hour messaging system or e-mail complaint system may be instituted in addition to the traditional phone service to ensure that no complaint is missed. The property manager should be sure to investigate every complaint, but he or she must be able to prioritize the complaints based on the information provided as well as the type of tenant involved. The property manager should keep a payment record for each tenant to assist in characterizing the tenant and also as evidence should court actions become necessary. The lease or rental agreement should clearly spell out the terms for occupying the property as well as the terms for eviction. The property manager should provide timely notices of intent, with clearly defined reasoning.

Tenant Selection

The tenant-selection process involves analyzing the tenant from the information provided through conversation as well as information provided in the rental application. Some tenants will be gracious enough to disqualify themselves through conversation. Prospective tenants who are argumentative about the rules that have been established for a rental property will probably be just as argumentative as tenants. A property manager has the power to pick and choose among prospective tenants.

Property managers may be tempted to search out the perfect tenant, but the time expended in trying to qualify the best possible tenant may prove to be wasted time. Property managers are encouraged to save the time and expense of maintaining a vacant property by choosing among the good tenants. "Good" implies tenants who are not necessarily perfect. The property manager should require all prospective tenants over the age of 18 to fill out a rental application. A typical rental application should contain the following information about the prospective tenant:

- Name

- Social Security number

- Phone number

- Driver's license number

- Make, model, and tag number of vehicles

- Information about the age and relationship of spouses, children, and other relatives or friends who will be occupying the rental unit

- The previous two addresses of the applicant with the property manager's name and phone number, if the previously held address was a rental property

- Employer's name, address, and phone number

- Length of employment

- Income

- Other sources of income

Credit History

A property manager must always ensure that the prospective tenant signs and agrees to allow the property manager to obtain a credit report. The property manager may also require that the applicant list credit card, checking, savings, and other types of accounts along with their balances. The credit report can be used to double-check the credit history supplied by the applicant. In order to obtain a credit report, the property manager must have the applicant's correct name, address, and Social Security number. This information will also allow the property manager to perform criminal and other background checks. These types of checks can be performed securely over the Internet in a matter of moments. If the applicant does not provide the correct information necessary to obtain these reports or if information from the reports is different from that provided by the applicant, the applicant is likely to be unqualified and the property manager may use that as grounds to select someone else.

References

Personal references should include at least three individuals who are familiar with the tenant and are able to vouch for his or her character and disposition.

Tenant Safety and Security

Rental property owners are responsible for providing reasonably safe and secure rental units for tenants and their guests. Security measures should be implemented to provide safety against both crime and natural disasters. The property manager should make the security of tenants a priority and establish methods and procedures that will reduce the likelihood of problems. The best security and safety measures are those that are easy to implement and difficult to disable. Property owners and managers are discouraged against installing illusive devices, such as security cameras that are not really operational. Fake security cameras may give tenants a false sense of security, and some jurisdictions may require that proper staff be put in place to operate such devices. Staff is required once the devices are installed, whether or not they are functional.

Access and Control

File Access and Control

The property manager maintains personal information for all tenants and has a responsibility to protect such information. Policy should be established to keep the information confidential by not providing it to anyone unless the tenant gives written permission to do so. The property manager should also lock and secure all physical and digital files from access to intruders. Digital files should be protected by secure software and hardware systems, and computer access to files that contain personal information should be limited to only those with a need to know. Perpetrators have been known to access such files to gain information about the vulnerability of potential victims, such as elderly residents, single women, and high-income residents. Property managers should also limit tenant identities to last names on rosters, directories, and mailboxes. Most postal carriers are aware of security and identity issues and will accommodate a system of posting tenant names on the inside of mailboxes.

Key-and-Lock Access Control

Property managers also maintain the keys or a master key to all rental units. In order for locks and keys to provide any type of security for a property, property managers need to establish control over the access to keys. Property managers are cautioned against having a master key to access multiple rental units. The reason is simple: If someone steals the master key, they are given access to all units accessible by the master key, and the property manager will have to re-key each of the compromised rental units. Property managers should adopt a key control system that allows for duplicates of individual keys, with a different key for each rental unit. The key control system should allow keys to be stored in a locked metal container or a key safe. Keys should be identifiable by code or some means other than a tenant's name, address, or unit number. The objective is to prevent lost and stolen keys from pointing the finder to the tenant or the tenant's rental unit.

Maintenance and repair workers should be provided access to units by an employee of the management company or someone trusted and authorized with access. Maintenance and repair workers should never be given unsupervised access to rental units.

When a tenant loses a key, the tenant should not be given a duplicate key unless the lost key is locked inside of the rental unit. In all other situations, the unit should be re-keyed for access. The lease or rental agreement should specify procedures and costs for lost or stolen keys. To avoid paying the rental management's cost, tenants may change or re-key their own locks. Some tenants may also add additional locks for safety. The property manager is required to have access to rental properties in emergency situations or to allow maintenance workers to make repairs. Tenants should be advised that the lease or rental agreement specifies the right of the property manager to have access the property, and modifying door-locking mechanisms creates a health and safety risk. If the tenant changes or adds additional locks, the tenant must provide the property manager with duplicate keys. If the tenant does not provide the property manager with duplicate keys, the tenant may be evicted.

Key Card Access and Control Systems

More modern properties may contain the technological

innovation of card key systems to provide access to rental units. When tenants make proper use of card keys, they offer effectiveness in controlling access, but these systems are more costly to implement than traditional lock-and-key systems. Card keys or "smart cards" are a technological innovation, which is commonplace in the banking industry with the use of ATM machines. Card keys have the approximate look, shape, and feel of ATM, debit, or credit cards. Smart cards have an embedded microchip that stores electronic information. When a smart card is inserted into a card reader, the reader interprets the information stored in the card's microchip. A lost or stolen card key is usually of no value to the possessor because card keys are not easily identifiable for their particular purpose or use and they also require the use of a PIN number or other method of confirmation before access is granted. Advancements in the use of smart cards require of the use of fingerprints or other biometric forms of identification for confirmation. When a card key is lost or stolen, technology allows card keys to be invalidated. The code necessary to gain access to a rental unit can be changed instantaneously and electronically from a central location, usually the rental office. No physical or mechanical modifications need to be made to the locking assembly. Smart cards offer the benefit of being able to store multiple forms of information. The same card may be used to access multiple entry points of a property, such as the laundry room and storage area.

Smart cards may also be programmed to perform monetary transactions, such as debits for laundry facilities and other amenities. Smart-card technology offers safety and security for tenants by not requiring them to engage in actual cash transactions. The cards may offer better security control than can be provided with key-and-lock systems, but smart-card systems are dependent upon tenants to be responsible for allowing, limiting, and denying access. The system is also dependant upon the real-time operation and functioning of a computer system. When the computer system fails or is comprised, so, too, is access.

Lighting Control Systems

One of the most effective methods of reducing the likelihood of injuries, criminal behavior, and nuisance behavior is to provide both effective interior and exterior lighting. Lighting also offers the benefit of providing curb appeal to rental properties. However, lighting is only effective if it is strategically placed, operational, and equipped with the proper type of bulb. Lighting in common areas should be inspected regularly, with immediate repair to broken fixtures or failed bulbs. When lighting is achieved with timers, the timers must be properly adjusted to account for daylight savings and other seasonal changes. A nighttime inspection offers the easiest method of detecting failed or malfunctioning lighting units. Lights equipped with photocells that detect darkness may be cost effective for property managers. Photocells eliminate the need to adjust the timing of lights when season changes occur. Also, testing photocells, by covering and uncovering photocell sensors, make photocells easy to test during both daylight and nighttime hours.

Professional Security Control Systems

For property managers who wish to implement manned security systems, two types of systems are available: standing guards and drive-through services. Standing guards are the most expensive of the two security systems, particularly when they are hired on a full-time basis. Drive-through guards make random checks of the property, either by foot and vehicle or strictly by vehicle. Guard services are best scheduled for various days and hours so that their procedures and processes are not easily monitored and compromised. It may also be cost effective to employ a combination of standing guards who are interspersed with drive-through services. Companies that provide such services should be thoroughly researched so that the property manager feels confident that the particular company is professional and can provide the type of security and surveillance that meets his or her needs. Not only should the company be screened, the individual guards should also be carefully screened for competence. The contract with guards and security services should clearly indicate that they are independent contractors to the property manager. The contract should also include language that allows for a short termination period. When a security firm or its guards cannot meet the expectations of the property manager, contract language should allow for a replacement as soon as possible. The property manager should insist that guards adhere to standards for behavior, particularly with regard to socializing with tenants of the property. Security guards should be subjected to the following:

- References

- Security-firm permits

- Status of all other state and local permits

- Status of all state and local licenses

- Proof of employer's workers' compensation insurance

- Proof of employer's liability insurance

- Current insurance with a minimum liability of $3 million

- Proof of automobile liability insurance

- Proof of a fidelity bond

The security guard's liability insurance should include both the property owner and property manager as named additional insured parties. Language of the contract with security guards must stipulate that the named parties be notified of any lapse of coverage 30 days prior to a lapse.

Property managers are cautioned against the hiring of armed guards. Some security firms may indicate that a community dictates armed guards be used to provide security of particular rental units. Property managers should consult with local law authority to validate such a claim. Proper research prior to the property's acquisition should have indicated the need for such extreme security procedures.

Safety Programs

Neighborhood Watch programs have been established around the country, with cooperation from local police departments. These programs are designed to train neighbors to recognize and report crime and other suspicious activity that they may witness. Neighborhood Watch programs have traditionally been established as a combined effort of local police and homeowners. Local police departments also engage in a program that is inclusive of rental property owners and their tenants. The Crime-Free Multi-Housing Program is an extension of the Neighborhood Watch program, designed to fight crime and raise the standard of living in neighborhoods that include multiple-unit housing. Like Neighborhood Watch, the Crime-Free Multi-Housing Program is supported by local law enforcement agencies that train property owners and property managers in effective ways of keeping illegal activities out of their housing units. The comprehensive training program includes:

- The preparation of safe rental properties

- The screening of applicants

- Crisis resolution

- Warning signs of drug activity

- How to identify criminal and suspicious behavior

- Ongoing management responsibilities

The Crime-Free Multi-Housing Program offers certification to property owners and managers who complete the required training and are able to demonstrate that they are following the prescribed procedures. Rental properties that are certified Crime-Free Multi-Housing Communities must include a Crime- and Drug-Free Housing Addendum in the lease agreement. Certified properties may be identified by signage that alerts prospective tenants to the property owner's commitment to providing a crime- and drug-free environment. Like the Neighborhood Watch program, the Crime-Free Multi-Housing Program achieves success by allowing law enforcement and residents to share information and ideas about criminal activities in their particular communities. Some local law enforcement may allow officers to patrol private property and make use of their patrol vehicles to perform off-duty services. The presence of official officers, in the standing guard or drive-through service capacity, offers a great deterrent against crime and criminal behavior. Tenants are often requested to pay for this type of security, and the presence, purpose, and cost of such services should be included in an addendum to the lease or rental agreement.

Informing Tenants of Crimes

The property manager should be prepared to respond to tenant inquires about the safety and security at their particular rental properties. The property manager has a responsibility to inform tenants of any known and confirmed incidents of criminal activity. There are no established rules regarding the reporting of crimes to tenants; however, tenants should be informed of any known incidents of serious or violent crime that may occur on or in the vicinity of the property. Tenants should be provided written notification of known crimes that involve bodily injury, physical attack, death, burglaries, and robberies along with any warnings or safety advice provided by law enforcement. Other isolated and petty crimes do not warrant notification unless they are persistent or directed toward the particular property. The notification should be dated with information that describes the type of crime and the extent of injury. The notice should not contain names and addresses of either party to the crime or any other information that may be used against the property owner or manager in legal actions. In some instances, victims may approve the use of their names in informing tenants of their victimization, but the skillful property manager should be able to provide tenants with the necessary information without such disclosure. Employees of the rental property management should also refrain from making statements about reported activities. The property manager who is not sure how to present such information should consult with legal counsel for directions.

Some tenants may become overly alarmed and respond to notification by vacating the rental property. This type of loss represents the risk that goes along with property management. The property owner's selection of good rental properties should be used to minimize this risk. The property manager has a responsibility both to warn tenants of criminal activity and to make them conscious of the security issues. Conscientious tenants practice better safety and are responsible enough to reduce further incidences of crime. In many instances, the property manager or owner is the last to find out about criminal activity in or around the rental property. The property manager has a responsibility to disclose any known incidents to inquisitive tenants and also to refer tenants to the local law enforcement agency responsible for the jurisdiction where the property is located for additional information.

Advertising Safety and Security

Property managers are discouraged from using such terms as "safe," "secure," and "crime-free," in advertising their rental properties. These terms are useful in attracting applicants, but the property manager increases his or her liability by offering such protection. No rental property is immune from crime, and once a crime is committed, the tenant may claim that the property manager or owner failed to live up to the expectations implied in advertisements. In fact, the property manager should inform tenants that there is no guarantee of safety or security for them, their families, their guests, or their possessions during tenure.

Security Devices

When alarms and security systems are included as part of the rental unit, they should not be advertised, orally or in print, as responsible for providing security or protection for the tenant. In fact, the tenant should be provided written documentation that states that such devices are subject to failure and malfunctioning. Security devices should be introduced to the tenant and the tenant should be shown the proper procedures for operating and maintaining them. The tenant should then be requested to sign documentation stating that he or she understands the limitations of such devices and that he or she will test such devices and report any failures or malfunctions immediately.

Sexual Offenders

Most states have adapted some version of Megan's Law, which requires convicted sexual offenders to register with law enforcement of the state. States are responsible for maintaining a database of such offenders, and most states make the information available to the public. States have three options for the distribution of information in their databases as follows:

1. States may present widespread notification with easy access, which allows the distribution of names and addresses in newspapers, on the Internet, or other means of widespread distribution.

2. States may opt for selective notification, with limited access to only entities thought to be at risk, such as schools and daycare centers.

3. States may allow only restricted notification, with narrow access that limits distribution to specific individuals, as determined by the state.

Unfortunately, many states have not been thorough in updating and maintaining sexual offender databases, particularly with respect to verifying and validating the locations of offenders. Offenders are required to reregister with the state every time they move, but many fail do to so. Some states require property owners to disclose the availability of Megan's Law databases.

Safety and Injuries

In the same fashion that rental properties are not immune from crime, tenants are not immune from injuries. Many property managers attempt to protect themselves from liability for tenant injuries by including disclaimers in their rental and lease agreements that void them of any responsibility for injuries to tenants. Most states, however, have laws that invalidate such disclaimers. Property managers have an obligation to present tenants with a habitable space that meets the minimum standards for health and safety. Rental property is legally bound by a warranty of implied habitability, which gives tenants the right to expect certain conditions and services in return for rental payments. Problems with lighting, broken windows, or door locks that malfunction are indications that the property manager fails to make reasonable repairs, and the property manager may be accused of causing or contributing to injury or victimization. The property owner should ensure that legal counsel has reviewed the lease or rental agreement and established language that limits the amount and extent of liability. The language should inform tenants that they are not guaranteed any level of security for themselves, their guests, or possessions. Furthermore, the language should inform tenants that there is no secure level of effectiveness or operability for attached security devices.

Fire Safety

Fire is a critical safety issue for property owners because fire spreads quickly and may destroy the rental property as well as adjacent properties. Fire also creates poisonous gases and smoke that can be deadly when inhaled. Property managers should get assistance from the local fire department in implementing a fire evacuation plan for tenants. Instructions should be documented and explained to each tenant prior to signing the lease agreement. Specific instructions should be documented for tenants with physical disabilities, mental challenges, and children. Emergency authorities should be notified in writing of challenged tenants so that specialized assistance is provided in case of an incident. Local fire departments are responsible for providing routine inspections of rental properties. Deficiencies are documented and they should be addressed immediately. Once corrections are instituted, a re-inspection should be requested, completed, and documented as meeting requested standards.

Some jurisdictions require that property owners provide tenants with fire extinguishers and to inspect, service, and recharge them when a new tenant moves in. Even in jurisdictions that do not require fire extinguishers, the property manager may find it cost effective to provide tenants with such devices. Tenants must be instructed on the use and maintenance of the device. The instruction should be documented with the signature of the tenant, indicating that the tenant understands the purpose and use of such a device. The documented instruction protects the property owner or manager's interest. The property owner or manager may be held liable in a legal suit if a tenant is injured because an issued fire extinguisher did not work or did not work properly. Some local fire departments may assist in teaching tenants how to use fire extinguishers.

Almost all states require property managers to install smoke detectors in rental units to alarm and waken tenants in the case of fire. Some local fire departments also provide free smoke detectors for residents who are not able to get them otherwise. Smoke detectors should be placed in hallways just outside of each bedroom, outside of the kitchen, and on each floor of the rental unit. Some jurisdictions have established regulations for the placement of fire detectors. Manufacturers also provide guidance on the proper placement of their units. Manufacturers also specify the frequency which the devices should be tested as well as the frequency with which batteries should be changed. The property owner or manager should be careful to perform routine inspections and testing of fire extinguishers. Requests by tenants to have smoke detectors repaired should be addressed immediately and documented with a signature by the tenant stating that the device is functional. As with a fire extinguisher, if a tenant is injured because the smoke detector did not work properly or did not work at all, the property owner or manager may be held liable in a legal suit.

Tony Drost
First Rate Property Management, Inc
7150 Potomac
Boise, ID 83704
208-321-1900
Tony@FRPMRentals.com
www.FRPMrentals.com

As newlyweds my wife and I rented an apartment. After nine months, it all became too much. The woman who lived below us set her couch on fire while she was smoking dope; the guy across the hall had an awful temper, and the couple directly behind us had loud, sex. On top of that, someone broke into my car, and my car was sustaining hits and dings every time the woman, in the assigned slot next to ours, slammed open her car door. Enough was enough. I became determined to buy a house. Unfortunately, we didn't qualify for a house. However, we did qualify for a duplex because we would receive rental income from the other half of the duplex. We began searching for a duplex, found one and purchased it. I've been a property manager ever since.

Residential real estate is my life. Not only do I own a property management company, but I also sell investment properties. Although property management can be very frustrating, doing my job and saving my clients from that frustration is very rewarding.

However, it takes time to build a solid company. When I first started in management, there was no source for procedures and forms. I basically had to create my own. That was until I found the National Association of Property Managers (NARPM). Through networking, education, and professional designations, my company has become a well-oiled machine.

While we specialize in four-plex management, I believe in keeping a good mix of properties to sustain market changes. Therefore, our portfolio consists of single family homes, duplexes, tri-plexes, four-plexes and several 12-unit apartment complexes. We currently manage 750 rental properties.

In our area, there is a surplus of rentals. Therefore, to determine the monthly rental rates, we pole the market, and because of the surplus of rentals, I have even more data to analyze. We use other available rentals to develop statistics on rental rates in the

area. With the data on hand and a quick onsite survey, we can recommend a rental rate with almost NASA-type precision.

We provide our tenants with a first-rate service, which starts from the first time we meet them and continues all the way until they move out. Our properties are very well-maintained. When a tenant calls for a plumbing leak, we don't argue who and how it got started. We simply go out and fix it and sort out fault later. We also offer cash incentives to our tenants. We pay them for every referral, and we pay them when they renew their leases.

The most common complaint we receive, however, is regarding our fees assessed to our tenants for paying their rent late. Our fees are steep, but their purpose is to deter late payments. Our jobs would be a lot easier if everyone paid their rent on the first of the month.

In fact, one way we minimize our risk is by carefully screening our potential tenants. Good tenants will make your job easier. Bad tenants are the first to put you and the property manager in jeopardy. Alternately, I maximize on our profits by being a part of NARPM; by charging fees in addition to management fees; and by providing consistent and first-rate service.

Furthermore, at no additional charge, First Rate Property Management is willing to pay property taxes or any other bills for our clients and post them to their account, as long as their account has sufficient funds. We also use a CPA and utilize specifically designed management software, MS Word, Excel and Outlook. I don't care what you use in your business, but don't use QuickBooks.

For those considering a career in residential property management or newcomers to the industry, I would advise you find and join the nearest NARPM chapter. It is much easier to start doing things right from the beginning. I have spent thousands of dollars fixing and changing procedure.

To be successful, you have to love the work, truly care about your clients' properties, and you have to have business savvy. If you only possess one of these qualities, you will fail and go out of business. If you only have two, you will always be frustrated, and you'll never be truly satisfied. If you possess all three, you will become successful, and you will truly enjoy your work.

The all-business property managers I have seen hate their jobs and provide terrible customer service. The property managers who are missing the business sense work very long hours, are burned out all of the time, and are almost always frustrated. I don't believe you can truly love your work, without the business part and the customer service part perfectly meshing.

CHAPTER NINE

Tenant Problems and Complaints

At some point, all property managers will have to deal with
problem tenants. Some problems amount to a one-time incident,
some problems are merely nuisance incidents, and other
problems may be severe, creating a threat to the safety and
security of the property and other tenants. Problem tenants
violate the lease or rental agreement and may necessitate
a notice from the landlord. Other problem tenants present
situations that are severe enough to warrant eviction. The
landlord's response to these tenants is dependent upon the
severity of the problem. The landlord should follow up on
problems presented and request feedback from tenants. The
problem, its resolution, and the tenant's feedback should
be stored in the tenant's file. When responding to tenant
complaints, property managers are encouraged to make
timely responses and to make note of any other visible signs
of maintenance needs. However, the property manager is
discouraged from making additional repairs at the tenant's
request because the tenant will come to expect such specialized
service all the time. Tenant complaints should follow the
procedures outlined in the lease or rental agreement so that they
are properly documented and accounted for.

The property manager must have strong people skills in order to diffuse problems with tenants. Landlords should address each problem, not necessarily with the same level of commitment, and keep open communication with tenants. The landlord may provide tenants with a suggestion box and thank tenants who provide good and useful feedback. Landlords may also provide tenants with a tenant bulletin board for posting notices, services, and other correspondence that should be shared with or among tenants. The landlord may also provide tenants with a regular newsletter that informs them of current, future, and planned activities. The newsletter should provide the best and most current method of contact with the landlord.

When a tenant presents a problem, the landlord should take the time to investigate the problem. This may require only a phone conversation to be sure the problem is in fact as the tenant presented it. The landlord may find the tenant has information regarding the business practices of his or her employees and contractors of which the landlord was not aware. If maintenance workers, for example, leave a jobsite before completing repairs, the tenant is often the first to know. Maintenance workers might skimp on a project and bill the landlord for services that were never completed. In this situation, the tenant's problem assists the landlord in identifying a fraudulent maintenance worker who could cost the landlord hundreds or thousands of dollars. In addition to the lost revenue, the landlord is left in the position of having to make repairs the fraudulent worker left undone.

Tenants have a right to disclose problems with authorities when they feel the problems are not resolved to their satisfaction. The landlord does not help the situation by resorting to threats and revenge. These types of actions make the landlord liable for even more damages. Tenants, particularly tenants who are behind on rent or otherwise in violation of their lease or rental agreement, are likely to confront the landlord in hopes of engaging the landlord, because the tenant benefits when the landlord loses his or her temper. Landlords are professionals, and courts hold them to a higher standard than tenants. Courts will likely side with the tenant who can prove harassment, retaliatory practices, or penalties.

Most states provide specific legal notices to issue to tenants who fail to pay rent. Other problems that warrant a notice, such as violations of noise restrictions or housing unauthorized pets, require a Lease or Rental Agreement Violation Letter as shown in Form 4.

Lease or Rental Agreement Violation Letter

_____
Date

_____
Name

_____
Street address

_____
City/state/zip code

Dear _____

This is a formal legal reminder that your lease or rental agreement does not allow:

_____

_____

It has come to our attention, that recently or beginning_____and continuing to the present, you have broken one or more terms of your tenancy by:

_____

_____

_____

It is our sincere desire that you will enjoy living in your rental unit, as will all of your neighbors. To make sure this happens, we enforce the Policies and Rules and all terms and conditions of your Lease or Rental Agreement. So please immediately:

_____

_____

_____

If you are unable to promptly resolve this matter, we will exercise our legal right to begin eviction proceedings.

Please feel free to contact us if you would like to discuss this issue.

Sincerely,

_____
Owner/Manager

Form 4: Lease or Rental Agreement Violation Letter (Griswold, p. 219)

Any violation of the lease or rental agreement should be documented and served to the tenant. This provides landlords with a time history of problems, particularly for tenants who continue to present minor problems or tenants who graduate to presenting bigger problems. Some of the most common problems that tenants create for landlords include failure to pay rent, disturbances, unsupervised children, unauthorized individuals and pets, storage, and other unusual circumstances.

Failure to Pay Rent

Some slow-paying tenants are consistently late with payment and willing to pay the additional fee that is attached to late payments. Other late payers will forget to include the additional fee with their late payment. Other tenants just refuse to pay rent for as long as they are allowed to do so. For all late payments, the landlords should issue a notice of Nonpayment of Rent, as shown in Form 5, to get the tenant to pay, even if no further action is planned. Slow-paying tenants who pay their rent and late fee and who do not cause any other problems may be cost effective to keep, particularly in a slow rental market. Though late, the payment is guaranteed each month with an additional bonus of the late fee. A landlord has no way of knowing whether the cost and expense of acquiring a new tenant will offer such a guarantee. The slow-paying tenant who neglects to include the late fee may continue the practice indefinitely. The landlord may need to supplement this tenant's notice with a notice that indicates consistent late payments and neglect of associated late fees is a violation of the lease or rental agreement as well as grounds for eviction. If the notices do not bring about a change in the tenant's payment pattern, the landlord should initiate eviction procedures. Tenants who are allowed to consistently pay late, without including a late charge and without being served notice, may argue that any rights to expect late payments are waived. Problem tenants who refuse to pay altogether should be issued a notice of Nonpayment of Rent as well as additional notices indicating the tenant's breach of lease prior to enforcing any eviction procedures. Notices should be issued with clearly defined reasons and explanations. Tenants who refuse to pay are the most problematic of all tenants. These tenants are more likely to damage and destroy property when eviction is inevitable. The landlord should be sure to keep payment records for these problem tenants to use as evidence in court actions.

Tenant Late Rent Warning and Excuses

(Note: To be given to new, renewing, and late tenants)

Dear Resident:

Your rent is due on the_____day of the month. I'm sure you fully understand that we must start eviction proceedings instantly once a payment is late (no matter the reason) and report your late payment to both local and national tenant/credit reporting agencies. We still request, however, that you submit your reason for late payment for our records. For your convenience, and to avoid lengthy explanation, you may simply check the appropriate reason below and submit this form with your late payment. Hopefully, this form and your payment will be received before you're evicted. Even better, your payment will arrive on time and you will not need this form.

I'm sorry my rent is late but...

A.   The check I've been waiting for did not come in the mail or was late.
B.   I was in the hospital/jail and I couldn't get to you.
C.   I missed a week's work because I had to take care of my sick mother/son/daughter.
D.   I had to have some teeth pulled, and the dentist wouldn't start work until I gave some money.
E.   I was in an automobile accident and I won't have any money until my attorney works things out with the other guy's insurance.
F.   I had my billfold stolen when this guy jumped me on my way to the bank/ post office/my office.
G.   Someone broke into my apartment and took my money. No, I didn't file a police report. Should I?
H.   I had to have my car fixed so I could get to work, so I could pay you.
I.   My mother/sister/uncle hasn't mailed me my money yet.
J.   I couldn't find your address. I put the wrong address on the envelope.
K.   I got laid off from my job, and I won't get unemployment for a couple of weeks.
L.   I was unable to get a money order, and I know you didn't want me to send cash.
M.   You didn't come by when I had the money.
N.   My husband/wife/boyfriend/girlfriend/roommate left, and I didn't have all the money.
O.   They garnished my check, and I don't understand it, because the guy told me it would be okay to just pay so much per month and I only missed a couple of payments.
P.   I told my friend to bring it or send it to you while I was out of town.
Q.   I haven't received my tax refund yet.
R.   I got a new job, and I had to work three weeks before I got my first check.
S.   I didn't pay the rent because my_____is not fixed. No, I'm sorry I didn't tell you there was a problem before now. I didn't think about it until now.
T.   My car is broken, and I didn't have a ride to your office/the post office.
U.   I had to help my brother/sister/friend who had a serious problem.
V.   My grandmother died, and I had to go to the funeral.
W.   I didn't have, or I forgot to put, a stamp on the envelope.
X.   The check's in the mail. Didn't you get it?
Y.   I ran out of checks.
Z.   I'm dead!
      Please briefly explain if your excuse is not listed above:

      _____

Form 5: Notice of Nonpayment of Rent (Taylor, p. 105)

Creating a Disturbance

Tenants who create a disturbance, whether it be arguing or playing music too loudly, are more of a problem for other tenants and neighbors than for the landlord. Tenants and neighbors who complain about noisy tenants should be instructed to contact law enforcement and file a formal complaint. Neighbors and tenants may be reluctant to become involved in law enforcement and court actions unless they are extremely annoyed. They will likely contact law enforcement anonymously, if at all. The landlord should request that any complaining neighbors or tenants provide written documentation of their complaints to the landlord. Should eviction become necessary, the documented complaints and any documented police reports will serve as proof in a court hearing.

Unsupervised Children

When the landlord becomes aware that tenants are not providing sufficient supervision of their children, the landlord should make an effort to visit the property to witness the actions of the children. If the child causes damage during the neglect, the landlord should discuss the issue with both the child and the caregivers. The tenant/caregiver should be billed for damages created by a child. If the landlord witnesses an unsupervised child for a second time, the landlord should provide the tenant/ caregiver with a written notice indicating the seriousness and consequences of leaving children unattended. If written notice is ineffective, the landlord may contact law enforcement and/ or social services to investigate the problem. The landlord is encouraged to send notice to the caregiver before filing a formal complaint with authorities. The landlord may be accused of and sued for discrimination against families with children if complaints to authorities are not backed by evidence of neglect. At the same time, the landlord may be accused and sued for failing to take reasonable action when a neglected child is not addressed, particularly if the child is hurt while unsupervised or neglected. In either case, the courts will likely look favorably upon a landlord who proves that he or she was reasonable and consistent in dealing with both the caregiver and the child.

Housing Unauthorized Individuals

All tenants of rental properties are allowed to have guests. When guests stay for extended periods of time, they become occupants. The landlord must follow specific procedures when he or she believes that tenants are housing individuals who are not named on the lease or rental agreement. The landlord should first discuss the situation with the legal tenant to understand whether the guest has converted to an occupant. If the landlord presumes a tenant to have taken on an additional occupant, the landlord should issue the tenant a Notice of Lease or Rental Agreement Violation. The notice must request that the additional occupant either move or be added to the lease or rental agreement as a tenant. If the additional occupant is a child, that child must be properly added to the lease or rental agreement. A landlord cannot discriminate against tenants who have child occupants unless HUD specifically certifies the property as adult housing. If the additional occupant is an adult, the occupant should make application and be subjected to the same screening process as all other adult occupants. The landlord is guilty of discrimination if he or she allows an adult to be added to a lease without going through the same process as all other adult tenants. Should the adult occupant fail to meet requirements for occupancy or fail to make application for a screening, the occupant must be requested to leave. If the occupant refuses to leave, legal action may be necessary to force the occupant and/or other tenants to leave.

Housing Unauthorized Pets

As with long-term guests, housing unauthorized pets is a violation of the lease or rental agreement. The tenant who houses an unauthorized pet should be issued a Notice of Lease or Rental Agreement Violation. The notice must stipulate the landlord's position with respect to pets. If the landlord permits tenants to have pets, the lease or rental agreement must be modified to include language that addresses rules and regulations regarding pets. If the landlord does not permit pets, the notice should request that the pet be removed from the premises. The landlord is guilty of discrimination if he or she allows a tenant to keep a pet when all other tenants are prohibited from doing so.

Creating Surplus Storage

Language of the lease or rental agreement should stipulate the type and extent of storage that is allowed on the premises. The tenant who stores an abundance of junk, a collection of inoperable vehicles, or a warehouse of machinery, should be issued a Notice of Lease or Rental Agreement Violation. The notice should point the tenant to the specific clause of the lease or rental agreement that prohibits such storage and request that the tenant remove the surplus items immediately. If the tenant refuses to comply within the time frame designated on the notice, the landlord should begin eviction processes.

Unusual Situations

Sometimes tenants face unusual yet common situations that warrant some type of response and action by the landlord.

These peculiarities should be dealt with in a timely manner and be applied consistently to each tenant who faces such situations.

Subleasing

Language of the lease or rental agreement should prohibit the assignment of subleases. If the tenant is interested in moving before expiration of the lease or rental agreement, the tenant should notify the landlord of the intent to allow the landlord proper time to complete application, screening, and qualifying of the new prospective tenant. If the prospect meets the qualifications of tenancy, the old lease should be terminated and a new lease drafted for the new occupant.

Departing Roommates

When a rental property has multiple tenants named on the lease and one of the roommates decides to move before expiration of the lease agreement, the landlord should have a policy in place that prohibits the return of money held as a security deposit until all roommates named on the lease have vacated the property. The landlord should allow the roommates to sort out their own differences. If the roommates are replacing the departing tenant, the new tenant should pay the departing tenant a fair and agreed-upon amount for their share of the security deposit. Any other issues of money and responsibility should be handled among the roommates so that the landlord's only responsibility is to screen and approve the new tenant. To protect against liability for the security deposit, the landlord should insist that the departing tenant sign a Deposit Assignment and Release Agreement, shown in Form 6, as part of the release of tenancy. This agreement releases the departing tenant from any further obligation to pay rent and also assigns the departing tenant's share of the security deposit to a named party.

Deposit Assignment and Release Agreement

This agreement is entered into this_____day of_____, 20_____, between _____(Tenant) and_____(Owner).

WHEREAS, on or about_____, 20_____, Tenant delivered to Owner a written notice of termination stating an intention to vacate the Premises located at: _____, effective on the_____day of _____, 20_____.

In consideration for Owner releasing Tenant from the obligations under the Lease or Rental Agreement dated the__day of_____, 20_____, Tenant hereby assigns to_____ _____any and all right or claim to the security deposit held by Owner for said rental unit.

As further consideration for the execution of this Agreement by Owner, Tenant agrees to waive and release any and all right or claim to said security deposit.

_____   _____
Date   Owner/Manager   Date   Tenant

Form 6: Deposit Assignment and Release Form (Griswold, p. 229)

Death of a Tenant

In the event that a tenant should pass away during tenancy, the tenant's family will likely take responsibility for the tenant's arrangements, property, and other necessities. If the tenant lived alone and is suspected of being deceased, the landlord should first try to gain entry to the rental unit using the procedures established for gaining entry during an emergency. Once a death has been confirmed, the police department and the person listed on the rental agreement as an emergency contact should be called. The landlord is then responsible for protecting the property of the deceased and denying entry, with the exception of law enforcement and legally authorized persons. The landlord's attorney is able to define legally authorized persons so that the landlord is not liable for missing items.

Domestic Problems

When members of the same family and rental unit have disputes, the landlord must remain neutral. The landlord does not have the authority to side with either party. When the disputes reach the point of creating a disturbance, they should be treated as any other tenant disturbance. Law enforcement should be called and disturbed neighbors should be requested to document a signed and written complaint. If the dispute becomes violent, law enforcement should be called to intervene. The landlord has no responsibility to change locks, remove a party from the property, or remove a party from the lease unless a restraining order or other court order dictates such actions. The landlord may request that the disputing parties sign an Agreement of Consent to follow the instructions as outlined in the court order.

Tenant Notices

When a tenant fails to pay rent in a timely manner or violates the lease or rental agreement, the tenant must be provided written notice of the problem and offered sufficient time to resolve the issue. Generally, seven to ten days is considered sufficient time. When the tenant cannot or will not respond within the established time limit, the landlord has a responsibility to file a claim to bring the matter before the courts to get an eviction. Bringing the matter before the courts can be a costly and emotionally draining experience. The loss of rent, legal fees, possibility of property damage, cost to acquire new tenants, and impact on the reputation of the landlord or property management are all at stake. A good property manager will try to avoid the time and expense of eviction procedures and implement an alternative plan of getting the tenant to leave. A long-term and expensive eviction process may be nonproductive if the problem tenant has no assets. The primary objective of the property manager should be to regain control of the rental unit and find another, more suitable tenant as quickly as possible in order to maintain or recreate cash flow. The property manager may engage more cost-effective alternatives to terminating the lease of problem tenants. As an alternative to eviction, the property manager may pursue one of the following avenues:

- **Negotiate a voluntary move-out**
  The property manager or owner may engage in negotiation with the problem tenant to move out voluntarily. The negotiation might include an offer to forgive any due money so long as the tenant moves by a specified date. The offer may include reimbursement of the security deposit even though the terms of the lease or rental agreement dictate that the tenant is not entitled to the amount. The offer may also include releasing the tenant from paying for any existent damages so long as the tenant leaves the property. In all negotiations with problem tenants, the resulting outcome should be documented and signed by the tenant. The documentation should clearly indicate a move-out date and specify that no due refunds or reimbursements be paid until the tenant actually moves out.

- **Engage a mediator or arbitrator**
  As an alternative to eviction and negotiation, the property manager may engage the services of a neutral third-party arbitrator. The lease or rental agreement should indicate that dispute resolution be provided through mediation or arbitration. Mediation and arbitration are often confused as being one and the same;

they are not. Mediation is an informal process where the tenant and landlord argue their case to the mediator and the mediator assists in resolving the issue. Arbitration is a more formal process, inclusive of attorneys, witnesses, and subject matter experts. The results of arbitration are legally binding and enforceable. Many companies exist for the purpose of providing mediation, arbitration, or both services.

- **Rent court**
  All states have small claims or municipal courts that serve local jurisdictions. Small claims court, however, may only be used to resolve disputes that do not involve eviction. Issues of responsibility for property damage, for example, may be handled in small claims court. Some states also have rent courts at the local municipality level that are designed to resolve tenant/landlord disputes, such as evictions. Other states require evictions to be handled in higher and more costly courts.

Tenant Evictions

When all other options have failed, eviction is inevitable. The court processes for eviction vary by state. The property manager who partners with a competent attorney skilled in real estate law may turn to the attorney to represent his or her interest. The attorney will be knowledgeable in laws and processes that are applicable to the particular property.

Before a landlord can evict a tenant from a rental property, the landlord must provide the tenant with an appropriate Notice to Terminate Tenancy, as shown in Form 7. The landlord must then file an appropriate claim with the courts and then follow the prescribed court procedures. The tenant will receive a copy of the complaint as filed with the court and be summoned to appear before a judge of the court. There are different types of evictions:

- Actual evictions occur when either a court order or law enforcement is obtained to remove tenants from a property and regain possession of the property.

- Constructive evictions occur when the landlord allows the physical structure to deteriorate to the point that it cannot serve the purpose for which it was rented.

- Partial evictions occur when the tenant is deprived of the use of a portion of the rental property as the property is defined in the lease or rental agreement. Partial evictions usually mean that the landlord is entitled to only a portion of the rent.

Notice to Terminate Tenancy

To _____

          Tenant(s) in Possession

You are hereby required within thirty (30) days from this date to vacate, remove your belongings, and deliver up possession of the premises, now held and occupied by you, being those premises located at:

House No_____Street_____Apt #_____

City_____State_____Zip_____

This notice is intended for the purpose of terminating the lease/rental agreement by which you now hold possession of the above-described premises. Should you fail to vacate and comply, legal proceedings will be instituted against you to recover possession, to declare said lease/rental forfeited, and to recover rents, damages attorney fees, and court costs for the period of the unlawful detention.

Please be advised that your rent for said premises is due and payable up to and including the date of termination of your tenancy under this notice. This notice complies with the terms and conditions of the lease or rental agreement under which you presently hold said property. Please contact the office of the landlord/manager if you have questions regarding this notice or the requirements and procedure for getting back any deposits to which you are entitled.

Dated this_____day of_____, 20_____

Owner/Manager

Proof of Service

I, the undersigned, being of legal age, declare under penalty of perjury that I served the notice to terminate tenancy, of which this is a true copy, on the above-mentioned tenant in possession, in the manner indicated below:

On_____, 20_____, I served the notice to the tenant in the following

manner:_____

Executed on_____, 20_____, at_____

By_____Title_____

Form 7: Notice of Termination (Taylor, p. 127)

An attorney should handle tenant evictions, particularly contested evictions, which would otherwise be prolonged and delayed processes. Attorneys are skilled in interpreting the precise and detailed rules governing the filing and serving of evictions. Mistakes in the eviction process can be very costly, and courts have ruled against landlords who do not present substantiating evidence of their claim. An eviction case that is lost because of technicalities creates a financial loss for the landlord as well as a continued relationship with the problem tenant who fails to pay or otherwise violates the lease or rental agreement.

The eviction process is emotionally draining and frustrating. The landlord must be competent and dedicated to withstand the lengthy process and not resort to constructive evictions, where illegal behavior and activities are used to force the tenant to vacate the property. Changing locks, shutting off utilities, and denying tenant services are illegal practices for which the landlord could be sued.

Landlords must respond to the tenant's request for maintenance and repairs during the eviction process. The landlord is still responsible to maintain a safe and habitable rental property during the eviction process. If a tenant is hurt or injured due to neglect, the neglect and subsequent injuries will be used against the landlord in court actions.

The landlord needs to provide proper notice of the intent to evict the tenant. There are four primary reasons for evicting tenants:

1. **The tenant fails to pay rent.**
   The tenant who fails to pay rent should be issued a Pay Rent or Quit Notice, as shown in Form 8. The notice informs the tenant that he or she must pay the rent or vacate the property. Dependent upon state law, the tenant is allowed three to seven days to pay in full.

Notice to Pay Rent or Quit

Please note: Check your state statutes for the specified number of days residents must be allowed to pay rent or deliver up possession, which should be stated in notice below. Also check to see if any additional or specific wording format is required by your city or state for this notice to be valid and enforceable.

TO _____
and all other residents in possession of the premises at the following address:

_____

PLEASE TAKE NOTICE that according to the terms of your rental agreement, the rent is now due and payable for the above stated address which you currently hold and occupy. Our records indicate that your rental account is delinquent in the amount itemized as follows:

Rental Period (dates)_____Rent Due $ _____
Rental Period (dates)_____Rent Due $ _____
Rental Period (dates)_____Rent Due $ _____
TOTAL RENT DUE $_____
Less partial payment of $_____
TOTAL BALANCE DUE of $_____

You are hereby required to pay said rent in full within_____days or to remove from and deliver up possession of the above address, or legal proceedings will be instituted against you to recover possession of said premises, and to recover all rents due and damages, together with court costs, legal and attorney fees, according to the terms of you Lease or Rental Agreement.

Date this_____day of_____, 20_____

Owner/Manager

Proof of Service

I, the undersigned being at least 18 years of age, declare under penalty of perjury that I served the above notice, of which this is a true copy, on the above-mentioned tenant(s) in possession in the manner(s) indicated below:

_____On_____, 20_____, I handed the notice to the tenant(s) personally.

_____On_____, 20_____, after attempting personal service, I handed the notice to a person of suitable age and discretion at the residence/business of the tenant(s), AND I deposited a true copy in the U.S. Mail, in a sealed envelope with postage fully prepaid, addressed to the tenant(s) at his/her/their place of residence (date mailed, if different from above date_____).

_____On_____, 20_____, after attempting service in both manners indicated above, I posted the notice in a conspicuous place at the residence of the tenant(s), AND I deposited a true copy in the U.S. Mail, in a sealed envelope with postage fully prepaid, addressed to the tenant(s) at his/her/their place of residence (date mailed, if different from above date_____).

Executed on_____, 20_____, at the County/City of

State of_____Served by_____

Form 8: Pay Rent or Quit (Taylor, p. 117)

2. **The tenant violates the lease or rental agreement.**
   The tenant who violates other terms of the lease or rental
   agreement should be issued a Cure or Quit Notice, as
   shown in Form 9. The notice informs the tenant that he
   or she must cure the violation, vacate the property, or
   be evicted. Dependent upon the state law, the tenant is
   allowed a limited number of days to comply with the
   notice. Tenants who are involved in illegal activities,
   have repeatedly violated the terms of the lease or rental
   agreement, or have subjected the property to extreme
   damage may be issued a Notice to Quit or Unconditional
   Quit Notice. This notice differs from the Cure or Quit
   notice because the tenant is not allowed an opportunity
   to cure the violation. The tenant is informed that he or
   she either must vacate the property or be evicted.

Notice to Cure or Quit
(Correct Rental Violation)

To _____
Tenant(s) in Possession

Address _____

_____

1. You are hereby notified that you have violated or failed to perform the following terms in your rental/lease agreement, which states that resident(s) agrees to:

2. You are in violation of that provision for the following reason(s):

3. You must perform or correct this violation within ____ days after service of this notice. The violation can be corrected by immediately doing the following:

   Or if you fail to perform or correct the terms of the rental/lease agreement within the specified time, you must vacate and deliver possession of the premises to the landlord/manager.

4. **If you fail to correct or vacate within _____days, legal proceedings will be initiated against you to recover possession, rent owed, damages, court costs, and attorney fees.**

5. It is not our intention to terminate the rental/lease agreement. However, all tenants must follow guidelines stated in the agreement. If you are unable to comply, the landlord elects to declare a forfeiture of your rental or lease agreement. You will also be subject to forfeit any security deposit given by you to cover any costs you are still liable for, and the landlord reserves the right to pursue collection of any future rental losses. We may be contacted at

Thank you for your prompt cooperation in correcting this matter

Owner/Manager_____Date_____

Form 9: Cure or Quit (Taylor, p. 110)

3. **The tenant vacates the property.**
   The tenant who abandons a property will do so without providing notice. Policy should be established in the lease or rental agreement that requires tenants to inform the property manager when extended absences of two or more weeks are anticipated. If no such notice is provided and the landlord suspects that the tenant

may have abandoned the property, the property manager must first determine that the property is in fact abandoned. The landlord should make reasonable efforts to ensure that the abandonment is not the result of an unexpected hospitalization or delay in returning from vacation. States have their own rules regarding abandonment. The landlord must follow state and local laws regarding gaining entry and disposing of personal property. When the landlord determines that the rental unit has been abandoned before the terms of the lease have been satisfied, the tenant's financial obligation to the lease is broken. Generally, if the landlord is already in the process of evicting the tenant, the landlord may continue with the eviction process until the court allows the landlord to gain possession of the rental property. This reduces the liability of landlords for tenants who may show up later and claim to be still occupying the property. If the property manager is not in the process of evicting the tenant, the landlord should issue Notice of Belief to Abandonment, in compliance with state laws. The issuance of this notice, along with completion of other state requirements, will allow the landlord to take possession of the rental unit and market it for re-rent.

Landlords have an obligation to mitigate rent loss damages by renting the unit to another tenant. The landlord must properly advertise, market, show, and select qualified tenants just as if the tenant had moved legally. When the landlord finds another suitable tenant to occupy the property, the abandoning tenant is released of any further financial obligations to the landlord. The landlord is not required to lower the rent or selection criteria in order to secure new tenants. Also, the landlord is not obligated to give the particular rental unit priority over other rental units in an effort to mitigate damages. The law requires that landlords make reasonable efforts to mitigate losses due to the former tenant. The landlord must be able to prove to the court that he or she was reasonable in mitigating damages. Courts place the burden of proof on the tenant to prove that the landlord was unreasonable in mitigating damages. The courts require tenants to present legitimate reasons for breaking the lease and abandoning the property. The courts may rule that harassment or uninhabitable conditions are legitimate reasons to break the lease on a property and provide the landlord no compensation under such circumstances. Some courts have allowed tenants to avoid the financial obligation in part or in whole by requesting the court's leniency for a hardship. Some state laws also allow tenants to avoid payment because of special circumstances, such as military transfers, job transfers, or health complications. The landlord should check the applicable laws that apply to the particular rental unit.

Once the landlord has possession of the rental unit, the property manager has a responsibility to try to locate the abandoning tenant with regard to his or her personal possessions. If the tenant cannot be located or the tenant refuses to take possession of the items, the landlord should photograph and itemize the abandoned items. The items should be securely stored until the landlord is able to either sell or dispose of the items. A third party should be present to witness to the handling of the tenant's items. When abandoned personal property is extensive, the landlord may consider choosing an outside company that specializes in the appraisal, sale, or disposition of such items. Some states allow the landlord to place liens against personal property to recover losses. After all appropriate notices have been issued and the time frame for the tenant to comply has expired, the landlord may sell the tenant's personal property to recover the cost of unpaid rent, removing personal property, storage fees, and sale of personal property. Any remaining balance should be refunded to the tenant. Some states allow for an automatic lien against personal property, others require the landlord to obtain a court order before taking possession of personal property. The landlord must understand and comply with laws applicable to the particular state.

4. **The tenant holds over at the property**
   The tenant who refuses to leave at the expiration of his or her lease or rental agreement is a holdover tenant. These tenants may continue to make payment on the lease or rental agreement. The landlord has the option of not accepting the payment. The payment is only considered rent if the landlord accepts it. Most states require the landlord to issue holdover tenants a notice to vacate or be evicted. Some states allow the landlord to begin eviction processes immediately.

If, after serving the tenant with appropriate notices, the tenant fails to pay the rent, cure the lease or rental agreement violation, or take possession of the abandoned property, eviction processes must be enforced. The landlord must first file the appropriate forms required of the particular state and have the tenant served a summons to appear in court. States offer pre-printed eviction forms that allow the landlord to specify the damages that he or she is seeking from the problem tenant. The damages must be limited to rent and actual damages. Late charges and other fees are not included in the eviction.

Serving Notice

A person authorized by the court to serve legal notice by hand delivery or another constructive service, such as certified mail, must serve the tenant. States have their own definitions of "proper legal service," and the landlord should follow the rules established by the state where the property is located. The state establishes rules governing who is authorized to serve notice, the method of delivering notice, the parties to be served, and the time frame for a response.

Involving the Courts

Tenants are usually aware that they have violated the conditions of a lease or rental agreement. In response to an eviction notice, the tenant may either leave voluntarily or opt for a settlement agreement outside of court. In either case, the landlord should dismiss the court eviction case. The busy court system expects landlords who are able to reach out-of-court settlements to dismiss their court actions in a timely fashion to save the courts the expense of further processing documentation for the case.

States impose a time limitation for tenants to respond to the eviction complaint. If the tenant does not respond within the specified time frame, the eviction will proceed as an uncontested eviction. The landlord is expected to prove his or her case. If the tenant is not present in court to respond to or deny the charges, the landlord usually prevails if sufficient documentation is presented to back the landlord's claim. If the tenant does respond to the eviction notice or appears in court to contest the allegations of the eviction, the case will proceed as a contested eviction. The tenant will be given a chance to present his or her defense to the allegations. The tenant may respond with a denial to the complaint or an affirmative defense for his or her actions. In some courts, the tenant has been successful in requesting the court to allow additional time for the tenant to engage in a payment plan or requesting the court's leniency for a hardship. Courts have also granted tenants extended time to appeal a ruling or extended time to overcome a hardship.

Taking Possession

Usually, if the landlord is able to provide documentation and justification for the eviction, the court will rule in the landlord's favor. However, the court will impose harsh penalties and fines against landlords who present situations that are perceived as illegal, retaliatory, or discriminatory. Once the court rules in the favor of the landlord, the landlord must present the ruling to law enforcement. Law enforcement will issue the tenant one final notice to vacate the premises. If the tenant does not vacate the premises, law enforcement may intervene in the process to remove the illegally housed tenants and their possessions and hand over legal possession of the property to the landlord. The landlord should accompany law enforcement in evicting the tenants and change locks to the property.

Enforcing Judgments

Getting the problem tenant to vacate the property and gaining possession of the property offers the landlord an opportunity to establish a new tenant-landlord relationship to create or recreate cash flow. However, judgments against problem tenants require more work of the landlord. When courts determine that evicted and problem tenants are responsible for paying rent, damages, and/or legal fees, the landlord is responsible for collecting the judgment. The landlord has several options with regard to collecting judgment amounts. Proper screening of tenants before signing leases or rental agreements should ensure that the tenant's Social Security number, employer, bank accounts, credit card accounts, vehicle information, and other personal information are accurate as of the day of lease or rental agreement signing. The landlord may make use of this information to:

- Locate the tenant.

- Make application for a court order to garnish the wages or salary of the tenant.

- Provide the information to a hired and licensed collection agency to collect the debt on behalf of the landlord. Licensed collection agencies receive part of the collected debt as a fee for services rendered. The amount of the fee is dependent upon the amount of the debt as well as the age of the debt. Landlords who are intent upon using this option should engage the services of the collection agency as soon as possible.

Even after completing all the work necessary to gain an eviction and collect a judgment, the tenant may still be able to stop payment to the landlord by filing bankruptcy. Current federal bankruptcy laws prohibit the landlord from proceeding with court evictions. The landlord is required to stop any collection or eviction efforts as soon as the bankruptcy is known. Federal laws impose strict penalties against landlords who violate the stay of bankruptcies. The landlord is required to file pleadings with the bankruptcy court to request an issuance of Relief from Stay before proceeding with eviction processes. The attorney is best suited to deal with tenant bankruptcies as they apply to evictions.

Tenant Move-Out

The lease or rental agreement should be supplemented with documentation that describes the procedures put into place when a tenant decides to move out of the rental unit. Tenants should follow the processes outlined, including giving appropriate notice of the intent to move. Upon receipt of a communication to vacate the property, the landlord should deliver to the tenant a Move-Out Information Letter, as shown in Form 10, that details the processes to follow. The checklist of conditions that was completed at move-in and modified during the tenancy should be used to checklist an inspection during move-out. The biggest issue to be resolved during a move-out is the return of the security deposit. The security deposit is held as liability against damages and unpaid rent. Damages do not include ordinary wear and tear. Disputes arise when the tenant and landlord disagree over the meaning of ordinary wear and tear.

Move-Out Information Letter

Tenant Name(s) _____

Rental Unit Address _____

Dear: _____

We are pleased that you selected our property for your home and hope that you enjoyed living here. Although we are disappointed to lose you as a tenant, we wish you good luck in the future. We want your move-out to go smoothly and end our relationship on a positive note.

Moving time is always chaotic and you have many things on your mind, including getting the maximum amount of your security deposit back. Contrary to some rental property owners, we want to be able to return you security deposit promptly and in full. Your security deposit is $_____. Note that your security deposit shall not be applied to your last month's rent as the deposit is to ensure the fulfillment of lease conditions and is to be used only as a contingency against any damages to the rental unit.

This move-out letter describes how we expect your rental unit to be left and what our procedures are for returning your security deposit. Basically, we expect you to leave your rental unit in the same condition it was in when you moved in, except for ordinary wear and tear that occurred during your tenancy. To refresh your memory, a copy of your signed Move-in/Move-out Inspection Checklist is attached reflecting the condition of the rental unit at the beginning of your tenancy. We will be using this same detailed checklist when we inspect your rental unit upon move-out and will deduct the cost of any necessary cleaning and the costs of repairs, not considered ordinary wear and tear, from your security deposit.

To maximize your chances of a full and prompt refund, we suggest that you go through the Move-in/Move-out Inspection Checklist line by line and make sure that all items are clean and free from damage, except for ordinary wear and tear. All closets, cabinets, shelves, drawers, countertops, storage, refrigerator, and exterior areas should be completely free of items. Feel free to check off completed items on this copy of the Move-in/Move-out Inspection Checklist, as we will use the original for your final inspection.

Some of our tenants prefer to let professionals complete these items. You can contact your own professional or, upon request, we will be glad to refer you to our service providers so that you can focus on other issues of your move. You will work directly with the service provider on costs and payment terms, knowing that you are working with someone who can prepare the unit for the walk-through inspection. Call us if you would like contact information or for any questions as to the type of cleaning we expect.

Please be sure to remove all personal possessions, including furniture, clothes, household items, food, plants, cleaning supplies, and any bags of garbage or loose items that belong to you. Of course, please do not remove any appliances, fixtures, or other items installed or attached to your rental unit unless you have our prior written approval.

Form 10: Move-Out Information Letter (Griswold, p. 234)

Move-Out Information Letter

continued

Please contact the appropriate companies and schedule the disconnection or transfer of your phone, cable, and utility services in your name. Also, cancel any newspaper subscriptions and provide the U.S. Postal Service with a change of address form.

Please contact us when all the conditions have been satisfied to arrange an inspection of your rental unit during daylight hours. To avoid being assessed a key replacement charge; please return all keys at the time you vacate.

You have listed_____as the move-out date in your notice. Please be reminded that you will be assessed holdover rent of $_____per day of each partial or full day after the above move-out date that you remain in the rental unit or have possession of the keys. If you need to extend your tenancy for any reason, you must contact us immediately. Please be prepared to provide your forwarding address where we may mail your security deposit.

It is our policy to return all security deposits either in person or to an address you provide within _____after you move out and return all keys. If any deductions are made for past due rent or other unpaid charges, for damages beyond ordinary wear and tear, or for failure to properly clean, an itemized explanation will be included with the security deposit accounting.

If you have any questions, please contact us at_____

Thank you again for making our property your home. We have enjoyed serving you, and we hope that you will recommend our rental properties to your friends, family, and colleagues. Please let us know if we can provide you with a recommendation letter. Good luck!

Sincerely,

_____
Owner/Manager

Form 10: Move-Out Information Letter (Griswold, p. 234)

Wear and Tear

Ordinary wear and tear is defined in most states to mean the deterioration or damage to property that is expected to occur from normal usage. The real discrepancy lies in the definition of the phrase "normal usage." Different individuals, courts, judges, and landlords have differing interpretations of the phrase. There are no rules regarding the definition, but the landlord is expected to be able to determine the difference between ordinary wear and tear and more serious damage that can be deducted from the security deposit. The landlord must be able to explain why the deducted damages exceed ordinary wear and tear. Some common examples that differentiate ordinary wear and tear from damage are provided in Table 1.

Ordinary Wear and Tear	Damage Beyond Ordinary Wear and Tear
Wall smudges, particularly around light switches	Pencil, pen, and crayon marks
Small marks on doors and walls	Large marks, scraps, graffiti, and holes in the doors or walls
Tack and nail holes	Large holes that require spackling or dry walling
Faded, peeling, and cracked paint	Large areas of dirty, smudged, and scuffed paint
Worn carpet	Torn or ripped carpet
Dirt and spots on carpet	Bleached, dyed, or urine-stained and smelly carpet
Faded curtains, drapes, and carpet	Cigarette burns, food, and drink stains in carpet, drapes, or curtains
Dirty blinds and shades	Bent and missing blinds, malfunctioning blinds and shades
Sticking doors and windows	Broken hinges and frames, missing window and door screens

Table 1: Ordinary Wear and Tear versus Damages

When documenting and accounting for damages, the landlord must be specific in the itemization. The documentation should include:

- Each damaged item, listed separately.

- The location of the damaged item using compass directions.

- The type and extent of damage; that is, excessive, minor,

ripped, cracked, burned, etc.

- The type and extent of repair; that is, spackle, paint, deodorize, refinish, etc.

- The cost of repair or replacement.

To avoid discrepancies in defining ordinary wear and tear, some landlords have successfully implemented a process of supplying tenants with a pricing chart that itemizes the charges that will be required to perform various services, replacement, or repairs. The tenant is able to see how expensive certain items and services are in advance of putting themselves in the position to cause damage. The problem with this process is that some items increase in value over time while others decrease in value. Also, different contractors have differing pricing for the same work. The landlord must be careful to update the pricing chart to reflect changes in the market. If the landlord's deductions are challenged in court, the courts will only consider actual invoices, not estimates of repair, replacement, or service. If the amounts charged, based on the pricing chart, exceed those provided to the court as invoices, the tenant may be awarded damages for the landlord's attempt to fraud both the tenant and the court.

Refunding Security Deposits

Most states will accept any form of oral or written communication, provided 30 days in advance, to serve as proper notification of the tenant's intent to move out. Some states require tenants to provide a written notice. If the landlord requires a more formal notice with a specific format, he or she should provide the tenant with such a form to be completed upon learning of the tenant's intent to move out. All states require the landlord to provide the tenant with a written accounting of the security deposit deductions within a maximum of three to four weeks of moving out. Some states require the accounting to be provided within 3 days, while others require it to be provided within 14 days. In any case, time is of essence in determining the amount of security deposit to refund to tenants.

Many tenants fear that the landlord will try to cheat them out of their security deposit and fail to pay the last month's rent. The language of the Move-Out Information Letter should clearly indicate that the security deposit is not to be substituted for the last month's rent payment. Unless the lease or rental agreement specifies that the deposit be applied to the last month's rent, the landlord is not legally obligated to apply the security deposit toward payment of rent. The landlord may initiate court action for failure to pay rent, particularly if other damages exist and the security deposit is not sufficient to cover the repairs. However, the courts are not likely to look favorably on such a case introduced as a matter of principle. Typically, the courts will only allow for damages outside of ordinary wear and tear, cleaning, keys, and unpaid rent. These expenses are often not excessive enough to incur the cost of engaging in a legal dispute. Also, the courts have a tendency to rule in favor of providing the tenant compensation for the aggravation of having to go to court. The landlord's efforts are better spent in encouraging the tenant to recover the full security deposit. The landlord, for example, may offer to provide tenants with a letter of recommendation for their next move. The offer encourages tenants to make an effort to leave the rental unit in good condition. This means that the landlord has to spend less money on renovating the unit for the next tenant and may begin to market and show the unit sooner. This method of supporting the tenant in the move-out results in more cash flow for the landlord than could ever be obtained through court actions.

Move-Out Inspection

The best time to conduct a move-out inspection is after the rental unit has been vacated. The landlord should conduct the walk-through as soon as possible, preferably with the tenant so that the tenant may not claim that damages were caused after his or her move-out. Since it is not always possible to conduct the move-out inspection with the tenant, the landlord may choose to do the inspection with a witness. The move-in checklist should be used at move-out to note any damages that have incurred.

During the walk-through, the landlord may not be able to correctly determine the cost of repairs or replacement. The landlord should note the damage and reserve the right to deduct the actual cost of repairs once they are determined. The actual costs must be determined and documented within the time frame specified by the particular state for providing tenants with an accounting of security deposits. Some tenants will request that the landlord allow them an opportunity to clean or make repairs in an effort to secure all of the security deposit. The landlord is cautioned against engaging in this type of arrangement. An unskilled tenant may create problems that will be even more costly at some later date. The landlord has a responsibility to provide a safe and habitable environment for the new tenant. Skilled maintenance and repair personnel should be employed to make repairs, and the landlord should refuse the tenant's request to fix the rental unit on his or her own.

Security Deposit Accounting

The tenant must be presented an accounting of the security

deposit within 30 days or less of move-out, dependent upon state statute. Failure to provide the tenant with an itemized accounting of the security deposit could result in the forfeiture of the security deposit or, in some instances, punitive damages against the landlord. Deductions must be clearly defined and any balance due the tenant should be returned. The walk-through should provide for a thorough accounting of damages. Pictures and videotapes are the landlord's best defense against disputes over damages. The landlord is cautioned to ensure that pictures and videotapes are acquired when the rental unit is empty or properly acquired during authorized visits to the rental unit. Any refund should be provided promptly. Tenants who are made to wait for their refund are more likely to get upset by the delay and challenge the expenses being charged. Although no laws or regulations prohibit the landlord from seeking reimbursement for damages discovered after providing a tenant an accounting and refund, courts are not likely to side with the landlord under such circumstances.

Depending upon the landlord-tenant relationship, a tenant may or may not disclose a forwarding address to mail the security deposit accounting and refund. The tenant's notice to vacate may contain a forwarding address. If not, the landlord should request that the tenant provide a forwarding address to mail the security deposit accounting and/or refund. Tenants may also offer to pick up their refunds personally. When the landlord has no other method of reaching the vacated tenant, the landlord may send the accounting and refund to the address of the vacated rental unit. If the tenant has submitted a change of address with the local post office, mail will be forwarded to the tenant's newly established address. If the tenant has not submitted a change of address, the correspondence will simply be returned to the landlord. The landlord should keep the returned envelope as proof that he or she tried in good faith to deliver the security deposit refund and accounting to the tenant. Different states have differing laws regarding undeliverable security deposit refunds. The landlord is required to determine the laws that apply to the particular rental property. As an alternative, the landlord may send the correspondence via certified mail or request that the post office provide a certificate of mailing when the correspondence is mailed. A certificate of mailing indicates the date on which correspondence is mailed, but unlike certified mail, a certificate of mailing does not require the signature of the receiving party.

When the vacating tenants include more than one adult, all of the adult tenants may believe that they are entitled to the security deposit, either in part or whole. Most state laws provide for the security deposit to be divided equally among the adult tenants whose signatures appear on the lease or rental agreement, unless specified otherwise. Written instructions, signed by each adult tenant or a court order may be used to determine the distribution of the security deposit refund. Otherwise, the landlord is required to split the security deposit among all adult tenants. The landlord should make the payment payable to all of the adult tenants to guard against liability to any of the tenants for payment. The landlord should mail the payment and accounting for the security deposit to just one of the adult tenants. The other adult tenants should be provided a copy of the check and a copy of the security deposit accounting. Correspondence should be mailed to each adult tenant at his or her respective forwarding address. The tenants would then handle the endorsement of the payment.

When unpaid rent and damages exceed the amount held as security deposit, the landlord should allocate the security deposit to the damages and then seek payment for the unpaid rent. When the security deposit is properly applied to damages, future court actions will only be necessary to address rent payments. This benefits the landlord because unpaid rent is easier to prove than damages in court hearings. The landlord must be able to research and evaluate the amounts involved when and if a tenant challenges deductions from a security deposit. If the expense involved in disputing deductions in court is more than the amount in dispute, the landlord should consider negotiating with the tenant outside of court proceedings.

10

CHAPTER TEN

Selling Management Property

The sale of management property is dependent upon its existing location, growth trends, interest rates, demographics, and zoning. Investors of management properties may use leverage in any existing properties to acquire new properties for investment purposes. The acquisition of new properties is often preceded by the sale of existing properties. The sale of management properties requires the ability to properly market the property as well as engage professional services to assist with the sale and closing.

Marketing

Investors in real estate who intend to buy and sell properties should consider the factors that will affect the sale of acquired properties before the purchase is made. The investor is cautioned to spend time developing an exit or sales strategy to put into place when the time comes to dispose of property. The investor must be able to anticipate market factors that will affect both the purchase and sale of acquired properties. This method of "beginning with the end in mind" is one method of increasing the property's marketability. The same factors that should be researched and understood before acquiring management property should be applied to the marketing and sale of management property:

- Location

- Growth trends

- Demographics

- Zoning ordinances

- Interest rates

Other methods used to increase marketability include maximizing exposure to the property, providing property that a buyer wants, pricing the property to sell, and "sweetening the pot." (Berges, 2004)

The marketing plan should include all economically feasible methods of maximizing exposure to the property. Buyers cannot buy unless they know that the property is for sale. The more individuals who know that a property is for sale, the better the chance a seller has in selling the property. Marketing should include all forms of advertisement, include the following:

- Newspapers

- Radio

- Real estate magazines

- Television

- Internet

- Signage

- Real estate agents

- Multiple listing services

- Professional affiliations

- Handouts and flyers

- Direct mailings

- Word-of-mouth

Property owners should provide the potential buyer with a property that presents the best characteristics of the neighborhood. The property should characterize the highest level of neatness and cleanliness; prospective buyers are not likely to invest in the ruins of the neighborhood. The property should be priced to sell within the average market price of the neighborhood in which it is located. Overpriced properties take longer to sell, whereas properties priced at or a little below market value offer a quicker sale. Properties that are vacant and also being financed incur monthly fees. These fees, tied to a non-income-producing property, could be better leveraged in an income-producing property. Property owners may "sweeten the pot" by offering credits, contributions to the closing costs, or other amenities such as appliances. These types of incentives may make the difference for potential buyers in choosing this property or moving on to other properties. Mortgage companies may allow the seller to give the buyer a credit of up to 3 percent of the selling price, to be used at the will of the buyer.

Hired Help

Some property owners are competent to sell property on their own; others engage the services of real estate professionals.

Many management property owners start out selling on their own with the belief that it would be more cost effective than paying the fees associated with hiring professionals. They will eventually turn to professionals because time is of essence in the sale of property, and many property owners and managers do not have the necessary skills to negotiate the sale. Realtors are trained and prepared to provide essential skills, such as:

- Preparing and printing advertisements

- Placing signage

- Changing advertisements

- Answering phone inquiries

- Conducting walk-throughs

- Negotiating terms and amounts

- Preparing documents

- Filing and submitting documents

The seller should also engage the services of an attorney to review the contract and other applicable documents used in the selling process. The seller must be sure to hire a real estate lawyer, trained in real estate law and contracts. Though most sellers would like to sell property as is, state laws and regulations require that sellers provide documentation and disclosures to reveal all known and suspect defects, environmental conditions, or other conditions that may be detrimental to the property and included structures. States have differing requirements for the disclosure of defects and conditions. Some jurisdictions go as far as requiring the seller to disclose any known suspected ghostly or physic phenomena.

Though these requirements are extreme, attempts to hide problems are illegal and could result in costly lawsuits for the property owner.

Taxes and Section 1031

The IRS established Section 1031 of the IRS code to allow property owners to defer paying capital gains taxes on the sale of property if the property is properly exchanged for other real property. The exchange must be for like-kind property, acquired within a specified time frame. Like-kind does not require that the properties be of equal value, though they could be. The exchanged property may be of equal or greater value than the owner's currently held property. This provides an investor the opportunity to increase the value of his or her assets. For management properties, the exchange property can be any real property held for business, trade, or investment purposes, so long as the property is of equal or greater value than the owner's property. A facilitator or registered exchange company must be retained to assist the exchange. The facilitator, who must be retained prior to the closing of either property in the exchange, is bound by a written agreement to hold the proceeds of the exchange. Since the owner is not allowed access to proceeds from the sale of his or her property, the owner retains no capital gain or profit. Section 1031 does allow for expenses of the property, such as the balance of the mortgage, title fees, and attorney's fee, to be paid from the proceeds of the property sale. The remaining proceeds are secured in an escrow account to be exchanged for the purchase of another property.

Within 45 days of the closing date, the property manager must identify no more than three potential properties to be used in the exchange. The owner is then given another six months to close on one of the three properties specified. There are instances in which the owner is not able to sell the existing property or acquire capital needed to buy the replacement property. The owner may hire the services of a replacement property exchange company, which will make the purchase on behalf of the owner for a fee. The fees vary by company and can be costly. The rules, regulations governing the purchase, and owner's equity in the purchase will also vary by company. The IRS allows for a reverse 1031 exchange, which allows the owner to first purchase the new property and then follow the established guidelines of Section 1031, requiring the close of the owner's existing property within six months of the purchase. (Griswold, 2001)

Sales Techniques

The art of negotiations is the key to sale of rental property. Negotiation is the exchange of items, which the negotiating parties agree are of equivalent value. In real estate, two parties can negotiate the exchange of money for property. Expert negotiations, however, will allow for the exchange of property for the best possible price and terms. There are techniques for negotiating rental property that allow both parties to receive the best possible price or terms. The six most successful techniques are as follows (Berges, 2004):

1. **Psychology**
   Not all property owners are professionals in real estate or the buying and selling processes. Buying and selling involves emotional and psychological transitions. Most people do not engage in real estate transactions on the spot. They need time to make comparisons, consult with others, or a number of other things that postpone

the decision to buy or sell. To reduce the decision time, the expert negotiator will offer the indecisive potential buyer an opportunity to put a hold on the property for a relatively small, refundable fee. The expert seller then allows the buyer a window of opportunity to make a decision about actually buying the property. The window could be a week or some other agreed-upon time frame. If the buyer agrees to the offer, the psychological transition begins. The buyer takes a step in the acquisition process, so the buyer transitions from deciding whether to purchase the property to reinforcing the decision to buy the property. As such, fear and negativity are transformed into rationalization and justification for taking the initial step. The psychological sales technique requires an understanding of people and working with them to overcome objections. The seller engages the buyer in the first step of the buying process and allows the buyer's psyche to lead him or her to secure the purchase.

2. **Market knowledge**

   This strategy requires the seller to know property values in a particular market as well or better than the buyer. When the seller is able to present the buyer with price comparisons of similar properties, the seller presents an unbiased evaluation of the price differentials in the particular market. When the buyer is able to investigate the market and draw similar conclusions, he or she gains confidence in the seller's ability to judge and valuate properties. That confidence leads to trust and a willingness to do business with the perceived expert in the market.

3. **Trial balloon**

    The trial balloon technique involves testing an idea or concept to gauge the reaction to it. When the reaction is favorable, the tester may implement the concept or launch additional trial balloons in an effort to test and negotiate other limits. Trial balloons may be launched to gauge a buyer's maximum and minimum limits on a property and then to negotiate a price within those bounds. Trial balloons are used to gauge the buyer's willingness to negotiate a number of issues related to the buying and selling of real estate, such as acceptable limits on interest rates, closing dates, and down payments. A seller may offer a property priced at the top of market values. If the seller gauges a negative response, the seller may choose to launch a trial balloon that reduces the price to a lower value. If the response is favorable or indifferent, the seller may launch additional trial balloons to negotiate a higher price.

4. **Blame game**

    The blame game is used to negotiate by shifting focus to someone or something else. Sellers and buyers may choose to blame the lender, appraiser, government, or any entity other than self for raising, lowering, or maintaining costs requested for a property. The buyer, for example, may indicate to the seller that his or her market research indicates that the property is not able to achieve the appraised value that the seller is asking in effort to negotiate a lower price. Though the blame game works most effectively for the buyer, a seller may allude to his or her market research to convince the buyer that similar properties appraise at or above the requested value. In both cases, focus is shifted to data provided by others, under the auspices of market research.

5. **In writing**

    The "in writing" technique is most effective as a closing technique. Buyers will attempt to float as many balloons as possible to negotiate the cost of a property. Once the buyer has shown enough interest in the property to begin floating balloons, the seller requests that the buyer establish his or her terms of acceptance in writing through a formalized offer of sale.

6. **Chess player**

    The chess player strategy involves carefully executing each step of the negotiation process by revealing to the other party only what he or she needs to know without disclosing any information that would be of benefit to them. The chess player incorporates all of the above techniques to negotiate the best price. The chess player engages the prospective buyer by obtaining a financial commitment to secure the property. Though the commitment is small, it changes the psychological and emotional attitude of the prospective buyer. The chess player uses market knowledge to float trial balloons using the blame game. When negotiations fall within acceptable limits, the seller insists upon a written offer to close out the verbal negotiation stage and move forward to contract negotiations.

In all negotiations, the seller has a responsibility to:

- Ask questions of the buyer in an effort to understand his or her needs and possibly the motivation behind those needs. The questioning should not be handled as though it were an interrogation, but as friendly inquiries as part of normal conversation.

- After asking questions, the seller should really listen to see if the response brings him or her any closer to understanding the needs of the buyer. The response may require the seller to use conversation to shift the focus of the buyer to those things that describe his or her needs. Many buyers are amateur negotiators and will follow the seller's lead in conversation.

- Establish a rapport with potential buyers by showing professionalism and by allowing the buyer to trust in his or her ability to be of assistance.

- Qualify the prospect as an actual buyer. The seller must be able to glean enough information from the prospect to determine if he or she is someone actually looking to buy or someone on a fact-finding mission. The seller must then determine how much time should be spent in meeting the prospect's goals versus meeting his or her own needs.

- Present the property as the best choice to meet the specific needs of the prospect.

- Handle objections to the sales presentation, particularly when objections are expressed before completing the presentation. Many prospects will want very specific information; the seller must be competent to address those specifics. The seller must be familiar enough with the presentation to switch the order in which it is presented to address the prospect's specific questions.

- Request that the prospect engage in the contract and provide a payment.

- Stay in touch with the prospect. Sellers require a network of individuals in order to advertise their properties and keep them abreast of new opportunities.

The seller is cautioned against holding out on a reasonable offer in an effort to acquire more profits. All sellers believe they should have gotten more, and all buyers believe they should have paid less. Some sellers have managed to hold out and increase their profit margins. However, there have been many instances in which the seller held out and had one or more of the following events to occur: the property sat empty, debts continued to accumulate, additional fees were incurred, and/or the profit margin was reduced to a level below that which the seller would have acquired if he or she had accepted an earlier offer.

Closing

The closing of a sale is the point at which the actual transfer of property takes place. A closing specifies that all parties of the sale have been satisfied and all paperwork has been properly processed. The closing is the final signage of documents and forms, which must accurately reflect costs, terms, and conditions agreed upon during negotiations. They must be thoroughly reviewed and checked for accuracy because mistakes can be very costly. The primary forms under consideration during closing include the title report, the settlement statement, the deed, and the promissory note.

The title report outlines the history of ownership, liens, judgments, and other outstanding covenants recorded and held against the property. A title insurance company provides title insurance to both the buyer and lender involved in the sale to ensure that the title to the property is clean and free. Title insurance provided to the buyer protects the buyer from any outstanding covenants that may be discovered after the closing. Title insurance provided to the lender or homeowner selling his or her own property protects them against loss of interest in the property due to defects in the title. Title insurance benefits are paid to named parties on the insurance document.

The title company also prepares the settlement statement, which outlines all debits and credits to the parties of the sale. Typical items included in the settlement statement include:

- Contract sale price

- Earnest money deposit

- Principal amounts of new loans

- Principal amounts of existing loans

- Seller financing

- Prorated cost adjustments

- Prorated income adjustments

- Lender charges and fees

- Title insurance charges

- Inspections, appraisals, surveys, and environmental audits

- Legal fees

- Recording fees

The deed is the formal document that transfers ownership from one party to another. The deed must be signed and witnessed by all parties to the sale according to laws established in the state where the property is located. The deed, which should be delivered on the closing day, uses specific terms to refer to the parties of the sale. The seller is termed the grantor and the buyer is termed the grantee. There are several types of deeds; the most common include the following:

- **Deed of Trust**
  A deed of trust assigns real property as security against a debt. A deed of trust requires that a third party be involved to hold the deed in trust for the borrower and lender. A third party, or trustee, holds the deed in trust until the debt to the lender is satisfied. Once the debt is satisfied, the deed becomes null and void. If the borrower defaults on the debt payments, the lender is the beneficiary of the property specified in the deed. As the beneficiary, the lender may sell the property as specified in the terms of the deed of trust. Some states treat a deed of trust as though it were a mortgage. The property may be sold without necessitating legal proceedings.

- **Special Warranty Deed**
  A special warranty deed protects the buyer or grantee by stipulating that the grantor did nothing during his or her ownership or will do nothing in the future that would impair the title of the grantee.

- **Quitclaim Deed**
  A quitclaim deed is used to transfer ownership of interest in a deed. Quitclaim deeds are usually issued to clear title to a property. The deed makes no warranties regarding the title; it only transfers any existing interest to the grantee. The grantee assumes all risk associated with the newly acquired interest.

The promissory note details the terms and conditions required of the lender in making a loan. Lenders that issue promissory notes include issuers of bank loans, mortgage companies, or sellers who finance the sale of their own properties. A promissory note can either be secured by something of mutually agreed-upon value or unsecured. The sale property is generally the collateral being secured, but it could be secured by other assets, property, or anything to which the parties of the financing agree. When no collateral is used to secure a promissory note, the lender is reliant upon good faith in establishing that the borrower will be able to repay the borrowed amount. A promissory note specifies the terms of repayment to include the amount borrowed, the interest rate, amortization period, and any pre-payment or late payment penalties imposed. The promissory note may also include conditions that warrant immediate payment, escrow requirements, minimum insurance requirements, standards for the care of the property, provisions for loan defaults, or a due-on-sale clause.

The seller is required to reveal any known defects of the property in the contract of sale. If the property was built before 1978, the seller is required to disclose any known or suspected surfaces treated with lead-based paint. The seller is required to complete all known repairs prior to the closing unless it is otherwise stipulated. If the buyer is using lender financing, the lender may require the seller to complete repairs prior to providing the financing; if the repairs exceed 5 percent of the sale price, the buyer is allowed to terminate the contract agreement. The seller of commercial and industrial properties is obligated to provide the buyer with an environmental audit of the property. An environmental audit specifies the presence of any known and detected environmental problems. The existence of environmental conditions would greatly increase the cost of developing such properties. Such an audit varies in cost depending upon the market, but a typical environmental audit costs $1,000.

The seller may be required to complete a "seller's disclosure of property condition" form. This form, which is used to specify all defects and conditions in need of repair, specifies the following:

- Defects of the property, appliances, and other items included in the sale, such as heating systems, air-conditioning systems, pools, fences, decks, and garages.

- Defects in the structure, such as the roof, foundation, fireplace, walls, ceilings, and windows.

- Damage caused by termites, water, or waste.

- Modifications to the structure, such as room additions.

- Association or maintenance fees.

- Pending legal suits against the seller.

The seller is responsible for casualty damages that may occur before the actual transfer of ownership or closing. The seller is required to make repairs necessitated by casualty losses by the closing date or some other mutually agreed-upon date. If repairs are not made timely and to the satisfaction of the buyer, the buyer may break the contract and also receive a refund of the earnest money vested in the sale of the property.

A seller-financing addendum is added to the sale contract when the seller is financing the sale of his or her own property. The addendum allows the seller to investigate the creditworthiness of the buyer and outlines the terms and conditions of the promissory note that is used to bind this type of sale. The promissory note may provide for any of the following:

- A single balloon payment.

- Payments amortized over some specified period of time.

- Interest-only payments that convert to interest-plus-principal payments until the note is satisfied.

- Other terms that are defined and agreed upon by both parties to the contract.

The promissory note and deed of trust that bind the financing may specify the requirements for reselling a seller-financed property. The buyer may sell the property without prior consent from the seller or the seller may require consent before resale of the property. The seller is recommended to make use of the following established practices used by lenders and mortgage companies:

- Add a due-on-sale clause that requires the total sale price be paid in full before a resale.

- Establish criteria for loan assumptions.

- Require the buyer to pay the taxes and insurance for the property into an escrow account unless the borrower has invested at least 20 percent of the property's value into the property.

Winston Rego

Winston T. Rego is a multi-millionaire real estate investor. In the last four years he has increased his net worth 1600%. He is also a licensed commercial Realtor with Open House Realty and assists investors increase their income and grow their wealth through investing in real estate. His phone number is 864-235-5600.

I was a very successful attorney in Chicago, Illinois, making a very good income. At the same time, I was looking for a better return on my money than what I could get from traditional stocks, mutual funds, and savings accounts. So, I turned to real estate.

I started by buying a four-unit apartment building in Chicago for $500,000. The tenants were good and paid on time. The maintenance was minimal, and we did fine. I then bought a 13-unit apartment complex in a poorer neighborhood of Chicago for $860,000. The tenants were horrible. They trashed their apartments and failed to pay rent on time. I had to spend a lot of time away from my busy law practice to manage that property. Fortunately, we managed to sell that property in nine months for $1,000,000, and we came out ahead. We then bought a 23-unit apartment complex in South Carolina. By that time, I had developed some ideas on how to run an apartment complex well. Again, this latest complex was in a poorer area, and the tenants were horrible. Using good management techniques, I turned the property around to where I had good tenants, and the property was making a profit.

In my opinion, residential rental properties are the worst investment. If mismanaged they cost you a lot. If managed perfectly, they give you a maximum return of about five percent. If you factor in your time, and even if the complex is managed perfectly, you will get a lower return than what you will get from putting your money in a CD in the bank. I managed residential rental property for three years. Now I own triple net commercial rental property that requires almost no management.

If you're a property manager or a prospective property manager, you must realize the market is the best way to determine rental rates. Check out what your competitors near your property are charging. Factor in whether those properties are better than yours, and that should help you figure out what to charge. Lower the rate if you have a lot of vacancies, and raise it if you have a waiting list.

I believe in keeping my tenants very happy, so I do not receive many complaints. However, it's expected that maintenance issues will crop up from time to time. I try to make my tenants understand that we have a partnership. If they treat me fairly, I will treat them fairly. I expect them to pay their rent on time and take care of the property as if it is their own home. In return, I fix all reasonable maintenance problems immediately. If it cannot be fixed immediately, I keep them informed as I am trying to get the problem fixed as soon as possible. The flip of this is, if the tenants fail to live up to this agreement, I will aggressively collect late fees and evict them.

Collecting rent and evicting nonpaying tenants were the biggest challenge I faced when I first started managing properties. Tenants are very smart and will take advantage of every weakness the landlord has. I am a kind-hearted person and believe in treating people fairly. It was hard for me to be strict with tenants when they gave me their sob stories on why they could not pay their rent, but I learned.

Accounting is another critical component of property management. While I have a CPA for accounting purposes, I use QuickBooks for in-house accounting needs. It's also important that you set up a reserve fund for payments that are annual or semi-annual, such as taxes and insurance.

If you're new to property management, you can start by having a good lease. Learn the local landlord and tenant laws and the process for evicting tenants. Immediately start the process for evicting nonpaying tenants when the grace period for paying the rent is up. Collect at least one month's security deposit. Treat tenants fairly, and fix all reasonable repairs promptly. If you treat the tenants well, they will reward you by paying their rent on time and by taking care of the property.

Having a professional rent collection, maintenance, and eviction system in place, and maintaining good documentation is the best way to minimize your risks. It is better to have a unit vacant than to put a bad tenant in there. Always do a credit check, and call references before you lease a unit to a tenant.

Bibliography

Berges, Steve. *The Complete Guide to Investing in Rental Properties.* New York, NY: McGraw-Hill, 2004.

Thomas, Suzanne P. *Rental Houses for the Successful Small Investor.* Boulder, CO: Gemstone House Publishing, 2005.

Griswold, Robert S. *Property Management for Dummies.* New York, NY: Hungry Minds, Inc., 2001.

Taylor, Jeff. *The Landlord's Kit.* Chicago, IL: Dearborn Trade Publishing, 2002.

Weiss, Mark B., and Dan Baldwin. *Streetwise Landlording & Property Management.* Avon, MA: Streetwise Publication, 2003.

Index

Glossary

401(k)/403(b) An investment plan sponsored by an employer which enables individuals to set aside pre-tax income for retirement or emergency purposes. 401(k) plans are provided by private corporations. 403(b) plans are provided by non-profit organizations.

401(k)/403(b) loan A type of financing using a loan against the money accumulated in a 401(k)/403(b) plan.

Abatement Sometimes referred to as free rent or early occupancy. A condition that could happen in addition to the primary term of the lease.

Above Building Standard Finishes and specialized designs that have been upgraded in order to accommodate a tenant's requirements.

Absorption Rate The speed and amount of time at which rentable space, in square feet, is filled.

Abstract or Title Search The process of reviewing all transactions that have been recorded publicly in order to determine whether any defects in the title exist which could interfere with a clear property ownership transfer.

Accelerated Cost Recovery System A calculation for taxes to provide more depreciation for the first few years of ownership.

Accelerated Depreciation A method of depreciation where the value of a property depreciates faster in the first few years after purchasing it.

Acceleration Clause A clause in a contract that gives the lender the right to demand immediate payment of the balance of the loan if the borrower defaults on the loan.

Acceptance An approval of a buyer's offer written by the seller.

Ad Valorem A Latin phrase which translates as "according to value." Refers to a tax that is imposed on a property's value which is typically based on the local government's evaluation of the property.

Addendum An addition or update for an existing contract between parties.

Additional Principal Payment Additional money paid to the lender, apart from the scheduled loan payments, to pay more of the principal balance, shortening the length of the loan.

Adjustable Rate Mortgage (ARM) A home loan with an interest rate that is adjusted periodically in order to reflect changes in a specific financial resource.

Adjusted Funds From Operations (AFFO) The rate

of REIT performance or ability to pay dividends which is used by many analysts who have concerns about the quality of earnings as measured by Funds From Operations (FFO).

Adjustment Date The date at which the interest rate is adjusted for an Adjustable-Rate Mortgage (ARM).

Adjustment Period The amount of time between adjustments for an interest rate in an ARM.

Administrative Fee A percentage of the value of the assets under management, or a fixed annual dollar amount charged to manage an account.

Advances The payments the servicer makes when the borrower fails to send a payment.

Adviser A broker or investment banker who represents an owner in a transaction and is paid a retainer and/or a performance fee once a financing or sales transaction has closed.

Agency Closing A type of closing in which a lender uses a title company or other firm as an agent to finish a loan.

Agency Disclosure A requirement in most states that

agents who act for both buyers or sellers must disclose who they are working for in the transaction.

Aggregation Risk The risk that is associated with warehousing mortgages during the process of pooling them for future security.

Agreement of Sale A legal document the buyer and seller must approve and sign that details the price and terms in the transaction.

Alienation Clause The provision in a loan that requires the borrower to pay the total balance of the loan at once if the property is sold or the ownership transferred.

Alternative Mortgage A home loan that does not match the standard terms of a fixed-rate mortgage.

Alternative or Specialty Investments Types of property that are not considered to be conventional real estate investments, such as self-storage facilities, mobile homes, timber, agriculture, or parking lots.

Amortization The usual process of paying a loan's interest and principal via scheduled monthly payments.

Amortization Schedule A chart or table which shows the percentage of each payment that will be applied toward principal and interest over the life of the mortgage and how the loan balance decreases until it reaches zero.

Amortization Tables The mathematical tables that are used to calculate what a borrower's monthly payment will be.

Amortization Term The number of months it will take to amortize the loan.

Anchor The business or individual who is serving as the primary draw to a commercial property.

Annual Mortgagor Statement A yearly statement to borrowers which details the remaining principal balance and amounts paid throughout the year for taxes and interest.

Annual Percentage Rate (APR) The interest rate that states the actual cost of borrowing money over the course of a year.

Annuity The regular payments of a fixed sum.

Application The form a borrower must complete in

order to apply for a mortgage loan, including information such as income, savings, assets, and debts.

Application Fee A fee some lenders charge that may include charges for items such as property appraisal or a credit report unless those fees are included elsewhere.

Appraisal The estimate of the value of a property on a particular date given by a professional appraiser, usually presented in a written document.

Appraisal Fee The fee charged by a professional appraiser for his estimate of the market value of a property.

Appraisal Report The written report presented by an appraiser regarding the value of a property.

Appraised Value The dollar amount a professional appraiser assigned to the value of a property in his report.

Appraiser A certified individual who is qualified by education, training, and experience to estimate the value of real and personal property.

Appreciation An increase in the home's or property's value.

Appreciation Return The amount gained when the value of the real estate assets increases during the current quarter.

Arbitrage The act of buying securities in one market and selling them immediately in another market in order to profit from the difference in price.

ARM index A number that is publicly published and used as the basis for interest rate adjustments on an ARM.

As-Is Condition A phrase in a purchase or lease contract in which the new tenant accepts the existing condition of the premises as well as any physical defects.

Assessed Value The value placed on a home which is determined by a tax assessor in order to calculate a tax base.

Assessment (1) The approximate value of a property. (2) A fee charged in addition to taxes in order to help pay for items such as water, sewer, street improvements, etc.

Assessor A public officer who estimates the value of a property for the purpose of taxation.

Asset A property or item of value owned by an individual or company.

Asset Management Fee A fee that is charged to investors based on the amount of money they have invested into real estate assets for the particular fund or account.

Asset Management The various tasks and areas around managing real estate assets from the initial investment until the time it is sold.

Asset Turnover The rate of total revenues for the previous 12 months divided by the average total assets.

Assets Under Management The amount of the current market value of real estate assets which a manager is responsible to manage and invest.

Assignee Name The individual or business to whom the lease, mortgage or other contract has been re-assigned.

Assignment The transfer of rights and responsibilities from one party to another for paying a debt. The original party remains liable for the debt should the second party default.

Assignor The person who transfers the rights and interests of a property to another.

Assumable Mortgage A mortgage that is capable of being transferred to a different borrower.

Assumption The act of assuming the mortgage of the seller.

Assumption Clause A contractual provision that enables the buyer to take responsibility for the mortgage loan from the seller.

Assumption Fee A fee charged to the buyer for processing new records when they are assuming an existing loan.

Attorn To agree to recognize a new owner of a property and to pay rent to the new landlord.

Average Common Equity The sum of the common equity for the last five quarters divided by five.

Average Downtime The number of months that are expected between a lease's expiration and the beginning of a replacement lease under the current market conditions.

Average Free Rent The number of months the rent abatement concession is expected to be granted to a tenant as part of an incentive to lease under current market conditions

Average Occupancy The average rate of each of the previous 12 months that a property was occupied.

Average Total Assets The sum of the total assets of a company for the previous five quarters divided by five.

Back Title Letter A letter that an attorney receives from a title insurance company before examining the title for insurance purposes.

Back-End Ratio The calculation lenders use to compare a borrower's gross monthly income to their total debt.

Balance Sheet A statement that lists an individual's assets, liabilities and net worth.

Balloon Loan A type of mortgage in which the monthly payments are not large enough to repay the loan by the end of the term, and the final payment is one large payment of the remaining balance.

Balloon Payment The final huge payment due at the end of a balloon mortgage.

Balloon Risk The risk that a borrower may not be able to come up with the funds for the balloon payment at maturity.

Bankrupt The state an individual or business is in if they are unable to repay their debt when it is due.

Bankruptcy A legal proceeding where a debtor can obtain relief from payment of certain obligations through restructuring their finances.

Base Loan Amount The amount which forms the basis for the loan payments.

Base Principal Balance The original loan amount once adjustments for subsequent fundings and principal payments have been made without including accrued interest or other unpaid debts.

Base Rent A certain amount that is used as a minimum rent, providing for rent increases over the term of the lease agreement.

Base Year The sum of actual taxes and operating expenses during a given year, often that in which a lease begins.

Basis Point A term for 1/100 of one percentage point.

Before-Tax Income An individual's income before taxes have been deducted.

Below-Grade Any structure or

part of a structure that is below the surface of the ground that surrounds it.

Beneficiary An employee who is covered by the benefit plan his company provides.

Beta The measurement of common stock price volatility for a company in comparison to the market.

Bid The price or range an investor is willing to spend on whole loans or securities.

Bill of Sale A written legal document that transfers the ownership of personal property to another party.

Binder (1) A report describing the conditions of a property's title. (2) An early agreement between seller and buyer.

Biweekly Mortgage A mortgage repayment plan that requires payments every two weeks to help repay the loan over a shorter amount of time.

Blanket Mortgage A rare type of mortgage that covers more than one of the borrower's properties.

Blind Pool A mixed fund that accepts capital from investors without specifying property assets.

Bond Market The daily buying and selling of thirty-year treasury bonds which also affects fixed rate mortgages.

Book Value The value of a property based on its purchase amount plus upgrades or other additions with depreciation subtracted.

Break-Even Point The point at which a landlord's income from rent matches expenses and debt.

Bridge Loan A short-term loan for individuals or companies that are still seeking more permanent financing.

Broker A person who serves as a go-between for a buyer and seller.

Brokerage The process of bringing two or more parties together in exchange for a fee, commission, or other compensation.

Buildable Acres The portion of land that can be built on after allowances for roads, setbacks, anticipated open spaces, and unsuitable areas have been made.

Building Code The laws set forth by the local government regarding end use of a given piece of property. These law codes may dictate the design, materials used, and/or types of improvements that will be allowed.

Building Standard Plus Allowance A detailed list provided by the landlord stating the standard building materials and costs necessary to make the premises inhabitable.

Build-Out Improvements to a property's space that have been implemented according to the tenant's specifications.

Build-to-Suit A way of leasing property, usually for commerical purposes, in which the developer or landlord builds to a tenant's specifications.

Buydown A term that usually refers to a fixed-rate mortgage for which additional payments can be applied to the interest rate for a temporary period, lowering payments for a period of one to three years.

Buydown Mortgage A style of home loan in which the lender receives a higher payment in order to convince them to reduce the interest rate during the initial years of the mortgage.

Buyer's Remorse A nervousness first-time homebuyers tend to feel after signing a sales contract or closing the purchase of a house.

Call Date The periodic or continuous right a lender has to call for payment of the total remaining balance prior to the date of maturity.

Call Option A clause in a loan agreement that allows a lender to demand repayment of the entire principal balance at any time.

Cap A limit on how much the monthly payment or interest rate is allowed to increase in an adjustable-rate mortgage.

Capital Appreciation The change in a property's or portfolio's market value after it has been adjusted for capital improvements and partial sales.

Capital Expenditures The purchase of long-term assets, or the expansion of existing ones which prolongs the life or efficiency of those assets.

Capital Gain The amount of excess when the net proceeds from the sale of an asset are higher than its book value.

Capital Improvements Expenses that prolong the life of a property or add new improvements to it.

Capital Markets Public and private markets where individuals or businesses can raise or borrow capital.

Capitalization The mathematical process that investors use to derive the value of a property using the rate of return on investments.

Capitalization Rate The percentage of return as it is estimated from the net income of a property.

Carryback Financing A type of funding in which a seller agrees to hold back a note for a specified portion of the sales price.

Carrying Charges Costs incurred to the landlord when initially leasing out a property and then during the periods of vacancy.

Cash Flow The amount of income an investor receives on a rental property after operating expenses and loan payments have been deducted.

Cashier's Check A check the bank draws on its own resources instead of a depositor's account.

Cash-on-Cash Yield The percentage of a property's net cash flow and the average amount of invested capital during the specified operating year.

Cash-Out Refinance The act of refinancing a mortgage for an amount that is higher than the original amount for the purpose of using the leftover cash for personal use.

Certificate of Deposit A type of deposit that is held in a bank for a limited time and pays a certain amount of interest to the depositor.

Certificate of Deposit Index (CODI) A rate that is based on interest rates of six-month CDs and is often used to determine interest rates for some ARMs.

Certificate of Eligibility A type of document that the Veterans Administration issues to verify the eligibility of a veteran for a VA loan.

Certificate of Occupancy (CO) A written document issued by a local government or building agency that states that a home or other building is inhabitable after meeting all building codes.

Certificate of Reasonable Value (CRV) An appraisal presented by the Veterans Administration that shows the current market value of a property.

Certificate of Veteran Status A document veterans or reservists receive if they have served 90 days of continuous active duty (including training time).

Chain of Title The official record of all transfers of ownership over the history of a piece of property.

Chapter 11 The part of the federal bankruptcy code that deals with reorganizations of businesses.

Chapter 7 The part of the federal bankruptcy code that deals with liquidations of businesses.

Circulation Factor The interior space that is required for internal office circulation and is not included in the net square footage.

Class A A property rating that is usually assigned to those that will generate the maximum rent per square foot, due to superior quality and/or location.

Class B A good property that most potential tenants would find desirable but lacks certain attributes that would bring in the top dollar.

Class C A building that is physically acceptable but offers few amenities, thereby becoming cost-effective space for tenants who are seeking a particular image.

Clear Title A property title that is free of liens, defects, or other legal encumbrances.

Clear-Span Facility A type of building, usually a warehouse or parking garage, consisting of vertical columns on the outer edges of the structure and clear spaces between the columns.

Closed-End Fund A mixed fund with a planned range of investor capital and a limited life.

Closing The final act of procuring a loan and title in which documents are signed between the buyer and seller and/or their respective representation, and all money, concerned in the contract, changes hands.

Closing Costs The expenses that are related to the sale of real estate including loan, title, and appraisal fees and are beyond the price of the property itself.

Closing Statement See: Settlement Statement.

Cloud on Title Certain conditions uncovered in a title search that present a negative impact to the title for the property.

Commercial Mortgage-Backed Securities (CMBS) A type of securities that is backed by loans on commercial real estate.

Collateralized Mortgage Obligation (CMO) Debt that is fully based on a pool of mortgages.

Co-Borrower Another individual who is jointly responsible for the loan and is on the title to the property.

Cost of Funds Index (COFI) An index used to determine changes in the interest rates for certain ARMs.

Co-Investment Program A separate account for an insurance company or investment partnership in which two or more pension funds may co-invest their capital in an individual property or a portfolio of properties.

Co-Investment The condition that occurs when two or more pension funds or groups of funds are sharing ownership of a real estate investment.

Collateral The property for which a borrower has obtained a loan, thereby assuming the risk of losing the property if the loan is not repaid according to the terms of the loan agreement.

Collection The effort on the part of a lender, due to a borrower defaulting on a loan, which involves mailing and recording certain documents in the event that the foreclosure procedure must be implemented.

Commercial Mortgage A loan used to purchase a piece of commercial property or building.

Commercial Mortgage Broker A broker specialized in commercial mortgage applications.

Commercial Mortgage Lender A lender specialized in funding commercial mortgage loans.

Commingled Fund A pooled fund that enables qualified employee benefit plans to mix their capital in order to achieve professional management, greater diversification, or investment positions in larger properties.

Commission A compensation to salespeople that is paid out of the total amount of the purchase transaction.

Commitment The agreement of a lender to make a loan with given terms for a specific period.

Commitment Fee The fee a lender charges for the guarantee of specified loan terms, to be honored at some point in the future.

Common Area Assessments Sometimes called Homeowners' Association Fees. Charges paid to the Homeowners' Association by the individual unit owners, in a condominium or Planned Unit Development (PUD), that are usually used to maintain the property and common areas.

Common Area Maintenance The additional charges the tenant must pay in addition to the base rent to pay for the maintenance of common areas.

Common Areas The portions of a building, land, and amenities, owned or managed by a planned unit development (PUD) or condominium's homeowners' association, that are used by all of the unit owners who share in the common expense of operation and maintenance.

Common Law A set of unofficial laws that were originally based on English customs and used to some extent in several states.

Community Property Property that is acquired by a married couple during the course of their marriage and is considered in many states to be owned jointly, unless certain circumstances are in play.

Comparable Sales Also called Comps or Comparables. The recent selling prices of similar properties in the area that are used to help determine the market value of a property.

Compound Interest The amount of interest paid on the principal balance of a mortgage in addition to accrued interest.

Concessions Cash, or the equivalent, that the landlord pays or allows in the form of rental abatement, additional tenant finish allowance, moving expenses, or other costs expended in order to persuade a tenant to sign a lease.

Condemnation A government agency's act of taking private property, without the owner's consent, for public use through the power of eminent domain.

Conditional Commitment A lender's agreement to make a loan providing the borrower meets certain conditions.

Conditional Sale A contract to sell a property which states that the seller will retain the title until all contractual conditions have been fulfilled.

Condominium A type of ownership in which all of the unit owners own the property, common areas, and buildings jointly, and have sole ownership in the unit to which they hold the title.

Condominium Conversion Changing an existing rental property's ownership to the condominium form of ownership.

Condominium Hotel A condominium project that involves registration desks, short-term occupancy, food and telephone services, and daily cleaning services, and is generally operated as a commercial hotel even though the units are individually owned.

Conduit A strategic alliance between lenders and unaffiliated organizations that acts as a source of funding by regularly purchasing loans, usually with a goal of pooling and securitizing them.

Conforming Loan A type of mortgage that meets the conditions to be purchased by Fannie Mae or Freddie Mac.

Construction Documents The drawings and specifications an architect and/or engineer provides to describe construction requirements for a project.

Construction Loan A short-term loan to finance the cost of construction, usually dispensed in stages throughout the construction project.

Construction Management The process of ensuring that the stages of the construction project are completed in a timely and seamless manner.

Construction-to-Permanent Loan A construction loan that can be converted to a longer-term traditional mortgage after construction is complete.

Consultant Any individual or company that provides the services to institutional investors, such as defining real estate investment policies, making recommendations to advisors or managers, analyzing existing real estate portfolios, monitoring and reporting on portfolio performance, and/or reviewing specified investment opportunities.

Consumer Price Index (CPI) A measurement of inflation, relating to the change in the prices of goods and services that are regularly purchased by a specific population during a certain period of time.

Contiguous Space Refers to several suites or spaces on a floor (or connected floors) in a given building that can be combined and rented to a single tenant.

Contingency A specific condition that must be met before either party in a contract can be legally bound.

Contract An agreement, either verbal or written, to perform or not to perform a certain thing.

Contract documents See: Construction Documents.

Contract Rent Also known as Face Rent. The dollar amount of the rental obligation specified in a lease.

Conventional Loan A long-term loan from a nongovernmental lender that a borrower obtains

for the purchase of a home.

Convertible Adjustable-Rate Mortgage A type of mortgage that begins as a traditional ARM but contains a provision to enable the borrower to change to a fixed-rate mortgage during a certain period of time.

Convertible Debt The point in a mortgage at which the lender has the option to convert to a partially or fully owned property within a certain period of time.

Convertible Preferred Stock Preferred stock that can be converted to common stock under certain conditions which have been specified by the issuer.

Conveyance The act of transfering a property title between parties by deed.

Cooperative Also called a Co-op. A type of ownership by multiple residents of a multi-unit housing complex, in which they all own shares in the cooperative corporation that owns the property, thereby having the right to occupy a particular apartment or unit.

Cooperative Mortgage Any loan that is related to a cooperative residential project.

Core Properties The main types

of property, specifically office, retail, industrial, and multi-family.

Co-Signer A second individual or party who also signs a promissory note or loan agreement, thereby taking responsibility for the debt in the event that the primary borrower cannot pay.

Cost-Approach Improvement Value The current expenses for constructing a copy or replacement for an existing structure, but subtracting an estimate of the accrued depreciation.

Cost-Approach Land Value The estimated value of the basic interest in the land, as if it were available for development to its highest and best use.

Cost-of-Sale Percentage An estimate of the expenses of selling an investment that represents brokerage commissions, closing costs, fees, and other necessary sales costs.

Coupon The token or expected interest rate the borrower is charged on a promissory note or mortgage.

Courier Fee The fee that is charged at closing for the delivery of documents between all parties concerned in a real estate transaction.

Covenant A written agreement, included in deeds or other legal documents, that defines the requirements for certain acts or use of a property.

Credit An agreement in which a borrower promises to repay the lender at a later date and receives something of value in exchange.

Credit Enhancement The necessary credit support, in addition to mortgage collateral, in order to achieve the desired credit rating on mortgage-backed securities.

Credit History An individual's record which details his current and past financial obligations and performance.

Credit Life Insurance A type of insurance that pays the balance of a mortgage if the borrower dies.

Credit Rating The degree of creditworthiness a person is assigned based on his credit history and current financial status.

Credit Report An individual's record detailing an individual's credit, employment, and residence history used to determine the individual's creditworthiness.

Credit Repository A company that records and updates credit applicants' financial and credit information from various sources.

Credit Score Sometimes called a Credit Risk Score. The number contained in a consumer's credit report that represents a statistical summary of the information.

Creditor A party to whom other parties owe money.

Cross-Collateralization A group of mortgages or properties that jointly secures one debt obligation.

Cross-Defaulting A provision that allows a trustee or lender to require full payment on all loans in a group, if any single loan in the group is in default.

Cumulative Discount Rate A percentage of the current value of base rent with all landlord lease concessions taken into account.

Current Occupancy The current percentage of units in a building or property that is leased.

Current Yield The amount of

the coupon divided by the price.

Deal Structure The type of agreement in financing an acquisition. The deal can be unleveraged, leveraged, traditional debt, participating debt, participating/convertible debt, or joint ventures.

Debt Any amount one party owes to another party.

Debt Service Coverage Ratio (DSCR) A property's yearly net operating income divided by the yearly cost of debt service.

Debt Service The amount of money that is necessary to meet all interest and principal payments during a specific period.

Debt-to-Income Ratio The percentage of a borrower's monthly payment on long-term debts divided by his gross monthly income.

Dedicate To change a private property to public ownership for a particular public use.

Deed A legal document that conveys property ownership to the buyer.

Deed in Lieu of Foreclosure A situation in which a deed is given to a lender in order to satisfy a mortgage debt and to avoid the foreclosure process.

Deed of Trust A provision that allows a lender to foreclose on a property in the event that the borrower defaults on the loan.

Default The state that occurs when a borrow fails to fulfill a duty or take care of an obligation, such as making monthly mortgage payments.

Deferred Maintenance Account A type of account that a borrower must fund to provide for maintenance of a property.

Deficiency Judgment The legal assignment of personal liability to a borrower for the unpaid balance of a mortgage, after foreclosing on the property has failed to yield the full amount of the debt.

Defined-Benefit Plan A type of benefit provided by an employer that defines an employee's benefits either as a fixed amount or a percentage of the beneficiary's salary when he retires.

Defined-Contribution Plan A type of benefit plan provided by an employer in which an employee's retirement benefits are determined by the amount

that has been contributed by the employer and/or employee during the time of employment, and by the actual investment earnings on those contributions over the life of the fund.

Delinquency A state that occurs when the borrower fails to make mortgage payments on time, eventually resulting in foreclosure, if severe enough.

Delinquent Mortgage A mortgage in which the borrower is behind on payments.

Demising Wall The physical partition between the spaces of two tenants or from the building's common areas.

Deposit Also referred to as "Earnest Money." The funds that the buyer provides when offering to purchase property.

Depreciation A decline in the value of property or an asset, often used as a tax deductible item.

Derivative Securities A type of securities that has been created from other financial instruments.

Design/Build An approach in which a single individual or business is responsible for both the design and construction.

Disclosure A written statement, presented to a potential buyer, that lists information relevant to a piece of property, whether positive or negative.

Discount Points Fees that a lender charges in order to provide a lower interest rate.

Discount Rate A figure used to translate present value from future payments or receipts.

Discretion The amount of authority an adviser or manager is granted for investing and managing a client's capital.

Distraint The act of seizing a tenant's personal property when the tenant is in default, based on the right the landlord has in satisfying the debt.

Diversification The act of spreading individual investments out to insulate a portfolio against the risk of reduced yield or capital loss.

Dividend Yield The percentage of a security's market price that represents the annual dividend rate.

Dividend Distributions of cash or stock that stockholders receive.

Dividend-Ex Date The initial date on which a person purchasing the stock can no longer receive the most recently announced dividend.

Document Needs List The list of documents a lender requires from a potential borrower who is submitting a loan application.

Documentation Preparation Fee A fee that lenders, brokers, and/or settlement agents charge for the preparation of the necessary closing documents.

Dollar Stop An agreed amount of taxes and operating expenses each tenant must pay out on a prorated basis.

Down Payment The variance between the purchase price and the portion that the mortgage lender financed.

DOWNREIT A structure of organization that makes it possible for REITs to purchase properties using partnership units.

Draw A payment from the construction loan proceeds made to contractors, subcontractors, home builders, or suppliers.

Due Diligence The activities of a prospective purchaser or mortgager of real property for the purpose of confirming that the property is as represented by the seller and is not subject to environmental or other problems.

Due on Sale Clause The standard mortage language that states the loan must still be repaid if the property is resold.

Earnest Money See: Deposit.

Earthquake Insurance A type of insurance policy that provides coverage against earthquake damage to a home.

Easement The right given to a non-ownership party to use a certain part of the property for specified purposes, such as servicing power lines or cable lines.

Economic Feasibility The viability of a building or project in terms of costs and revenue where the degree of viability is established by extra revenue.

Economic Rent The market rental value of a property at a particular point in time.

Effective Age An estimate of the physical condition of a building presented by an appraiser.

Effective Date The date on which the sale of securities can commence once a registration statement becomes effective.

Effective Gross Income (EGI) The total property income which rents and other sources generate after subtracting a vacancy factor estimated to be appropriate for the property.

Effective Gross Rent (EGR) The net rent that is generated after adjusting for tenant improvements and other capital costs, lease commissions and other sales expenses.

Effective Rent The actual rental rate that the landlord achieves after deducting the concession value from the base rental rate a tenant pays.

Electronic Authentication A way of providing proof that a particular electronic document is genuine, has arrived unaltered, and came from the indicated source.

Eminent Domain The power of the governement to pay the fair market value for a property, appropriating it for public use.

Encroachment Any improvement or upgrade that illegally intrudes onto another party's property.

Encumbrance Any right or interest in a property that

interferes with using it or transfering ownership.

End Loan The result of converting to permanent financing from a construction loan.

Entitlement A benefit of a VA home loan. Often referred to as eligibility.

Environmental Impact Statement Legally required documents that must accompany major project proposals where there will likely be an impact on the surrounding environment.

Equal Credit Opportunity Act (ECOA) A federal law that requires a lender or other creditor to make credit available for applicants regardless of sex, marital status, race, religion, or age.

Equifax One of the three primary credit-reporting bureaus.

Equity The value of a property after existing liabilities have been deducted.

Employee Retirement Income Security Act (ERISA) A legislation that controls the investment activities, mainly of corporate and union pension plans.

Errors and Omissions Insurance A type of policy that insures against the mistakes of a builder or architect.

Escalation Clause The clause in a lease that provides for the rent to be increased to account for increases in the expenses the landlord must pay.

Escrow A valuable item, money or documents deposited with a third party for delivery upon the fulfillment of a condition.

Escrow Account Also referred to as an Impound Account. An account established by a mortgage lender or servicing company for the purpose of holding funds for the payment of items, such as homeowners insurance and property taxes.

Escrow Agent A neutral third party who makes sure that all conditions of a real estate transaction have been met before any funds are transfered or property is recorded.

Escrow Agreement A written agreement between an escrow agent and the contractual parties which defines the basic obligations of each party, the money (or other valuables) to be deposited in escrow, and how the escrow agent is to dispose of the money on deposit.

Escrow Analysis An annual investigation a lender performs to make sure they are collecting the appropriate amount of money for anticipated expenditures.

Escrow Closing The event in which all conditions of a real estate transaction have been met, and the property title is transferred to the buyer.

Escrow Company A neutral company that serves as a third party to ensure that all conditions of a real estate transaction are met.

Escrow Disbursements The dispensing of escrow funds for the payment of real estate taxes, hazard insurance, mortgage insurance, and other property expenses as they are due.

Escrow Payment The funds that are withdrawn by a mortgage servicer from a borrower's escrow account to pay property taxes and insurance.

Estate The total assets, including property, of an individual after he has died.

Estimated Closing Costs An estimation of the expenses relating to the sale of real estate.

Estimated Hazard Insurance An estimation of hazard insurance, or homeowners' insurance, that will cover physical risks.

Estimated Property Taxes An estimation of the property taxes that must be paid on the property, according to state and county tax rates.

Estoppel Certificate A signed statement that certifies that certain factual statements are correct as of the date of the statement and can be relied upon by a third party, such as a prospective lender or purchaser.

Eviction The legal removal of an occupant from a piece of property.

Examination of Title A title company's inspection and report of public records and other documents for the purpose of determining the chain of ownership of a property.

Exclusive Agency Listing A written agreement between a property owner and a real estate broker in which the owner promises to pay the broker a commission if certain property is leased during the listing period.

Exclusive Listing A contract that allows a licensed real estate agent to be the only agent who can sell a property for a given time.

Executed Contract An agreement in which all parties involved have fulfilled their duties.

Executor The individual who is named in a will to administer an estate. Executrix is the feminine form.

Exit strategy An approach investors may use when they wish to liquidate all or part of their investment.

Experian One of the three primary credit-reporting bureaus.

Face Rental Rate The rental rate that the landlord publishes.

Facility Space The floor area in a hospitality property that is dedicated to activities, such as restaurants, health clubs, and gift shops that interactively service multiple people and is not directly related to room occupancy.

Funds Available for Distribution (FAD) The income from operations, with cash expenditures subtracted, that may be used for leasing commissions and tenant improvement costs.

FAD Multiple The price per share of a REIT divided by its funds available for distribution.

Fair Credit Reporting Act (FCRA) The federal legislation that governs the processes credit reporting agencies must follow.

Fair Housing Act The federal legislation that prohibits the refusal to rent or sell to anyone based on race, color, religion, sex, family status, B268, or disability.

Fair Market Value The highest price that a buyer would be willing to pay, and the lowest a seller would be willing to accept.

Fannie Mae See: Federal National Mortgage Association.

Fannie Mae's Community Home Buyer's Program A community lending model based on borrower income in which mortgage insurers and Fannie Mae offer flexible underwriting guidelines in order to increase the buying power for a low- or moderate-income family and to decrease the total amount of cash needed to purchase a home.

Farmer's Home Administration (FMHA) An agency within the U.S. Department of Agriculture that provides credit to farmers and other rural residents.

Federal Home Loan Mortgage Corporation (FHLMC) Also known as Freddie Mac. The company that buys mortgages from lending institutions, combines them with other loans, and sells shares to investors.

Federal Housing Administration (FHA) A government agency that provides low-rate mortgages to buyers who are able to make a down payment as low as three percent.

Federal National Mortgage Association (FNMA) Also known as Fannie Mae. A congressionally chartered, shareholder-owned company that is the nation's largest supplier of home mortgage funds. The company buys mortgages from lenders and resells them as securities on the secondary mortgage market.

Fee Simple The highest possible interest a person can have in a piece of real estate.

Fee Simple Estate An unconditional, unlimited inheritance estate in which the owner may dispose of or use the property as desired.

Fee Simple Interest The state of owning all the rights in a real estate parcel.

Funds From Operations (FFO) A ratio that is meant to highlight the amount of cash a company's real estate portfolio generates relative to its total operating cash flow.

FFO Multiple The price of a REIT share divided by its funds from operations.

FHA Loans Mortgages that the Federal Housing Administration (FHA) insures.

FHA Mortgage Insurance A type of insurance that requires a fee to be paid at closing in order to insure the loan with the Federal Housing Administration (FHA).

Fiduciary Any individual who holds authority over a plan's asset management, administration or disposition, or renders paid investment advice regarding a plan's assets.

Finance Charge The amount of interest to be paid on a loan or credit card balance.

Firm Commitment A written agreement a lender makes to loan money for the purchase of property.

First Mortgage The main mortgage on a property.

First Refusal Right/ Right of First Refusal A lease clause that gives a tenant the first opportunity to buy a property or to lease additional space in a property at the same price and terms as those contained in an offer from a third-party that the owner has expressed a willingness to accept.

First-Generation Space A new space that has never before been occupied by a tenant and is currently available for lease.

First-Loss Position A security's position that will suffer the first economic loss if the assets below it lose value or are foreclosed on.

Fixed Costs Expenses remain the same despite the level of sales or production.

Fixed Rate An interest rate that does not change over the life of the loan.

Fixed Time The particular weeks of a year that the owner of a timeshare arrangement can access his accommodations.

Fixed-Rate Mortgage A loan with an unchanging interest rate over the life of the loan.

Fixture Items that become a part of the property when they are permanently attached to the property.

Flat Fee An amount of money that an adviser or manager receives for managing a portfolio of real estate assets.

Flex Space A building that provides a flexible configuration of office or showroom space combined with manufacturing, laboratory, warehouse, distribution, etc.

Float The number of freely traded shares owned by the public.

Flood Certification The process of analyzing whether a property is located in a known flood zone.

Flood Insurance A policy that is required in designated flood zones to protect against loss due to flood damage.

Floor Area Ratio (FAR) A measurement of a building's gross square footage compared to the square footage of the land on which it is located.

For Sale By Owner (FSBO) A method of selling property in which the property owner serves as the selling agent and directly handles the sales process with the buyer or buyer's agent.

Force Majeure An external force that is not controlled by the contractual parties and prevents them from complying with the provisions of the contract.

Foreclosure The legal process in which a lender takes over ownership of a property once the borrower is in default in a mortgage arrangement.

Forward Commitments Contractual agreements to perform certain financing duties according to any stated conditions.

Four Quadrants of the Real Estate Capital Markets The four market types that consist of Private Equity, Public Equity, Private Debt, and Public Debt.

Freddie Mac See: Federal Home Loan Mortgage Corporation.

Front-End Ratio The measurement a lender uses to compare a borrower's monthly housing expense to gross monthly income.

Full Recourse A loan on which the responsibility of a loan is transferred to an endorser or guarantor in the event of default by the borrower.

Full-Service Rent A rental rate that includes all operating expenses and real estate taxes for the first year.

Fully Amortized ARM An ARM with a monthly payment that is sufficient to amortize the remaining balance at the current interest accrual rate over the amortization term.

Fully Diluted Shares The number of outstanding common stock shares if all convertible securities were converted to common shares.

Future Proposed Space The space in a commercial development that has been proposed but is not yet under construction, or the future phases of a multi-phase project that has not yet been built.

General Contractor The main person or business that contracts for the construction of an entire building or project, rather than individual duties.

General Partner The member in a partnership who holds the authority to bind the partnership and shares in its profits and losses.

Gift Money a buyer has received from a relative or other source.

Ginnie Mae See: Government National Mortgage Association.

Going-In Capitalization Rate The rate that is computed by dividing the expected net operating income for the first year by the value of the property.

Good Faith Estimate A lender's or broker's estimate that shows all costs associated with obtaining a home loan including loan processing, title, and inspection fees.

Government Loan A mortgage that is insured or guaranteed by the FHA, the Department of Veterans Affairs (VA), or the Rural Housing Service (RHS).

Government National Mortgage Association (GNMA) Also known as Ginnie Mae. A government-owned corporation under the U.S. Department of Housing and Urban Development (HUD) which performs the same role as Fannie Mae and Freddie Mac in providing funds to lenders for making home loans, but only purchases loans that are backed by the federal government.

Grace Period A defined time period in which a borrower may make a loan payment after its due date without incurring a penalty.

Graduated Lease A lease, usually long-term, in which rent payments vary in accordance with future contingencies.

Graduated Payment Mortgage A mortgage that requires low payments during the first years of the loan, but eventually requires larger monthly payments over the term of the loan that become fixed later in the term.

Grant To give or transfer an interest in a property by deed or other documented method.

Grantee The party to whom an interest in a property is given.

Grantor The party who is transferring an interest in a property.

Gross Building Area The sum of areas at all floor levels, including the basement, mezzanine, and penthouses included in the principal outside faces of the exterior walls without allowing for architectural setbacks or projections.

Gross Income The total income of a household before taxes or expenses have been subtracted.

Gross Investment in Real Estate (Historic Cost) The total amount of equity and debt that is invested in a piece of real estate minus proceeds from sales or partial sales.

Gross Leasable Area The amount of floor space that is designed for tenants' occupancy and exclusive use.

Gross Lease A rental arrangement in which the tenant pays a flat sum for rent, and the landlord must pay all building expenses out of that amount.

Gross Real Estate Asset Value The total market value of the real estate investments under management in a fund or individual accounts, usually including the total value of all equity positions, debt positions, and joint venture ownership positions.

Gross Real Estate Investment Value The market value of real estate investments that are held in a portfolio without including debt.

Gross Returns The investment returns generated from operating a property without adjusting for adviser or manager fees.

Ground Rent A long-term lease (e.g. 99 years) in which rent is paid to the land owner, normally to build something on that land.

Growing-Equity Mortgage A fixed-rate mortgage in which payments increase over a specified amount of time with the extra funds being applied to the principal.

Guarantor The part who makes a guaranty.

Guaranty An agreement in which the guarantor promises to satisfy the debt or obligations of another, if and when the debtor fails to do so.

Hard Cost The expenses attributes to actually constructing property improvements.

Hazard Insurance Also known as Homeowners' Insurance or Fire Insurance. A policy that provides coverage for damage from forces, such as fire and wind.

Highest and Best Use The most reasonable, expected, legal use of a piece of vacant land or improved property that is physically possible, supported appropriately, financially feasible, and that results in the highest value.

High-Rise In a suburban district, any building taller than six stories. In a business district, any building taller than 25 stories.

Holdbacks A portion of a loan funding that is not dispersed until an additional condition is met, such as the completion of construction.

Holding Period The expected length of time, from purchase to sale, that an investor will own a property.

Hold-Over Tenant A tenant who retains possession of the leased premises after the lease has expired.

Home Equity Conversion Mortgage (HECM) Also referred to as a Reverse Annuity Mortgage. A type of mortgage in which the lender makes payments to the owner, thereby enabling older homeowners to convert equity in their homes into cash in the form of monthly payments.

Home Equity Line An open-ended amount of credit based on the equity a homeowner has accumulated.

Home Equity Loan A type of loan that allows owners to borrow against the equity in their homes up to a limited amount.

Home Inspection A pre-purchase examination of the condition a home is in by a certified inspector.

Home Inspector A certified professional who determines the structural soundness and operating systems of a property.

Home Price The price that a buyer and seller agree upon, generally based on the home's appraised market value.

Homeowners' Association (HOA) A group that governs a community, condominium building, or neighborhood and enforces the covenants, conditions, and restrictions set by the developer.

Homeowners' Association Dues The monthly payments that are paid to the homeowners' association for maintenance and communal expenses.

Homeowners' Insurance A policy that includes coverage for all damages that may affect the value of a house as defined in the terms of the insurance policy.

Homeowner's Warranty A type

of policy homebuyers often purchase to cover repairs, such as heating or air conditioning, should they stop working within the coverage period.

Homestead The property an owner uses as his primary residence.

Housing Expense Ratio The percentage of gross income that is devoted to housing costs each month.

HUD Housing and Urban Development. A federal agency that oversees a variety of housing and community development programs, including the FHA.

HUD Median Income The average income for families in a particular area, which is estimated by HUD.

HUD-1 Settlement Statement Also known as the Closing Statement or Settlement Sheet. An itemized listing of the funds paid at closing.

HUD-1 Uniform Settlement Statement A closing statement for the buyer and seller that describes all closing costs for a real estate transaction or refinancing.

HVAC Heating, Ventilating,

and Air Conditioning.

Hybrid Debt A position in a mortgage that has equity-like features of participation in both cash flow and the appreciation of the property at the point of sale or refinance.

Implied Cap Rate The net operating income divided by the sum of a REIT's equity market capitalization and its total outstanding debt.

Impounds The part of the monthly mortgage payment that is reserved in an account in order to pay for hazard insurance, property taxes, and private mortgage insurance.

Improvements The upgrades or changes made to a building to improve its value or usefulness.

Incentive Fee A structure in which the fee amount charged is based on the performance of the real estate assets under management.

Income Capitalization Value The figure derived for an income-producing property by converting its expected benefits into property value.

Income Property A particular property that is used to generate income but is not occupied by the owner.

Income Return The percentage of the total return generated by the income from property, fund, or account operations.

Index A financial table that lenders use for calculating interest rates on ARMs.

Indexed Rate The sum of the published index with a margin added.

Indirect Costs Expenses of development other than the costs of direct material and labor that are related directly to the construction of improvements.

Individual Account Management The process of maintaining accounts that have been established for individual plan sponsors or other investors for investment in real estate, where a firm acts as an adviser in obtaining and/or managing a real estate portfolio.

Inflation Hedge An investment whose value tends to increase at a greater rate than inflation, contributing to the preservation of the purchasing power of a portfolio.

Inflation The rate at which consumer prices increase each year.

Initial Interest Rate The original interest rate on an ARM which is sometimes subject to a variety of adjustments throughout the mortgage.

Initial Public Offering (IPO) The first time a previously private company offers securities for public sale.

Initial Rate Cap The limit specified by some ARMs as the maximum amount the interest rate may increase when the initial interest rate expires.

Initial Rate Duration The date specified by most ARMs at which the initial rate expires.

Inspection Fee The fee that a licensed property inspector charges for determining the current physical condition of the property.

Inspection Report A written report of the property's condition presented by a licensed inspection professional.

Institutional-Grade Property A variety of types of real estate properties usually owned or financed by tax-exempt institutional investors.

Insurance Binder A temporary insurance policy that is implemented while a permanent policy is drawn up or obtained.

Insurance Company Separate Account A real estate investment vehicle only offered by life insurance companies, which enables an ERISA-governed fund to avoid creating unrelated taxable income for certain types of property investments and investment structures.

Insured Mortgage A mortgage that is guaranteed by the FHA or by private mortgage insurance (PMI).

Interest Accrual Rate The rate at which a mortgage accrues interest.

Interest Only Loan A mortgage for which the borrower pays only the interest that accrues on the loan balance each month.

Interest Paid over Life of Loan The total amount that has been paid to the lender during the time the money was borrowed.

Interest Rate The percentage that is charged for a loan.

Interest Rate Buy-Down Plans A plan in which a seller uses funds from the sale of the home to buy down the interest rate and reduce the buyer's monthly payments.

Interest Rate Cap The highest interest rate charge allowed on the monthly payment of an ARM during an adjustment period.

Interest rate ceiling The maximum interest rate a lender can charge for an ARM.

Interest Rate Floor The minimum possible interest rate a lender can charge for an ARM.

Interest The price that is paid for the use of capital.

Interest-Only Strip A derivative security that consists of all or part of the portion of interest in the underlying loan or security.

Interim Financing Also known as Bridge or Swing Loans. Short-term financing a seller uses to bridge the gap between the sale of one house and the purchase of another.

Internal Rate of Return (IRR) The calculation of a discounted cash-flow analysis which is used to determine the potential total return of a real estate asset during a particular holding period.

Inventory The entire space of a certain proscribed market without concern for its availability or condition.

Investment Committee The governing body that is charged with overseeing corporate pension investments and developing investment policies for board approval.

Investment Manager An individual or company that assumes authority over a specified amount of real estate capital, invests that capital in assets using a separate account, and provides asset management.

Investment Policy A document that formalizes an institution's goals, objectives, and guidelines for asset management, investment advisory contracting, fees, and utilization of consultants and other outside professionals.

Investment Property A piece of real estate that generates some form of income.

Investment Strategy The methods used by a manager in structuring a portfolio and selecting the real estate assets for a fund or an account.

Investment Structures Approaches to investing that include unleveraged acquisitions, leveraged acquisitions, traditional debt, participating debt, convertible debt, triple-net leases, and joint ventures.

Investment-Grade CMBS Commercial Mortgage-Backed Securities that have ratings of AAA, AA, A, or BBB.

Investor Status The position an investor is in, either taxable or tax-exempt.

Joint Liability The condition in which responsibility rests with two or more people for fulfilling the terms of a home loan or other financial debt.

Joint Tenancy A form of ownership in which two or more people have equal shares in a piece of property, and rights pass to the surviving owner(s) in the event of death.

Joint Venture An investment business formed by more than one party for the purpose of acquiring or developing and managing property and/or other assets.

Judgment The decision a court of law makes.

Judicial Foreclosure The usual foreclosure proceeding some states use, which is handled in a civil lawsuit.

Jumbo Loan A type of mortgage that exceeds the required limits set by Fannie Mae and Freddie Mac each year.

Junior Mortgage A loan that is a lower priority behind the primary loan.

Just Compensation The amount that is fair to both the owner and the government when property is appropriated for public use through Eminent Domain.

Landlord's Warrant The warrant a landlord obtains to take a tenant's personal property to sell at a public sale to compel payment of the rent or other stipulation in the lease.

Late Charge The fee that is imposed by a lender when the borrower has not made a payment when it was due.

Late Payment The payment made to the lender after the due date has passed.

Lead Manager The investment banking firm that has primary responsibility for coordinating the new issuance of securities.

Lease A contract between a property owner and tenant that defines payments and conditions under which the tenant may occupy the real estate for a given period of time.

Lease Commencement Date The date at which the terms of the lease are implemented.

Lease Expiration Exposure Schedule A chart of the total square footage of all current leases that expire in each of the next five years, without taking renewal options into account.

Lease Option A financing option that provides for homebuyers to lease a home with an option to buy, with part of the rental payments being applied toward the down payment.

Leasehold The limited right to inhabit a piece of real estate held by a tenant.

Leasehold State A way of holding a property title in which the mortgagor does not actually own the property but has a long-term lease on it.

Leasehold Interest The right to hold or use property for a specific period of time at a given price without transfering ownership.

Lease-Purchase A contract that defines the closing date and solutions for the seller in the event that the buyer defaults.

Legal Blemish A negative

325

count against a piece of property such as a zoning violation or fraudulent title claim.

Legal Description A way of describing and locating a piece of real estate that is recognized by law.

Legal Owner The party who holds the title to the property, although the title may carry no actual rights to the property other than as a lien.

Lender A bank or other financial institution that offers home loans.

Letter of Credit A promise from a bank or other party that the issuer will honor drafts or other requests for payment upon complying with the requirements specified in the letter of credit.

Letter of Intent An initial agreement defining the proposed terms for the end contract.

Leverage The process of increasing the return on an investment by borrowing some of the funds at an interest rate less than the return on the project.

Liabilities A borrower's debts and financial obligations, whether long- or short-term.

Liability Insurance A type of policy that protects owners against negligence, personal injury, or property damage claims.

LIBOR Acronym for "London Interbank Offered Rate." An index used to determine interest rate changes for adjustable rate mortgages. Very popular index for interest-only mortgage programs.

London InterBank Offered Rate (LIBOR) The interest rate offered on Eurodollar deposits traded between banks and used to determine changes in interest rate for ARMs.

Lien A claim put by one party on the property of another as collateral for money owed.

Lien Waiver A waiver of a mechanic's lien rights that is sometimes required before the general contractor can receive money under the payment provisions of a construction loan and contract.

Life Cap A limit on the amount an ARM's interest rate can increase during the mortgage term.

Lifecycle The stages of development for a property:

pre-development, development, leasing, operating, and rehabilitation.

Lifetime Payment Cap A limit on the amount that payments can increase or decrease over the life of an ARM.

Lifetime Rate Cap The highest possible interest rate that may be charged, under any circumstances, over the entire life of an ARM.

Like-Kind Property A term that refers to real estate that is held for productive use in a trade or business or for investment.

Limited Partnership A type of partnership in which some partners manage the business and are personally liable for partnership debts, but some partners contribute capital and share in profits without the responsibility of management.

Line of Credit An amount of credit granted by a financial institution up to a specified amount for a certain period of time to a borrower.

Liquid Asset A type of asset that can be easily converted into cash.

Liquidity The ease with which an individual's or company's

assets can be converted to cash without losing their value.

Listing Agreement An agreement between a property owner and a real estate broker which authorizes the broker to attempt to sell or lease the property at a specified price and terms in return for a commission or other compensation.

Loan An amount of money that is borrowed and usually repaid with interest.

Loan Application A document that presents a borrower's income, debt, and other obligations to determine credit worthiness, as well as some basic information on the target property.

Loan Application Fee A fee lenders charge to cover expenses relating to reviewing a loan application.

Loan Commitment An agreement by a lender or other financial institution to make or insure a loan for the specified amount and terms.

Loan Officer An official representative of a lending institution who is authorized to act on behalf of the lender within specified limits.

Loan Origination The process of obtaining and arranging new loans.

Loan Origination Fee A fee lenders charge to cover the costs related to arranging the loan.

Loan Servicing The process a lending institution goes through for all loans it manages. This involves processing payments, sending statements, managing the escrow/impound account, providing collection services on delinquent loans, ensuring that insurance and property taxes are made on the property, handling pay-offs and assumptions, as well as various other services.

Loan Term The time, usually expressed in years, that a lender sets in which a buyer must pay a mortgage.

Loan-to-Value (LTV) The ratio of the amount of the loan compared to the appraised value or sales price.

Lock-Box Structure An arrangement in which the payments are sent directly from the tenant or borrower to the trustee.

Lock-In A commitment from a lender to a borrower to guarantee a given interest rate for a limited amount of time.

Lock-In Period The period of time during which the borrower is guaranteed a specified interest rate.

Lockout The period of time during which a loan may not be paid off early.

Long-Term Lease A rental agreement that will last at least three years from initial signing to the date of expiration or renewal.

Loss Severity The percentage of lost principal when a loan is foreclosed.

Lot One of several contiguous parcels of a larger piece of land.

Low-Documentation Loan A mortage that requires only a basic verification of income and assets.

Low-Rise A building that involves fewer than four stories above the ground level.

Lump-Sum Contract A type of construction contract that requires the general contractor to complete a building project for a fixed cost that is usually established beforehand by competitive bidding.

Magic Page A story of projected

growth which describes how a new REIT will achieve its future plans for funds from operations or funds available for distribution.

Maintenance Fee The charge to homeowners' association members each month for the repair and maintenance of common areas.

Maker One who issues a promissory note and commits to paying the note when it is due.

Margin A percentage that is added to the index and fixed for the mortgage term.

Mark to Market The act of changing the original investment cost or value of a property or portfolio to the level of the current estimated market value.

Market Capitalization A measurement of a company's value that is calculated by multiplying the current share price by the current number of shares outstanding.

Market Rental Rates The rental income that a landlord could most likely ask for a property in the open market, indicated by the current rents for comparable spaces.

Market Study A forecast of the demand for a certain type of real estate project in the future which includes an estimate of the square footage that could be absorbed and the rents that could be charged.

Market Value The price a property would sell for at a particular point in time in a competitive market.

Marketable Title A title that is free of encumbrances and can be marketed immediately to a willing purchaser.

Master Lease The primary lease that controls other subsequent leases and may cover more property than all subsequent leases combined.

Master Servicer An entity that acts on behalf of a trustee for security holders' benefit in collecting funds from a borrower, advancing funds in the event of delinquencies and, in the event of default, taking a property through foreclosure.

Maturity Date The date at which the total principal balance of a loan is due.

Mechanic's Lien A claim created for securing payment priority for the price and value of work performed and materials furnished in constructing, repairing, or improving a building or other structure.

Meeting Space The space in hotels that is made available to the public to rent for meetings, conferences, or banquets.

Merged Credit Report A report that combines information from the three primary credit-reporting agencies including: Equifax, Experian, and Trans Union.

Metes and Bounds The surveyed boundary lines of a piece of land described by listing the compass directions (bounds) and distances (metes) of the boundaries.

Mezzanine Financing A financing position somewhere between equity and debt, meaning that there are higher-priority debts above and equity below.

Mid-Rise Usually, a building which shows four to eight stories above ground level. In a business district, buildings up to 25 stories may also be included.

Mixed-Use A term referring to space within a building or project which can be used for more than one activity.

Modern Portfolio Theory (MPT) An approach of quantifying risk and return in an asset portfolio which emphasizes the portfolio rather than the individual assets and how the assets perform in relation to each other.

Modification An adjustment in the terms of a loan agreement.

Modified Annual Percentage Rate (APR) An index of the cost of a loan based on the standard APR but adjusted for the amount of time the borrower expects to hold the loan.

Monthly Association Dues A payment due each month to a homeowners' association for expenses relating to maintenance and community operations.

Mortgage An amount of money that is borrowed to purchase a property using that property as collateral.

Mortgage Acceleration Clause A provision enabling a lender to require that the rest of the loan balance is paid in a lump sum under certain circumstances.

Mortgage Banker A financial institution that provides home loans using its own resources, often selling them to investors such as insurance companies or Fannie Mae.

Mortgage Broker An individual that matches prospective borrowers with lenders that the broker is approved to deal with.

Mortgage Broker Business A company that matches prospective borrowers with lenders that the broker is approved to deal with.

Mortgage Constant A figure comparing an amortizing mortgage payment to the outstanding mortgage balance.

Mortgage Insurance (MI) A policy, required by lenders on some loans, that covers the lender against certain losses that are incurred as a result of a default on a home loan.

Mortgage Insurance Premium (MIP) The amount charged for mortgage insurance, either to a government agency or to a private MI company.

Mortgage Interest Deduction The tax write-off that the IRS allows most homeowners to deduct for annual interest payments made on real estate loans.

Mortgage Life and Disability Insurance A type of term life insurance borrowers often purchase to cover debt that is left when the borrower dies or becomes too disabled to make the mortgage payments.

Mortgagee The financial institution that lends money to the borrower.

Mortgagor The person who requests to borrow money to purchase a property.

Multidwelling Units A set of properties that provide separate housing areas for more than one family but only require a single mortgage.

National Association of Real Estate Investment Trusts (NAREIT) The national, non-profit trade organization that represents the real estate investment trust industry.

National Council of Real Estate Investment Fiduciaries (NCREIF) A group of real estate professionals who serve on committees, sponsor research articles, seminars and symposiums, and produce the NCREIF Property Index.

NCREIF Property Index (NPI) A quarterly and yearly report presenting income and appreciation components.

Negative Amortization An event that occurs when the deferred interest on an ARM is added, and the balance increases instead of decreases.

Net Asset Value (NAV) The total value of an asset or property minus leveraging or joint venture interests.

Net Asset Value Per Share The total value of a REIT's current assets divided by outstanding shares.

Net Assets The total value of assets minus total liabilities based on market value.

Net Cash Flow The total income generated by an investment property after expenses have been subtracted.

Net Investment in Real Estate Gross investment in properties minus the outstanding balance of debt.

Net Investment Income The income or loss of a portfolio or business minus all expenses, including portfolio and asset management fees, but before gains and losses on investments are considered.

Net Operating Income (NOI) The pre-tax figure of gross revenue minus operating expenses and an allowance for expected vacancy.

Net Present Value (NPV) The sum of the total current value of incremental future cash flows plus the current value of estimated sales proceeds.

Net Purchase Price The gross purchase price minus any associated financed debt.

Net Real Estate Investment Value The total market value of all real estate minus property-level debt.

Net Returns The returns paid to investors minus fees to advisers or managers.

Net Sales Proceeds The income from the sale of an asset, or part of an asset, minus brokerage commissions, closing costs, and market expenses.

Net Square Footage The total space required for a task or staff position.

Net Worth The worth of an individual or company figured on the basis of a difference between all assets and liabilities.

No-Cash-Out Refinance Sometimes referred to as a Rate and Term Refinance. A refinancing transaction which is intended only to cover the balance due on the current loan and any costs associated with obtaining the new mortgage.

No-Cost Loan A loan for which there are no costs associated with the loan that are charged by the lender, but with a slightly higher interest rate.

No-Documentation Loan A type of loan application that requires no income or asset verification, usually granted based on strong credit with a large down payment.

Nominal Yield The yield investors receive before it is adjusted for fees, inflation, or risk.

Non-Assumption Clause A provision in a loan agreement that prohibits transfering a mortgage to another borrower without approval from the lender.

Non-Compete Clause A provision in a lease agreement that specifies that the tenant's business is the only one that may operate in the property in question, thereby preventing a competitor moving in next door.

Non-Conforming Loan Any loan that is too large or does not meet certain qualifications to be purchased by Fannie Mae or Freddie Mac.

Non-Discretionary Funds The funds that are allocated to an investment manager who must have approval from the investor for each transaction.

Non-Investment-Grade CMBS Also referred to as High-Yield CMBS. Commercial Mortgage-Backed Securities that have ratings of BB or B.

Non-Liquid Asset A type of asset that is not turned into cash very easily.

Non-Performing Loan A loan agreement that cannot meet its contractual principal and interest payments.

Non-Recourse Debt A loan that limits the lender's options to collect on the value of the real estate in the event of a default by the borrower.

Nonrecurring Closing Costs Fees that are only paid one time in a given transaction.

Note A legal document requiring a borrower to repay a mortgage at a specified interest rate over a certain period of time.

Note Rate The interest rate that is defined in a mortgage note.

Notice of Default A formal written notification a borrower receives once the borrower is in default stating that legal action may be taken.

Offer A term that describes a specified price or spread to sell whole loans or securities.

One-Year Adjustable Rate Mortgage An ARM for which the interest rate changes annually, generally based on movements of a published index plus a specified margin.

Open Space A section of land or water that has been dedicated for public or private use or enjoyment.

Open-End Fund A type of commingled fund with an infinite life, always accepting new investor capital and making new investments in property.

Operating Cost Escalation A clause that is intended to adjust rents to account for external standards such as published indexes, negotiated wage levels, or building-related expenses.

Operating Expense The regular costs associated with operating and managing a property.

Opportunistic A phrase that generally describes a strategy of holding investments in underperforming and/or undermanaged assets with the expectation of increases in cash flow and/or value.

Option A condition in which the buyer pays for the right to purchase a property within a certain period of time without the obligation to buy.

Option Arm Loan A type of mortgage in which the borrower has a variety of payment options each month.

Original Principal Balance The total principal owed on a mortgage before a borrower has made a payment.

Origination Fee A fee that most lenders charge for the purpose of covering the costs associated with arranging the loan.

Originator A company that underwrites loans for commercial and/or multi-family properties.

Out-Parcel The individual retail sites located within a shopping center.

Overallotment A practice in which the underwriters offer and sell a higher number of shares than they had planned to purchase from the issuer.

Owner Financing A transaction in which the property seller agrees to finance all or part of the amount of the purchase.

Parking Ratio A figure, generally expressed as square footage, that compares a building's total rentable square footage to its total number of parking spaces.

Partial Payment An amount paid that is not large enough to cover the normal monthly payment on a mortgage loan.

Partial Sales The act of selling a real estate interest that is smaller than the whole property.

Partial Taking The appropriating of a portion of an owner's property under the laws of eminent domain.

Participating Debt Financing that allows the lender to have participatory rights to equity through increased income and/or residual value over the balance of the loan or original value at the time the loan is funded.

Party in Interest Any party that may hold an interest, including employers, unions and, sometimes, fiduciaries.

Pass-Through Certificate A document that allows the holder to receive payments of principal and interest from the underlying pool of mortgages.

Payment Cap The maximum amount a monthly payment may increase on an ARM.

Payment Change Date The date on which a new payment amount takes effect on an ARM or GPM, usually in the month directly after the adjustment date.

Payout Ratio The percentage of the primary earnings per share, excluding unusual items, that are paid to common stockholders as cash dividends during the next 12 months.

Pension Liability The full amount of capital that is required to finance vested pension fund benefits.

Percentage Rent The amount of rent that is adjusted based on the percentage of gross sales or revenues the tenant receives.

Per-Diem Interest The interest that is charged or accrued daily.

Performance Bond A bond that contractor posts to guarantee full performance of a contract in which the proceeds will be used for completing the contract or compensating the owner for loss in the event of nonperformance.

Performance Measurement The process of measuring how well an investor's real estate has performed regarding individual assets, advisers/managers, and portfolios.

Performance The changes each quarter in fund or account values that can be explained by investment income, realized or unrealized appreciation, and the total return to the investors before and after investment management fees.

Performance-Based Fees The fees that advisers or managers receive which are based on returns to investors.

Periodic Payment Cap The highest amount that payments can increase or decrease during a given adjustment period on an ARM.

Periodic Rate Cap The maximum amount that the interest rate can increase or decrease during a given adjustment period on an ARM.

Permanent Loan A long-term property mortgage.

Personal Property Any items belonging to a person that is not real estate.

PITI Principal, Interest, Taxes, Insurance. The items that are included in the monthly payment to the lender for an impounded loan, as well as mortgage insurance.

PITI Reserves The amount in cash that a borrower must readily have after the down payment and all closing costs are paid when purchasing a home.

Plan Assets The assets included in a pension plan.

Plan Sponsor The party that is responsible for administering an employee benefit plan.

Planned Unit Development (PUD) A type of ownership where individuals actually own the building or unit they live in, but common areas are owned jointly with the other members of the development or association. Contrast with condominium, where an individual actually owns the airspace of his unit, but the buildings and common areas are owned jointly with the others in the development or association.

Plat A chart or map of a certain area showing the boundaries of individual lots, streets, and easements.

Pledged Account Mortgage (PAM) A loan tied to a pledged savings account for which the fund and earned interest are used to gradually reduce mortgage payments.

Point Also referred to as a Discount Point. A fee a lender charges to provide a lower interest rate, equal to one percent of the amount of the loan.

Portfolio Management A process that involves formulating, modifying, and implementing a real estate investment strategy according to an investor's investment objectives.

Portfolio Turnover The amount of time averaged from the time an investment is funded until it is repaid or sold.

Power of Attorney A legal document that gives someone the authority to act on behalf of another party.

Power of Sale The clause included in a mortgage or deed of trust that provides the mortgagee (or trustee) with the right and power to advertise and sell the property at public auction if the borrower is in default.

Pre-Approval The complete analysis a lender makes regarding a potential borrower's ability to pay for a home as well as a confirmation of the proposed amount to be borrowed.

Pre-Approval Letter The letter a lender presents which states the amount of money they are willing to lend a potential buyer.

Preferred Shares Certain stocks that have a prior distributions claim up to a defined amount before the common shareholders may receive anything.

Preleased A certain amount of space in a proposed building that must be leased before construction may begin or a certificate of occupancy may be issued.

Prepaid Expenses The amount of money that is paid before it is due, including including taxes, insurance, and/or assessments.

Prepaid Fees The charges that a borrower must pay in advance regarding certain recurring items, such as interest, property taxes, hazard insurance, and PMI, if applicable.

Prepaid Interest The amount of interest that is paid before its due date.

Prepayment The money that is paid to reduce the principal balance of a loan before the date it is due.

Prepayment Penalty A penalty that may be charged to the borrower when he pays off a loan before the planned maturity date.

Prepayment Rights The right a borrower is given to pay the total principal balance before the maturity date free of penalty.

Prequalification The initial assessment by a lender of a potential borrower's ability to pay for a home as well as an estimate of how much the lender is willing to supply to the buyer.

Price to Earnings Ratio The comparison that is derived by dividing the current share price by the sum of the primary earnings per share from continuing operations over the past year.

Primary Issuance The preliminary financing of an issuer.

Prime Rate The best interest rate reserved for a bank's preferred customers.

Prime Space The first-generation space that is available for lease.

Prime Tenant The largest or highest-earning tenant in a building or shopping center.

Principal The amount of money originally borrowed in a mortgage, before interest is included and with any payments subtracted.

Principal Balance The total current balance of mortgage principal not including interest.

Principal Paid over Life of Loan The final total of scheduled payments to the principal which the lender calculates to equal the face amount of the loan.

Principal Payments The lender's return of invested capital.

Principle of Conformity The concept that a property will probably increase in value if its size, age, condition, and style are similar to other properties in the immediate area.

Private Debt Mortgages or other liabilities for which an individual is responsible.

Private Equity A real estate investment that has been acquired by a noncommercial entity.

Private Mortgage Insurance (PMI) A type of policy that a lender requires when the borrower's down payment or home equity percentage is under 20 percent of the value of the property.

Private Placement The sale of a security in a way that renders it exempt from the registration rules and requirements of the SEC.

Private REIT A real estate investment company that is structured as a real estate investment trust and which places and holds shares privately rather than publicly.

Pro Rata The proportionate amount of expenses per tenant for the property's maintenance and operation.

Processing Fee A fee some lenders charge for gathering the information necessary to process the loan.

Production Acres The portion of land that can be used directly in agriculture or timber activities to generate income, but not areas used for such things as machinery storage or support.

Prohibited Transaction Certain transactions that may not be performed between a pension plan and a party in interest, such as the following: the sale, exchange or lease of any property; a loan or other grant of credit; and furnishing goods or services.

Promissory Note A written agreement to repay the specific amount over a certain period of time.

Property Tax The tax that must be paid on private property.

Prudent Man Rule The standard to which ERISA holds a fiduciary accountable.

Public Auction An announced public meeting held at a specified location for the purpose of selling property to repay a mortgage in default.

Public Debt Mortgages or other liabilities for which a commercial entity is responsible.

Public Equity A real estate investment that has been acquired by REITs and other publicly traded real estate operating companies.

Punch List An itemized list that documents incomplete or unsatisfactory items after the contractor has declared the space to be mostly complete.

Purchase Agreement The written contract the buyer and seller both sign defining the terms and conditions under which a property is sold.

Purchase Money Transaction A transaction in which property is acquired through the exchange of money or something of equivalent value.

Purchase-Money Mortgage (PMM) A mortgage obtained by a borrower which serves as partial payment for a property.

Qualified Plan Any employee benefit plan that the IRS has approved as a tax-exempt plan.

Qualifying Ratio The measurement a lender uses to determine how much they are willing to lend to a potential buyer.

Quitclaim Deed A written document that releases a party from any interest they may have in a property.

Rate Cap The highest interest rate allowed on a monthly payment during an adjustment period of an ARM.

Rate Lock The commitment of a lender to a borrower that guarantees a certain interest rate for a specific amount of time.

Rate-Improvement Mortgage A loan that includes a clause which entitles a borrower to a one-time-only cut in the interest rate without having to refinance.

Rating Agencies Independent firms that are engaged to rate securities' creditworthiness on behalf of investors.

Rating A figure that represents the credit quality or creditworthiness of securities.

Raw Land A piece of property that has not been developed and remains in its natural state.

Raw Space Shell space in a building that has not yet been developed.

Real Estate Agent An individual who is licensed to negotiate and transact the real estate sales.

Real Estate Fundamentals The factors that drive the value of property.

Real Estate Settlement Procedures Act (RESPA) A legislation for consumer protection that requires lenders to notify borrowers regarding closing costs in advance.

Real Property Land and anything else of a permanent nature that is affixed to the land.

Real Rate of Return The yield given to investors minus an inflationary factor.

Realtor A real estate agent or broker who is an active member of a local real estate board affiliated with the National Association of Realtors.

Recapture The act of the IRS recovering the tax benefit of a deduction or a credit that a taxpayer has previously taken in error.

Recorder A public official who records transactions that affect real estate in the area.

Recording The documentation that the registrar's office keeps of the details of properly executed legal documents.

Recording Fee A fee real estate agents charge for moving the sale of a piece of property into the public record.

Recourse The option a lender has for recovering losses against the personal assets of a secondary party who is also liable for a debt that is in default.

Red Herring An early prospectus that is distributed to prospective investors that includes a note in red ink on the cover stating that the SEC-approved registration statement is not yet in effect.

Refinance Transaction The act of paying off an existing loan using the funding gained from a new loan which uses the same property as security.

Regional Diversification Boundaries that are defined based on geography or economic lines.

Registration Statement The set of forms that are filed with the SEC (or the appropriate state agency) regarding a proposed offering of new securities or the listing of outstanding securities on a national exchange.

Regulation Z A federal legislation under the Truth in Lending Act that requires lenders to advise the borrower in writing of all costs that are associated with the credit portion of a financial transaction.

Rehab Short for Rehabilitation. Refers to an extensive renovation intended to extend the life of a building or project.

Rehabilitation Mortgage A loan meant to fund the repairing and improving of a resale home or building.

Real Estate Investment Trust (REIT) A trust corporation that combines the capital of several investors for the purpose of acquiring or providing funding for real estate.

Remaining Balance The amount of the principal on a home loan that has not yet been paid.

Remaining Term The original term of the loan after the number of payments made has been subtracted.

Real Estate Mortgage Investment Conduit (REMIC) An investment vehicle that is designed to hold a pool of mortgages solely to issue multiple classes of mortgage-backed securities in a way that avoids doubled corporate tax.

Renewal Option A clause in a lease agreement that allows a tenant to extend the term of a lease.

Renewal Probability The average percentage of a building's tenants who are expected to renew terms at market rental rates upon the lease expiration.

Rent Commencement Date The date at which a tenant is to begin paying rent.

Rent Loss Insurance A policy that covers loss of rent or rental value for a landlord due to any condition that renders the leased premises inhabitable, thereby excusing the tenant from paying rent.

Rent The fee paid for the occupancy and/or use of any rental property or equipment.

Rentable/Usable Ratio A total rentable area in a building divided by the area available for use.

Rental Concession See: Concessions.

Rental Growth Rate The projected trend of market rental rates over a particular period of analysis.

Rent-Up Period The period of time following completion of a new building when tenants are actively being sought and the project is stabilizing.

Real Estate Owned (REO)

The real estate that a savings institution owns as a result of foreclosure on borrowers in default.

Repayment Plan An agreement made to repay late installments or advances.

Replacement Cost The projected cost by current standards of constructing a building that is equivalent to the building being appraised.

Replacement Reserve Fund Money that is set aside for replacing of common property in a condominium, PUD, or cooperative project.

Request for Proposal (RFP) A formal request that invites investment managers to submit information regarding investment strategies, historical investment performance, current investment opportunities, investment management fees, and other pension fund client relationships used by their firm.

Rescission The legal withdrawing of a contract or consent from the parties involved.

Reserve Account An account that must be funded by the borrower to protect the lender.

Resolution Trust Corp. (RTC) The congressional corporation established for the purpose of containing, managing, and selling failed financial institutions, thereby recovering taxpayer funds.

Retail Investor An investor who sells interests directly to consumers.

Retention Rate The percentage of trailing year's earnings that have been dispersed into the company again. It is calculated as 100 minus the trailing 12-month payout ratio.

Return on Assets The measurement of the ability to produce net profits efficiently by making use of assets.

Return on Equity The measurement of the return on the investment in a business or property.

Return on Investments The percentage of money that has been gained as a result of certain investments.

Reverse Mortgage See: Home Equity Conversion Mortgage.

Reversion Capitalization Rate The capitalization rate that is used to derive reversion value.

Reversion Value A benefit that an investor expects to receive as a lump sum at the end of an investment.

Revolving Debt A credit arrangement which enables a customer to borrow against a predetermined line of credit when purchasing goods and services.

Revenue Per Available Room (RevPAR) The total room revenue for a particular period divided by the average number of rooms available in a hospitality facility.

Right of Ingress or Egress The option to enter or to leave the premises in question.

Right of Survivorship The option that survivors have to take on the interest of a deceased joint tenant.

Right to Rescission A legal provision that enables borrowers to cancel certain loan types within three days after they sign.

Risk Management A logical approach to analyzing and defining insurable and non-insurable risks while evaluating the availability and costs of purchasing third-party insurance.

Risk-Adjusted Rate of Return A percentage that is used to identify investment options that are expected to deliver a positive premium despite their volatility.

Road Show A tour of the executives of a company that is planning to go public, during which the executives travel to a variety cities to make presentations to underwriters and analysts regarding their company and IPO.

Roll-Over Risk The possibility that tenants will not renew their lease.

Sale-Leaseback An arrangement in which a seller deeds a property, or part of it, to a buyer in exchange for money or the equivalent, then leases the property from the new owner.

Sales Comparison Value A value that is calculated by comparing the appraised property to similar properties in the area that have been recently sold.

Sales Contract An agreement that both the buyer and seller sign defining the terms of a property sale.

Second Mortgage A secondary loan obtained upon a piece of property.

Secondary Market A market in which existing mortgages are bought and sold as part of a mortgages pool.

Secondary (Follow-On) Offering An offering of stock made by a company that is already public.

Second-Generation or Secondary Space Space that has been occupied before and becomes available for lease again, either by the landlord or as a sublease.

Secured Loan A loan that is secured by some sort of collateral.

Securities and Exchange Commission (SEC) The federal agency that oversees the issuing and exchanging of public securities.

Securitization The act of converting a non-liquid asset into a tradable form.

Security The property or other asset that will serve as a loan's collateral.

Security Deposit An amount of money a tenant gives to a landlord to secure the performance of terms in a lease agreement.

Seisen (Seizen) The ownership of real property under a claim of freehold estate.

Self-Administered REIT A REIT in which the management are employees of the REIT or similar entity.

Self-Managed REIT See: Self-Administered REIT.

Seller Carry-Back An arrangement in which the seller provides the financing to purchase a home.

Seller Financing A type of funding in which the borrower may use part of the equity in the property to finance the purchase.

Senior Classes The security classes who have the highest priority for receiving payments from the underlying mortgage loans.

Separate Account A relationship in which a single pension plan sponsor is used to retain an investment manager or adviser under a stated investment policy exclusively for that sponsor.

Servicer An organization that collects principal and interest payments from borrowers and manages borrowers' escrow accounts on behalf of a trustee.

Servicing The process of collecting mortgage payments from borrowers as well as related responsibilities.

Setback The distance required from a given reference point before a structure can be built.

Settlement or Closing Fees Fees that the escrow agent receives for carrying out the written instructions in the agreement between borrower and lender and/or buyer and seller.

Settlement Statement See: HUD-1 Settlement Statement.

Shared-Appreciation Mortgage A loan which enables a lender or other party to share in the profits of the borrower when the borrower sells the home.

Shared-Equity Transaction A transaction in which two people purchase a property, one as a residence and the other as an investment.

Shares Outstanding The number of shares of outstanding common stock minus the treasury shares.

Site Analysis A determination of how suitable a specific parcel of land is for a particular use.

Site Development The implementation of all improvements that are needed for a site before construction may begin.

Site Plan A detailed description and map of the location of improvements to a parcel.

Slab The flat, exposed surface that is laid over the structural support beams to form the building's floor(s).

Social Investing A strategy in which investments are driven in partially or completely by social or non-real estate objectives.

Soft Cost The part of an equity investment, aside from the literal cost of the improvements, that could be tax-deductible in the first year.

Space Plan A chart or map of space requirements for a tenant which include wall/door locations, room sizes, and even furniture layouts.

Special Assessment Certain charges that are levied against real estates for public improvements to benefit the property in question.

Special Servicer A company that is hired to collect on mortgages that are either delinquent or in default.

Specified Investing A strategy of investment in individually specified properties, portfolios, or commingled funds are fully or partially detailed prior to the commitment of investor capital.

Speculative Space Any space in a rental property that has not been leased prior to construction on a new building begins.

Stabilized Net Operating Income Expected income minus expenses that reflect relatively stable operations.

Stabilized Occupancy The best projected range of long-term occupancy that a piece of rental property will achieve after existing in the open market for a reasonable period of time with terms and conditions that are comparable to similar offerings.

Step-Rate Mortgage A loan which allows for a gradual interest rate increase during the first few years of the loan.

Step-Up Lease (Graded Lease) A lease agreement which specifies certain increases in rent at certain intervals during the complete term of the lease.

Straight Lease (Flat Lease) A lease agreement which specifies an amount of rent that should be paid regularly during the complete term of the lease.

Strip Center Any shopping area that is made up of a row of stores but is not large enough to be anchored by a grocery store.

Subcontractor A contractor who has been hired by the general contractor, often specializing in a certain required task for the construction project.

Subdivision The most common type of housing development created by dividing a larger tract of land into individual lots for sale or lease.

Sublessee A person or business that holds the rights of use and occupancy under a lease contract with the original lessee, who still retains primary responsibility the lease obligations.

Subordinate Financing Any loan with a priority lower than loans that were obtained beforehand.

Subordinate Loan A second or third mortgage obtained with the same property being used as collateral.

Subordinated Classes Classes that have the lowest priority of receiving payments from underlying mortgage loans.

Subordination The act of sharing credit loss risk at varying rates among two or more classes of securities.

Subsequent Rate Adjustments The interest rate for ARMs that adjusts at regular intervals, sometimes differing from the duration period of the initial interest rate.

Subsequent Rate Cap The maximum amount the interest rate may increase at each regularly scheduled interest rate adjustment date on an ARM.

Super Jumbo Mortgage A loan that is over $650,000 for some lenders or $1,000,000 for others.

Surety A person who willingly binds himself to the debt or obligation of another party.

Surface Rights A right or easement that is usually granted with mineral rights which enabling the holder to drill through the surface.

Survey A document or analysis containing the precise measurements of a piece of property as performed by a licensed surveyor.

Sweat Equity The non-cash improvements in value that an owner adds to a piece of property.

Synthetic Lease A transaction that is considered to be a lease by accounting standards but a loan by tax standards.

Taking Similar to condemning, or any other interference with rights to private property, but a physical seizure or appropriation is not required.

Tax Base The determined value of all property that lies within the jurisdiction of the taxing authority.

Tax Lien A type of lien placed against a property if the owner has not paid property or personal taxes.

Tax Roll A record, that contains the descriptions of all land parcels and their owners, that is located within the county.

Tax Service Fee A fee that is charged for the purpose of setting up monitoring of the borrower's property tax payments by a third-party.

Teaser Rate A small, short-term interest rate offered on a mortgage in order to convince the potential borrower to apply.

Tenancy by the Entirety A form of ownership held by spouses in which they both hold title to the entire property with right of survivorship.

Tenancy in Common A type of ownership held by two or more owners in an undivided interest in the property with no right of survivorship.

Tenant (Lessee) A party who rents a piece of real estate from another by way of a lease agreement.

Tenant at Will A person who possesses a piece of real estate with the owner's permission.

Tenant Improvement (TI) Allowance The specified amount of money that the landlord contributes toward tenant improvements.

Tenant Improvement (TI) The upgrades or repairs that are made to the leased premises by or for a tenant.

Tenant Mix The quality of the income stream for a property.

Term The length that a loan lasts or is expected to last before it is repaid.

Third-Party Origination A process in which another party is used by the lender to originate, process, underwrite, close,

fund, or package the mortgages it expects to deliver to the secondary mortgage market.

Timeshare A form of ownership involving purchasing a specific period of time or percentage of interest in a vacation property.

Time-Weighted Average Annual Rate of Return The regular yearly return over several years that would have the same return value as combining the actual annual returns for each year in the series.

Title The legal written document which provides someone ownership in a piece of real estate.

Title Company A business that determines that a property title is clear and that provides title insurance.

Title Exam An analysis of the public records in order to confirm that the seller is the legal owner, and there are no encumbrances on the property.

Title Insurance A type of policy that is issued to both lenders and buyers to cover loss due to property ownership disputes that may arise at a later date.

Title Insurance Binder A written promise from the title

insurance company to insure the title to the property, based on the conditions and exclusions shown in the binder.

Title Risk The potential impediments in transfering a title from one party to another.

Title Search The process of analyzing all transactions existing in the public record in order to determine whether any title defects could interfere with the clear transfer of property ownership.

Total Acres The complete amount of land area that is contained within a real estate investment.

Total Assets The final amount of all gross investments, cash and equivalents, receivables, and other assets as they are presented on the balance sheet.

Total Commitment The complete funding amount that is promised once all specified conditions have been met.

Total Expense Ratio The comparison of monthly debt obligations to gross monthly income.

Total Inventory The total amount of square footage commanded by property within

a geographical area.

Total Lender Fees Charges which the lender requires for obtaining the loan, aside from other fees associated with the transfer of a property.

Total Loan Amount The basic amount of the loan plus any additional financed closing costs.

Total Monthly Housing Costs The amount that must be paid each month to cover principal, interest, property taxes, PMI, and/or either hazard insurance or homeowners' association dues.

Total of All Payments The total cost of the loan after figuring the sum of all monthly interest payments.

Total Principal Balance The sum of all debt, including the original loan amount adjusted for subsequent payments and any unpaid items that may be included in the principal balance by the mortgage note or by law.

Total Retail Area The total floor area of a retail center that is currently leased or available for lease.

Total Return The final amount of income and appreciation returns per quarter.

Townhouse An attached home that is not considered to be a condominium.

Trade Fixtures Any personal property that is attached to a structure and used in the business but is removable once the lease is terminated.

Trading Down The act of purchasing a property that is less expensive than the one currently owned.

Trading Up The act of purchasing a property that is more expensive than the one currently owned.

Tranche A class of securities that may or may not be rated.

Trans Union Corporation One of the primary credit reporting bureaus.

Transfer of Ownership Any process in which a property changes hands from one owner to another.

Transfer Tax An amount specified by state or local authorities when ownership in a piece of property changes hands.

Treasury Index A measurement that is used to derive interest rate changes for ARMs.

Triple Net Lease A lease that requires the tenant to pay all property expenses on top of the rental payments.

Trustee A fiduciary who oversees property or funds on behalf of another party.

Truth-in-Lending The federal legislation requiring lenders to fully disclose the terms and conditions of a mortgage in writing.

Turn Key Project A project in which someone other than the owner is responsible for the construction of a building or for tenant improvements.

Two- to Four-Family Property A structure that provides living space for two to four families while ownership is held in a single deed.

Two-Step Mortgage An ARM with two different interest rates: one for the loan's first five or seven years and another for the remainder of the loan term.

Under Construction The time period that exists after a building's construction has started but before a certificate of occupancy has been presented.

Under Contract The period of time during which a buyer's offer to purchase a property has been accepted, and the buyer is able to finalize financing arrangements without the concern of the seller making a deal with another buyer.

Underwriter A company, usually an investment banking firm, that is involved in a guarantee that an entire issue of stocks or bonds will be purchased.

Underwriters' Knot An approved knot according to code that may be tied at the end of an electrical cord to prevent the wires from being pulled away from their connection to each other or to electrical terminals.

Underwriting The process during which lenders analyze the risks a particular borrower presents and set appropriate conditions for the loan.

Underwriting Fee A fee that mortgage lenders charge for verifying the information on the loan application and making a final decision on approving the loan.

Unencumbered A term that refers to property free of liens or other encumbrances.

Unimproved Land See: Raw Land.

Unrated Classes Usually the lowest classes securities.

Unrecorded Deed A deed that transfers right of ownership from one owner to another without being officially documented.

Umbrella Partnership Real Estate Investment Trust (UPREIT) An organizational structure in which a REIT's assets are owned by a holding company for tax reasons.

Usable Square Footage The total area that is included within the exterior walls of the tenant's space.

Use The particular purpose for which a property is intended to be employed.

VA Loan A mortgage through the VA program in which a down payment is not necessarily required.

Vacancy Factor The percentage of gross revenue that pro forma income statements expect to be lost due to vacancies.

Vacancy Rate The percentage of space that is available to rent.

Vacant Space Existing rental space that is presently being marketed for lease minus space that is available for sublease.

Value-Added A phrase advisors and managers generally use to describe investments in underperforming and/or undermanaged assets.

Variable Rate Mortgage (VRM) A loan in which the interest rate changes according to fluctuations in particular indexes.

Variable-Rate Also called adjustable-rate. The interest rate on a loan that varies over the term of the loan according to a predetermined index.

Variance A permission that enables a property owner to work around a zoning ordinance's literal requirements which cause a unique hardship due to special circumstances.

Verification of Deposit (VOD) The confirmation statement a borrower's bank may be asked to sign in order to verify the borrower's account balances and history.

Verification of Employment (VOE) The confirmation statement a borrower's employer may be asked to sign in order to verify the borrower's position and salary.

Vested Having the right to draw on a portion or on all of a pension or other retirement fund.

Veterans Administration (VA) A federal government agency that assists veterans in purchasing a home without a down payment.

Virtual Storefront A retail business presence on the Internet.

Waiting Period The period of time between initially filing a registration statement and the date it becomes effective.

Warehouse Fee A closing cost fee that represents the lender's expense of temporarily holding a borrower's loan before it is sold on the secondary mortgage market.

Weighted-Average Coupon The average, using the balance of each mortgage as the weighting factor, of the gross interest rates of the mortgages underlying a pool as of the date of issue.

Weighted-Average Equity The part of the equation that is used to calculate investment-level income, appreciation, and total returns on a quarter-by-quarter basis.

Weighted-Average Rental Rates The average ratio of unequal rental rates across two or more buildings in a market.

Working Drawings The detailed blueprints for a construction project that comprise the contractual documents which describe the exact manner in which a project is to be built.

Workout The strategy in which a borrower negotiates with a lender to attempt to restructure the borrower's debt rather than go through the foreclosure proceedings.

Wraparound Mortgage A loan obtained by a buyer to use for the remaining balance on the seller's first mortgage, as well as an additional amount requested by the seller.

Write-Down A procedure used in accounting when an asset's book value is adjusted downward to reflect current market value more accurately.

Write-Off A procedure used in accounting when an asset is determined to be uncollectible and is therefore considered to be a loss.

Yield Maintenance Premium A penalty the borrower must pay in order to make investors whole in the event of early repayment of principal.

Yield Spread The difference in income derived from a commercial mortgage and from a benchmark value.

Yield The actual return on an investment, usually paid in dividends or interest.

Zoning Ordinance The regulations and laws that control the use or improvement of land in a particular area or zone.

Zoning The act of dividing a city or town into particular areas and applying laws and regulations regarding the architectural design, structure, and intended uses of buildings within those areas.

Resources

A Vantage Properties
Wendy Frenzel, e-PRO®
372 Shasta Court
Kiowa, CO 80117
Phone: 303-621-9262
Fax: 303-621-9820
avp@avantageproperties.com
**http://www.avantageproperties
.com**

Acacia Property Management,
Inc.
Allen Houchins
555 116th Avenue N.E.
Suite 253
Bellevue, WA 98004
Phone: 425-451-1519
Fax: 425-642-8006
leaseahome@msn.com
http://www.acaciapmrealty.com

Ace Property Management, Llc
John Aceves
1085 N Main Street, Ste. N

Orange, CA 92867
Phone: 714-538-6117
Fax: 714-771-1890
john.acemgmt@mpowercom.net

AIM Realty Management
Donald Hay, RMP®
5250 Pacific Street
Rocklin, CA 95677
Phone: 916-624-4000
Fax: 916-630-2153
don@aimrealty.com
http://www.aimrealty.com

Allied Property Management
Group, Inc.
Anthony Marotta
P.O. Box 221674
West Palm Beach, FL 33422
Phone: 561-818-1184
Fax: 561-616-3454
anthony@alliedpmg.com
http://www.alliedpmg.com

Allvillage Realty
Nancy Steinmetz
106 S Old Dixie Highway
Lady Lake, FL 32159
Phone: 352-753-9828
Fax: 352-753-1311
steinmetz986@earthlink.net
**http://www.AllVillageRealty
.com**

American Management
Keli Henderson
104 Circle Way
Lake Jackson, TX 77566
Phone: 979-297-5555
Fax: 979-297-9847
keli@computron.net

Amerisouth Management, Inc.
Mark Vonder Meulen
PO Box 681722
Marietta, GA 30068
Phone: 678-245-4620
Fax: 678-298-9633
mark@goamerisouth.com
http://www.goamerisouth.com

Apollo Associates Realty
Shirley A. Harden
Support Specialist
1077 Ralph D. Abernathy Bd. SW
Atlanta, GA 30310
Phone: 404-753-7374
Fax: 404-753-8859
sharden@apolloassociatesrealty
.com
**http://www
.apolloassociatesrealty.com**

Arbour Real Estate Management,
Lambert Munz, RMP®
777 Campus Commons Road
Sacramento, CA 95825
Phone: 888-551-5114
Fax: 916-313-3424
arbourpm@comcast.net
http://www.arbourpm.com

Beaumont Property Management
Dick Beaumont, RMP®
PO Box 0429
Monterey, CA 93942
Phone: 831-643-2328
Fax: 831-643-2776
dick@beaumontpm.com
http://www.beaumontpm.com

Boardwalk Real Property
Management
Stephen Foster, MPM®
2141 NW Military Highway, #101
San Antonio, TX 78213
Phone: 210-340-1717
Fax: 210-342-4198
steve@boardwalkrpm.com
http://boardwalkrpm.com

Brw & Associates, Inc.
Bill Williamson
PO Box 33534
San Antonio, TX 78265
Phone: 210-590-0123
Fax: 210-946-7500
brwsatx@sbcglobal.net
http://www.brwproperties.com

Burleson Properties, LLC
Alanna Kay Burleson
PO Box 5464
Fredericksburg, VA 22403
Phone: 540-286-5258
Fax: 540-286-0746
kburleson1@adelphia.net

Camden Rei, Inc.
Felix Montez
3100 West Lake St.
Minneapolis, MN 55416
Phone: 612-529-8360
Fax: 612-983-60X4
NARPM@CamdenREI.com
http://www.CamdenREI.com

Cathy George Associates, Inc.
Helen Skov
850 W Hind Dr #210
Honolulu, HI 96821
Phone: 808-373-9844
Fax: 808-377-0834
cga@cgahawaii.com
http://www.cgahawaii.com

Century 21 Accent Homes, Inc.
Tom Sklopan
311 Telegraph Corner Lane
Alexandria, VA 22310
Phone: 800-368-3225
Fax: 703-971-5357
broker@c21accenthomes.com
http://www.c21accenthomes.com

Century 21 G-J Property
Management
Kathy Lohr

15201 Leffingwell Road
Whittier, CA 90604
Phone: 888-880-8680
Fax: 714-996-2792
klohr@c21gj.com
http://www.c21gj.com

Century 21 REP
Carolyn Wiegman
965 Chauncey Ct.
Ocoee, FL 34761
Phone: 321-306-7700
Fax: 321-380-7206
cwiegman@aol.com
http://www
.rentalhomesinorlando.com

Champion Group Realty
Albert Avitabile
8695 College Parkway
Suite 300
Fort Myers, FL 33919
Phone: 239-2926910
Fax: 239-225-9044
al@swfl-properties.com
www.swfl-properties.com

Champion Realty, Inc.
Molly Crafton
645 Baltimore-Annapolis Blvd
Suite 200
Severna Park, MD 21146
Phone: 410-975-3041
Fax: 410-384-9486
MollyCrafton@ChampionRealty
.com

Coast To Coast Real Estate
Bill McLaughlin
528 E. Tarpon Ave
Tarpon Springs, FL 34689
Phone: 727-937-0555
Fax: 727-934-0821
billpmc21@yahoo.com
http://www.ctocrg.com

Coldwell Banker Commercial
Linda Bryan, MPM®
Danforth & Associates, Inc. PM
33313 First Way So
Federal Way, WA 98003
Phone: 206-686-3850
Fax: 206-838-0760
bryanLL@msn.com
http://www.cbcdanforth.com
/property_mngt/index.html

Coldwell Banker Residential RE
Lisa Schmelzer
1633 Jefferson Avenue
Miami Beach, FL 33139
Phone: 305-604-8000
Fax: 305-532-0940
lisaeve@the-beach.net
http://www.floridamoves.com
/lisa.eve

Coldwell Banker Residential RE,
Inc.
Lisa Eve Schmelzer
1691 Michigan Ave
Miami Beach, FL 33139
Phone: 305-604-8000
Fax: 305-532-0940
lisaeve@floridamoves.com

http://www.floridamoves.com
/lisa.eve

Coldwell Banker Sunstar Realty
Diane Pfaehler
96 Harwich Circle
Englewood, FL 34223
Phone: 941-475-3108
Fax: 941-475-1812
pfaehlerd@sunstarrealty.com
http://www.sunstarrentals.com

Cornerstone Properties
Carl Frazier
99-082 Kauhale Street #c-17
Aiea, HI 96701
Phone: 808-484-1211
Fax: 808-485-1184
hawaiicarl@aol.com
http://www.cornerstonehawaii
.com

Cornerstone Property
Management
Brian Bonnifield, RMP®
2100 Curtner Avenue, Ste B
San Jose, CA 95124
Phone: 408-377-3000
Fax: 408-377-6280
brian@brianbonnifield.com
http://www.cornerstonepm.net

Diversified Property
Management LLC
Anne Pence
14618 W. Thorne Lane SW
Lakewood, WA 98498
Phone: 253-588-4447

Fax: 252-588-3365
annepence@msn.com
http://www
.diversifiedpropertymanagementllc
.com

Dominion Properties Virginia
Robert Kaltsounis
3420 Pump Road
Richmond, VA 23233
Phone: 804-937-4730
Fax: 804-364-2622
rkaltsounis@comcast.net
http://www.dpva.com

Don Asher & Associates
Jill Boles, RMP®
1801 Cook Avenue
Orlando, FL 32806
Phone: 407-425-4561
Fax: 407-843-5169
redhead1552@msn.com

Double Z, Inc.
Terri Patterson
14401 Pacific Avenue
Tacoma, WA 98444
Phone: 253-531-9431
Fax: 253-531-0184
terrimd1@msn.com
http://www.doublez.net

Enterprise Property Management
Aaron Ivey
3280 Chester St., Suite 101
Arlington, TN 38002
Phone: 901-451-5030
Fax: 901-451-5025

aaron@epmleasing.com
http://www.epmleasing.com

Farnsworth-Ricks Management
David Ricks
6001 E University Drive
Mesa, AZ 85205
Phone: 480-924-1300
Fax: 480-807-9762
dave@farnsworth-ricks.com
www.farnsworth-ricks.com

Flarent, Inc.
Geoffrey Hall
274 Wilshire Blvd, Suite 282
Casselberry, FL 32707
Phone: 407-339-5797
Fax: 407-339-6763
geoff@flarent.com
http://www.flarent.com

Hawaii Kai Realty
DemetriaWingfield
377 Keahole St, #211D
Honolulu, HI 96825
Phone: 808-395-8698
Fax: 808-395-2799
demetria@hawaiikairealty.com
http://www.hawaiikairealty.com

Henderson Properties, Inc.
Philip Henderson
919 Norland Road
Charlotte, NC 28205
Phone: 704-535-1122
Fax: 704-569-9669
phenderson
@hendersonproperties.com

http://hendersonproperties.com

Homefinders Plus
Lorne Sutherlin
2401 S Willis, Ste. 106
Abilene, TX 79605
Phone: 915-690-0222
Fax: 915-795-1662
sutherlin@abilene.com

Homeinvest Time, LLC
Dennis Murdock
3200 W Ray Road, #130
Chandler, AZ 85226
Phone: 480-786-5339
Fax: 480-821-0132
dcmurdock@cox.net

Homevest Realty
Corey Van Dyke
1300 E. Michigan St.
Orlando, FL 32806
Phone: 407-897-5400 ext. 208
Fax: 407-898-2911
corey@homevest.com
http://www.sellorbuyflorida.com

Horizon Properties
Janet S. Regan, RMP®
5941 San Juan Avenue, #12
Citrus Heights, CA 95610
Phone: 916-961-7368
Fax: 916-961-5368
janet@horizonproperties.com
http://www.horizonproperties
.com

Integrity Real Estate
Deidre Graybill
1801 East Colonial Drive, #206
Orlando, FL 32803
Phone: 407-541-2012
Fax: 407-541-0716
dgraybill@integrityrealestatemgt
.com
http://www
.integrityrealestatemgt.com

International Mgmt. Co
Lee Blackburn
118 Rebecca Dr.
Hendersonville, TN 37075
Phone: 615-226-1368
Fax: 615-822-5085
lee.blackburn@hotmail.com

Jubilee Real Estate Services Inc.
Nancy Ryan, MPM
3330 Mira Loma Court
Colorado Springs, CO 80918
Phone: 719-532-9377
Fax: 719-532-1053
Jresincnjr@aol.com

Lee S. Halyard & Associates
Lee Halyard
1133 North Battlefield Blvd
Chesapeake, VA 22320
Phone: 757-549-3700
Fax: 757-549-2887
lee@leehalyard.com
http://leehalyard.com

Management Masters Inc.
Donna Brandsey, MPM®
3370 N Hayden Road, #123-307
Scottsdale, AZ 85251
Phone: 480-990-1833
Fax: 480-990-1041
donna@mgmtmasters.com
http://www.mgmtmasters.com

Marchant Chapman Realtors
Jon Marchant
780 Sir Frances Drake Blvd.
San Anselmo, CA 94960
Phone: 415-451-1474
Fax: 415-456-8393
jon@marchantchapman.com
**http://www.marchantchapman
.com**

Marcie Emily Real Estate
Marcie Emily, RMP®
6410 W 44th Avenue, #3
Wheat Ridge, CO 80033
Phone: 303-456-5556
mere85@msn.com

McGinnis Property Management
Wayne Guthals
5353 N Union Boulevard
Colorado Springs, CO 80918
Phone: 719-584-7380
Fax: 719-534-7411
wayne.guthals@mcginnis.com
http://mcginnis.com

Metro Realty & Investments
Peter Polce
313 W Sycamore Valley Road

Danville, CA 94526
Phone: 925-556-1976
Fax: 925-556-1180
peter@metrorentals.net
http://www.metrorentals.net

Mike Hill Real Estate
Mike Hill
PO Box 1725
Valdosta, GA 31603
Phone: 229-242-1401
Fax: 229-242-1578
mike@mikehillrealestate.com

MKAT Properties
Cynthia Frigge
2412 E. Chicago Street
Caldwell, ID 83605
Phone: 208-455-4442
Fax: 208-455-4252
cyndy@mkatproperties.com
http://www.mkatproperties.com

Monterey Bay Property
Management
Jan Leasure
816 Wave Street
Monterey, CA 93940
Phone: 831-655-7840
Fax: 831-655-7845
jan@montereyrentals.com
**http://www.montereyrentals
.com**

Naper Realty, Property
Management
Daniel Satre
865 N Columbia Street

Naperville, IL 60563
Phone: 630-452-4074
Fax: 630-769-8380
narpm@alanarico.com
http://www.nrpm.net

Nelson-Rives Realty, Inc.
Patricia Bevis
2759 Chamblee-Tucker Road
Atlanta, GA 30341
Phone: 770-451-2323
Fax: 770-457-2511
patbevis@bellsouth.net
http://www.nelson-rives.com

Nickel Property
Earnestine Nickel
PO Box 2198
Cedar Hill, TX 75106
Phone: 972-296-9291
Fax: 972-723-2980
nickelprop@aol.com
http://www.Nickelproperty.com

Niels G. Nielsen Services Ltd.
Karin Harkness, RMP®
331 Bryan Avenue, #8
Bremerton, WA 98312
Phone: 360-377-4498
Fax: 360-479-3963
nielsen@telebyte.com
http://www.nielsenservices.com

Otero Realty Group, Inc.
Elise Otero, RMP®
1000 W. Apache Trail, #107
Apache Junction, AZ 85220
Phone: 428-983-9600

Fax: 480-983-9602
eliseotero@hotmail.com
**http://www.oterorealtygroup
.com**

P&L Property Management, Inc.
Rachel Lindsay
PO Box 50487
Summerville, SC 29485
Phone: 843-875-0444
Fax: 843-821-7561
rlindsay@sclandlord.com
http://www.sclandlord.com

Palm Beach First National
Dorothy Hamilton
P.O. Box 500
Virginia Beach, VA 23462
Phone: 075-534-6755
Fax: 075-598-2110
dorothyh@palmbeachfn.com.au
http://www.palmbeachfn.com.au

Parker Properties
Larry Parker
303 Partridge Run Drive
Duncanville, TX 75137
Phone: 972-780-0014
Fax: 972-709-7142
parkerproperties@charter.net
http://www.parkerproperties.us

Pre Management Co., Inc.
Chris Prefontaine
71 Elm Street, Suite 101
Worcester, MA 01609
Phone: 508-552-7109
Fax: 508-799-7511

chris@pre-co.com
http://www.pre-co.com

Premier Properties
Greg Jones
1035 Minnesota Avenue, #C
San Jose, CA 95125
Phone: 408-995-5900
Fax: 408-995-5901
prem-prop@sbcglobal.net
**http://www.pmpropertiesinc
.com**

Prime Time Properties
Management
JoDee Lucier
756 E University Drive
Mesa, AZ 85203
Phone: 480-833-7228
Fax: 480-962-6107
jodeelucier@aol.com
**http://www
.primetimeproperties.com**

Professional Property Mgmt
Patty McKinney
555 Oakdale St., Suite C
Folsom, CA 95630
Phone: 916-353-1900
Fax: 916-791-1991
patty@ppm4you.com
http://www.ppm4you.com

Professional Realty Group
Patricia Bonomo, RMP®
1660 Highway 260
Cottonwood, AZ 86326
Phone: 928-649-6306

Fax: 928-646-5800
patbonomo@hotmail.com
**http://www
.verdevalleyrealestate.net**

ProHome Rentals
Doug Wansley
PO Box 491893
Lawrenceville, GA 30049
Phone: 678-377-2567
Fax: 678-407-9471
doug@prohomerentals.com
http://prohomerentals.com

Properties Unlimited Of TN
Linda Dillon
403 N Walnut Street
Murfreesboro, TN 37130
Phone: 615-890-6565
Fax: 615-890-9325
linda@lindadillon.com
http://www.lindadillon.com

Property Network, Ltd.
Robert Smith
75-5799 B-3 Alii Drive
Kailua-Kona, HI 96740
Phone: 808-329-7977
Fax: 808-329-1200
rob@hawaii-kona.com
http://www.hawaii-kona.com

Property Profiles, Inc.
Lurline Johnson
98-030 Hekaha Street, #26
Aiea, HI 96701
Phone: 808-487-9500
Fax: 808-484-4051

lur@pixi.com
http://www.pprofiles.com

RAB Property Management
Richard Bieker
5234 50th Avenue NE
Seattle, WA 98105
Phone: 206-633-6060
Fax: 206-633-3030
RichBieker
@RABPropertyManagement.com
**http://www
.RABPropertyManagement.com**

RE/MAX Realty Associates
Angela Meyer
3119 Commercial Ave.
Anacortes, WA 98221
Phone: 360-293-8600
Fax: 360-293-7640
remax@cnw.com
**http://www.anacortesforrent
.com**

Realty Management Associates,
Conee Spano
4290 Chinden Boulevard, Ste A
Boise, ID 83714
Phone: 208-761-5517
Fax: 208-377-2966
rmaconee@cableone.net
http://www.rentalsinboise.com

Realty Masters Of Florida
Pamela Keen
6704 C Plantation Rd
Pensacola, FL 32504
Phone: 850-473-3983

Fax: 850-473-3975
pam@pensacolarealtymasters
.com
http://www.pamkeen.com

Realty Station Inc.
Janice Beam
2135 Sheridan Rd., suite F
Bremerton, WA 98310
Phone: 360-377-5699
Fax: 360-377-0608
realtystation@aol.com
http://www.realtystationinc.com

Realty Station Inc.
Renee Chester
2135 Sheridan Rd., suite F
Bremerton, WA 98310
Phone: 360-377-5699
Fax: 360-377-0608
realtystation@aol.com
http://www.realtystationinc.com

Recar & Associates, Realtors
Greg Fedro, MPM®
8400 N Mopac Expressway, #200
Austin, TX 78759
Phone: 512-345-9886
Fax: 512-345-2302
greg.fedro@recar-realtors.com
http://www.recar-realtors.com

Reid Property Management, LLC
Loren Johnson
9564 Silverdale Way, #200
Silverdale, WA 98383
Phone: 360-698-4026
Fax: 360-698-3584

lorenre@reidpm.com
http://reidpm.com

Reliable Property Management,
Inc.
Terrance Godbold, MPM® RMP®
ARM® GRI
3006 Bee Caves Road, B-180
Austin, TX 78746
Phone: 512-732-8388
Fax: 512-327-3283
terry@landlordaustin.com
http://www.landlordaustin.com

Roberts & Sons, LLC
Daren Roberts
PO Box 3517
Greenwood Village, CO 80155
Phone: 303-549-6179
Fax: 720-529-1599
daren.roberts@robertsandsons
.com
http://www.robertsandsons.com

Rosman Property Management
Stephen Rosman
24901 Northwestern Hwy #313B
Southfield, MI 48075
Phone: 248-355-4212
Fax: 248-355-9267
srosman@aol.com

Safeguard Property Management
Barney Christiansen
11075 S State Street, #5A
Sandy, UT 84070
Phone: 801-566-9339
Fax: 801-990-1799

sfgdpm@aol.com
http://www.safeguardproperty
.com

Seashore Real Estate, Inc.
Dean Jacobsen
PO Box 2026
Bluffton, SC 29910
Phone: 843-815-2447
Fax: 842-815-5812
dean@blufftonarearealestate.com

Skagit Tradition Realty LLC
Danya Wolf
2017 Continental Place, #8
Mount Vernon, WA 98273
Phone: 360-424-0300
Fax: 360-428-2919
danya@skagittraditionrealty.com
http://www
.skagittraditionrealty.com

Star Realty & Management, Inc
Judith Clark
4960 Horizon Drive
Cleveland, OH 44143
Phone: 216-469-4761
Fax: 216-453-2055
starrealtysales@sbcglobal.net
http://www.starrealtyohio.com

The Realty Shoppe Of Pasco, Inc.
Mary A. Rinaldi, GRI, RMP
PO Box 628
8924 US 19
Port Richey, FL 34673
Phone: 727-849-9844
Fax: 727-859-0590

maryr@sanctum.com
http://www.therealtyshoppe.com

http://www
.wrightpropertymanager.com

West Chapter: Realty of Prescott
Kristine Nelson
7900 E Florentine
Prescott Valley, AZ 86314
Phone: 928-759-3610
Fax: 928-759-3703
rentpv@hotmail.com

Young Fella Properties, Inc.
Vincent J. Lilly
106 W. Palisade Ave., Ste 201
Englewood, NJ 7631
Phone: 201-227-7649
Fax: 201-227-7640
veejaysbiznus@verizon.net

Willis Management Corp.
Keith Cowden ARM, GRI
2107 Global Court
Sarasota, FL 34240
Phone: 941-925-2100
Fax: 941-926-7774
willisrealty@cs.com

Windermere Property
Management
Lori Gill
700 112th Avenue NE, #203
Bellevue, WA 98004
Phone: 425-455-5515
Fax: 425-455-5537
lorigill@windermere.com
http://windermere.com

Wright Property Management
Kristine Williams
216 W State Street
Boise, ID 83702
Phone: 208-344-7662
Fax: 208-344-7663
info@wrightpropertymanager
.com

About the Author

Jamaine is a freelance writer that spent more than sixteen years as an Operations Research Systems Analyst for the U.S. Army. Her research skills, combined with knowledge acquired from a good friend who personally acquired, held, and managed more than 80 properties at any given time, were used to research and document the material presented in this book.

MONTH-TO-MONTH RENTAL AGREEMENT

Date: _____, 20 _____

RECEIPT IS HEREBY ACKNOWLEDGED by _____

hereinafter called Management, from _____

hereinafter called Resident, the sum of $_____ for the first month's rent of
the premises owned by said Management and located at _____

hereinafter called premises, said premises the Management hereby agrees to rent to said Resident on
a month-to-month basis at a rental of $_____ per month, payable in advance on
the _____ day of each and every succeeding calendar month.

In considered hereof and of the use or occupancy of the said premises, Resident agrees:

1. To maintain said premises in a clean, orderly, and law abiding manner and to keep the yards thereof
free of weeds, debris, and/or material that may become unsightly or a detriment to the appearance
of said premises. Management shall have the right to enter and inspect said premises at any and all
reasonable times.

2. No alterations or redecorating of any kind to the dwelling shall be made without the prior written
consent of Management.

3. To pay for all utility service furnished to the property.

4. To pay the cost of all repairs for any damage done to said premises and the cost of any cleaning up
of said premises which Management may consider necessary.

5. No birds, animals, or other pets shall be kept on the premises without the knowledge and
written consent from Management; any consent, so given may be withdrawn, if, in the opinion of
Management, such bird, animal, or other pet constitutes a nuisance, causes complaint from neighbors,
or adversely affects the normal maintenance of the property.

6. Not to let or sublet the whole or any part of the premises to anyone for any purpose whatsoever
without prior written permission from Management, and the number of persons to occupy said
premises shall not exceed _____ without written permission from Management.

7. To give thirty days written notice by registered mail to Management prior to vacating said premises
and to permit prospective tenants the opportunity of reasonable inspection.

8. To clean up said premises upon vacating and restore said premises to the same condition they are
now in, reasonable wear and tear and damage by the elements excepted.

9. That the violation of any of the covenants of this agreement or the nonpayment of any rent due
and unpaid shall be sufficient cause for eviction from said premises upon three (3) days written notice
thereof by registered mail or by personal service. If suit be brought to collect rent or damages, to cause
eviction from said premises, or to collect the costs of repairs to or cleaning of said premises, Resident
agrees to pay all costs of such action, including reasonable attorney fees as may be fixed by the Court.
No waiver by Management at any time of any of the terms of this agreement shall be deemed as a
subsequent waiver of the same, nor of the strict and prompt performance thereof by the Resident.

10. All rent shall be paid at the office of _____, or any other place
designated by Management. Each party hereto acknowledges receipt of a copy of this agreement.

_____ Signed
Management

_____ Signed
Resident

PET AGREEMENT

This agreement, dated _____ , is attached to and forms a part of the _____
_____ Agreement dated _____,
between _____, Management, and _____, Resident,
for the residential unit located at _____.

Resident desires to keep a pet named _____ and described as
_____ in the dwelling Tenant occupies under the Lease Agreement referred
to above, and because this agreement specifically prohibits keeping pets without Management's
permission, Resident agrees to:

- Keep the pet under control at all times.

- Keep the pet restrained, but not tethered, when it is outside Resident's dwelling.

- Not leave the pet unattended for any unreasonable periods.

- Dispose of the pet's droppings properly and quickly.

- Not leave food or water for the pet, or any other animal, outside the dwelling.

- Keep pet from causing any annoyance or discomfort to others and will remedy immediately any complaints made through the Management.

- Remove the pet's offspring from the premises within eight weeks of birth.

- Pay immediately for any damage, loss, or expense caused by the pet and, in addition, Resident will add $ _____ to Resident's security/cleaning deposit, any of which may be used for cleaning, repairs, or delinquent rent when Resident vacates. This added deposit, or what remains of it when pet damages have been assessed, will be returned to Resident within _____ days after Resident proves this pet is no longer kept on the premises.

- Management reserves the right to revoke permission to keep the pet should Resident violate this agreement.

_____ Signed
            Management

_____ Signed
            Resident

WATERBED AGREEMENT

This agreement, dated _____ , is attached to and forms a part of the
_____Agreement dated _____
between _____, Management and _____ ,
Resident, for the residential unit located at _____ .

Resident desires to keep a waterbed described as _____ in
the dwelling occupied under the Lease Agreement referred to above, and because this agreement
specifically prohibits keeping waterbeds without Management's permission, Resident agrees to:

1. Keep one waterbed approved by Management for this dwelling. Waterbed shall consist of a
    mattress at least 20 mil thick with lap seams, a safety liner at least 8 mil, and a frame enclosure
    which meets the Waterbed Manufacturers Association standards.

2. Consult with Management about the location of the waterbed. Resident agrees to hire a
    qualified professional to install and dismantle the bed according to the manufacturer's
    specifications and further agrees not to relocate it without the Management's consent.

3. Allow Management to inspect the waterbed installation at any and all reasonable times and
    Resident agrees to remedy any problems or potential problems immediately.

4. Furnish Management with a copy of a valid liability insurance policy for at least $100,000
    covering this waterbed installation and agrees to renew the policy as necessary for continuous
    coverage.

5. Pay immediately for any damage caused by the waterbed and, in addition, Resident will add
    $ _____ to the security/cleaning deposit, any of which may be used for
    cleaning, repairs, or delinquent rent when Resident vacates. This added deposit, or what remains
    of it when waterbed damages have been assessed, will be returned to Resident within _____
    _____ days after Resident proves the waterbed is no longer located on the premises.

6. In consideration of the additional time, effort, costs, and risks involved in this waterbed
    installation, Resident agrees to pay additional rent of $ _____, which [ ] includes [ ]
    does not include the premium for the waterbed liability insurance policy referred to in item 4.

7. Resident agrees that Management reserves the right to revoke this permission to keep a
    waterbed should the Resident break this agreement.

_____ Signed
                    Management

_____ Signed
                    Resident

NOTICE OF OVERDUE RENT

Date: _____

To: _____

      _____

      _____

      _____

Your rent of $_____ for the period of _____ has not been received as of the date listed above.

Please be reminded that your rent was due on _____.

In addition, our lease agreement provides for a late charge of _____.

Your rent, including applicable late charges, should be sent to:

      _____

      _____

      _____

      _____

By _____
                Landlord/Management

Phone _____

PAYMENT ARRANGEMENT

I am currently renting (address) _____ from
(owner) _____. I realize that I am currently $_____
behind in my rent. I promise that I will pay the above amount owed, in full, by the date of
_____ , 20 _____.

In the event that I, for any reason, do not follow through with the above promise, I shall vacate said
premises immediately and no later than the above mentioned date. If I fail to do the above, I give
my permission to said owner to change the locks and allow the same to re-rent said premises. If said
premises is unfurnished, I give said owner or agent permission to remove the furniture from said
premises and set it out on the street. The owner will return all personal clothing and belongings to me.
I realize it is my responsibility to pick up my personal belongings and articles no later than 48 hours
after the locks have been changed.

Dated this _____ day of _____ 20_____.

_____ Signed
          Management

_____ Signed
          Resident

30-DAY NOTICE TO TERMINATE TENANCY

To: _____   Address Of Premises:_____

                                                    Date: _____

Notice is hereby given that you are required, within thirty (30) days, to move from and deliver up possession of the above-referenced premises.

This notice is intended for the purpose of terminating the Lease/Rental Agreement by which you now hold possession of the above-described premises, and should you fail to comply, legal proceedings will be instituted against you to recover possession, to declare said Rental Agreement forfeited, and to recover rents and damages for the period of unlawful detention.

Please be advised that rent on said premises is due and payable up to and including the date of termination of your tenancy under this notice.

_____
Landlord/Managing Agent

State of S.S.	AFFIDAVIT OF SERVICE - When Served by a person not an officer
County of	

_____, being duly sworn, on oath deposes and says that on the _____ day of _____, _____ he/she served the within notice on the tenant named therein, as follows: (Initial applicable)

1. By delivering a copy thereof to the within named tenant, _____.

2. By delivering a copy thereof to _____, a person above the age of sixteen years, residing in or in charge of the within described premises.

3. By sending a copy thereof to said tenant by certified/registered mail, return receipt requested.

4. By posting a copy thereof on the main door of the within described premises, no one being in actual possession thereof.

_____
Signature of Notice Server

Subscribed and sworn to before me this _____ day of _____, 20_____

_____
Notary Public

REMODELING

Within _____ months from _____[year], lessee agrees to expend not less than $_____ in improving, repairing and remodeling building now standing on premises in order to put building in good condition and repair and to adapt the same for the purposes of the business to be conducted therein by lessee. Before letting any contract or commencing any work in connection with such improvements, repairs and remodeling, lessee agrees to furnish to lessor, and allow him to keep as lessor's own property, correct copies of all plans and specifications showing nature and extent of such work, together with a written statement by some reputable licensed architect showing estimated cost of such work, so that lessor may have an opportunity to determine in advance whether such plans, specifications and estimate conform to the requirements of this lease.

Lessee agrees to make and complete such improvements, repairs and remodeling as speedily as possible, and in any event prior to _____[year], substantially in accordance with plans and specifications to be submitted to lessor, as aforesaid, fully paid for and free and clear of and from any and all liens in the nature of mechanics' liens, or claims therefor, in connection with any work or labor performed or material, machinery or equipment furnished or installed in connection with the aforesaid work of improving, repairing and remodeling the present building on such premises.

During work of improving, repairing and remodeling building as aforesaid, lessee agrees, at lessee's own expense, to do any and all shoring up, and take all other necessary steps to protect building in connection with any excavation or any of building operations in, upon, over or under premises, or any adjoining premises, street or alley.

Lessee agrees before commencing any of such work to take out and keep in force until the completion thereof, adequate fire, public liability and casualty insurance in good and responsible insurance companies, and to an amount sufficient at all times to protect and save harmless lessor from and against any and all claims for loss or damage to any persons or property whatever, by reason of or in any way arising from or during the continuance of such work; and lessee agrees that all of such work shall and will be done by lessee in substantial accordance with the plans and specifications therefor, to be submitted to lessor as aforesaid, and also in conformity with all laws, ordinances, and building regulations of the city of _____, applicable thereto.

AGREEMENT TO EXECUTE LEASE

AGREEMENT is made by and between the following parties, _____ (hereinafter referred to as "Landlord") and _____ (hereinafter referred to as "Tenant"), on this _____ (Month & Day) _____ (Year).

IN CONSIDERATION OF THE PROMISES AND COVENANTS CONTAINED HEREIN, and in consideration of the amount of _____ ($_____) paid by the Tenant to the Landlord which shall be credited toward the first month's rent under a certain lease described below, and receipt of which is hereby acknowledged, the parties mutually agree as follows:

I.   A certain lease for the following subject premises more particularly described as: _____

shall be made, signed, executed, and delivered by the parties.

2.   The execution and delivery of said Lease shall take place on _____(Month & Day) _____ (Year), at a location specifically described as: _____ _____

_____ Signed
                        Landlord

_____ Signed
                        Tenant

AGREEMENT TO CANCEL LEASE

_____ is Landlord under the Lease Agreement, and _____; _____ Corp. ("Retailer") is the successor in interest to tenant; and

Retailer has ceased operating the premises and is desirous of obtaining a release from all of its obligations under the Lease Agreement; and

Landlord is willing to release Retailer from all of its obligations under the Lease Agreement upon the terms and conditions set forth herein.

Therefore, in consideration of the premises and other good and valuable consideration, the parties hereby agree as follows:

1.   Landlord agrees to execute, acknowledge and deliver at closing to Retailer: (i) a Surrender of Lease in the form annexed hereto and made a part hereof as Exhibit "A"; and (ii) Assignment of Lease and Assumption Agreements in the form annexed hereto and made a part hereof.

2.   Retailer agrees at closing to: (i) deliver to Landlord its check in the amount of $_____; (ii) execute, acknowledge and deliver to Landlord a Bargain and Sale Deed with Covenant Against Grantor's Acts in the form annexed and made a part hereof for property located at _____ Avenue, _____, _____ and more particularly described. As of the date of closing, title shall be good and marketable and such as would be insured by _____ Title Insurance Company, at regular rates, free and clear of all liens and encumbrances or objections except those set forth in Exhibit annexed hereto and made a part hereof; (iii) execute, acknowledge and deliver to Landlord an assignment of all of Retailer's right, title and interest as lessee in and to that certain lease dated _____ [year], by and between _____ and _____, as lessor, and _____, as lessee, in the form annexed hereto and made a part hereof, for property located at _____ Avenue, _____, _____, and more particularly described in such lease, a copy of which has been delivered to Landlord, and receipt of which is hereby acknowledged; and (iv) execute, acknowledge and deliver to Landlord an assignment of all of Retailer's right, title and interest as Landlord in and to that certain lease dated _____ [year], by and between Landlord, and _____, tenant, for property located at _____ Avenue, _____, _____, and more particularly described in such lease, a copy of which has been delivered to Landlord, and receipt of which is hereby acknowledged, together with the sum of $_____ representing the security delivered by tenant to Landlord on the making of the lease.

3.   Adjustments for each of the properties shall be made as of the date of closing and adjustments shall be made, where applicable, for real estate taxes, fuel and rents.

4.   The closing shall be held at 10:00 a.m. on _____ [year] at the office of _____ Corporation, _____ Drive, _____, _____.

5.   In the event that Landlord shall, on the tender by Retailer of all of the items required to be delivered by it pursuant to Paragraph 2, fail to execute, acknowledge and deliver the Surrender of Lease as provided in Paragraph 1 hereof, then Retailer shall be released of all of its obligations under the Lease Agreement as of the closing date provided for herein.

6.   In the event that Retailer shall fail to tender all of the items required of it pursuant to Paragraph 2 hereof then Landlord shall have the right to (i) sue for specific performance or (ii) cancel this Agreement and the parties hereunder shall have no further rights or obligations to each other with respect to this Agreement.

7. With respect to the property located at _____ Avenue, _____, _____, Landlord agrees to accept the premises in its as is condition as of the date hereof.

8. This Cancellation Agreement is subject to the approval of the Bank of _____, and no rights or obligations shall accrue hereunder until the Bank's approval has been secured provided, however, that unless such approval is obtained within ten (10) days from the date hereof Retailer shall have the right to terminate this Cancellation Agreement upon the giving of fifteen (15) days' notice and from and after the date specified in said notice this Cancellation Agreement shall be null and void and of no further force and effect.

9. This Cancellation Agreement contains the entire agreement between the parties with respect to the matters contained herein and cannot be changed, modified or amended unless in writing and executed by the party against whom the enforcement of the change, modification or amendment is sought.

10. This Cancellation Agreement shall be binding upon the parties hereto and their respective successors and assigns.

11. Any notices required to be given hereunder shall be in writing and shall be deemed given if sent by registered or certified mail, return receipt requested, postage prepaid, (a) to Landlord at the address hereinabove set forth, or such other address as Landlord may designate by notice to Retailer, or (b) to Retailer in duplicate under separate cover, one copy to the attention of the President of Retailer, and one copy to the attention of the Vice-President in charge of real estate, at the address of Retailer set forth above, or such other address as Retailer may designate by notice to Landlord. During the period of any postal strike or other interference with the mails, personal delivery shall be substituted for registered or certified mail.

In witness whereof, the parties hereto have caused this Agreement to be executed on the date first above written.

_____ Signed
                  Management

_____ Signed
                  Tenant

AGREEMENT TO TERMINATE LEASE

Date: _____

FOR GOOD CONSIDERATION, _____ (Landlord) and _____
_____ (Tenant) as of _____ (Date) hereby mutually
agree to terminate and cancel said lease dated _____ (Date) on premises known
as _____ (Address). Both
_____(Landlord) and _____ (Tenant) hereby agree that
this termination agreement cancels all rights and obligations under said lease excepting only for any
unpaid rent obligations accruing under the lease prior to the effective termination date.

_____ (Tenant) agrees to promptly surrender the premises by the
termination date and to return said premises to _____ (Landlord) in the same
condition received to the extent reasonably possible, free of _____ (Tenants)
goods and effects.

This agreement shall be binding upon the parties, their successors, assigns, personal agents and
representatives.

_____ Signed
                    Landlord

_____ Signed
                    Tenant

_____ Signed
                    Witness

NOTICE OF INTENT TO ENTER

To: _____

_____

_____

YOU ARE HEREBY NOTIFIED that on or about _____ a.m. or p.m. on _____ _____ (Month & Day), _____ (Year), the Owner, Manager, Owner's agent, or Owner's employees intend to enter the premises identified above which you hold and occupy. They will need to stay approximately _____ hours.

The purpose for entry is as follows:

_____

_____

_____

You are not required to be on the premises to provide access. Whoever comes to enter will knock first and after determining that no one is available to answer, will enter using a passkey.

This is intended to be a reasonable notice of at least twenty-four (24) hours.

This notice was personally served by the Owner/Manager at the following time:

_____a.m. or p.m., and _____(Month & Day), _____.

_____
Owner/Manager

APARTMENT SERVICE CALL

Date: _____

To Resident: _____ of Apartment No.: _____

____ Filter Changed Today

____ Heat Checked Today

____ Air Conditioning Checked Today

____ _____ Checked Today

____ _____ Checked Today

____ _____ Checked Today

____ _____ Checked Today

Please note that the following items were not completed:

_____

_____

_____

If you have question or require further assistance, please contact the office at:

_____

The office hours are: _____ a.m. - _____ p.m. Monday - Saturday

_____ a.m. - _____ p.m. Sunday.

Completed By: _____

NOTICE TO CHANGE RENT

To: _____

       _____

       _____

YOU ARE HEREBY NOTIFIED that the terms of tenancy under which you occupy the above-described premises are about to be changed.

Effective _____ (Month & Day), _____ (Year), your rent will be increased by _____ ($_____) per month from _____ ($_____) to _____ ($_____), payable in advance.

Dated this _____ (Month & Day), _____ (Year).

_____
Owner/Manager

This notice was served by the Owner/Manager in the following manner (check those which apply):

____ by personal delivery to the tenant,

____ by leaving a copy with someone on the premises other than the tenant,

____ by mailing,

____ by posting.

Americans with Disabilities Act—Addendum

Notwithstanding anything else in this lease to the contrary, this paragraph shall apply to all issues related to compliance with both the Americans with Disabilities Act ("ADA") and the _____ [state statute]. In the event of any conflict between the rest of the lease and this Paragraph, this Paragraph shall control.

(a). Any remodeling, construction, reconstruction, installation of improvements or other work done to the common areas or other portions of the property of which the Premises are a part (the "Property") shall be performed by Landlord, at Landlord's expense, in compliance with the requirements of the ADA and the _____ [state statute] and regulations promulgated pursuant to them.

(b). Any remodeling, construction, reconstruction, installation of improvements or other work done to the Premises shall be done in compliance with ADA and _____ [state statute] requirements, at the expense of the party who is performing the work.

(c). In the event that a regulatory agency, private party, organization or any other person or entity makes a claim under either the ADA or the _____ [state statute] against either (or both) parties, the party whose breach (or alleged breach) of responsibility under this lease gave rise to the claim shall promptly retain attorneys and other appropriate persons to advise the parties regarding the same, and shall in good faith and at that party's sole cost and expense take whatever actions are necessary to bring the Premises or the Property, as the case may be, into compliance with ADA or _____ [state statute] requirements. That party shall defend, save and hold harmless the other party from any and all expenses incurred in responding to such a claim, including without limitation the fees of attorneys and other advisors, court costs, and costs incurred for bringing the Property and/or the Premises into compliance. If the claim relates to an aspect of the Premises or the Property as it existed at the time of the execution of the lease, as opposed to work performed by either party after the execution of the lease, then Landlord shall be deemed to be the party whose breach of responsibility gave rise to the claim.

[Alternatives: if a claim is made, Tenant has the option of terminating the lease; the parties split the cost in an agreed-upon proportion (e.g., 50/50, 60/40, etc.); Tenant bears the cost if the claim pertains only or primarily to the Premises, while Landlord bears the cost if the claim relates only or primarily to the Property; etc.]

(d). Common area maintenance charges shall not include any costs or expenses incurred by Landlord in bringing the Premises or the Property into compliance with ADA or _____ [state statute] requirements, either voluntarily or in response to a claim of non-compliance.

[Alternatives: only a certain dollar amount or percentage may be included; all of the cost for such items may be included; those pertaining to the Premises could be passed on in CAM charges, but not those pertaining to common areas; etc.]

(e). Tenant shall not change its use of the Premises without the prior written consent of Landlord. If the proposed change in use would, in the good faith written opinion of Landlord's advisors, trigger expenditures to comply with ADA or _____ [state statute] requirements not applicable to the then-current use of the Premises by Tenant, Landlord may refuse the proposed change in use on that ground or condition approval of the change in use on Tenant's agreement to bear the expense of compliance with ADA and _____ [state statute] requirements triggered by Tenant's proposed change in use. This subparagraph shall also apply to proposed assignments or subleases which would change the use of the Premises.

[Alternatives: An outright prohibition on change of use; Landlord's options limited to approval or disapproval; Tenant bears the first $_____ of expenses; etc.]

(f). Notwithstanding the above, neither party shall be responsible for any costs or expenses relating to practices of the other which are deemed to be discriminatory under the ADA or _____ [state statute] and which relate solely to the conduct of such party (as opposed to physical barriers), and each party shall indemnify the other against costs or expenses relating to the other party's conduct.

(g). Notwithstanding the above, Tenant shall be solely responsible for expenses necessary to comply with ADA and _____ [state statute] requirements triggered solely by a disability of one or more of Tenant's employees.

[Alternative: if the expense to be incurred would be for an item which would become a fixture to the real estate, the cost might be shared in some proportion.]

(h). Both parties covenant with one another to cooperate reasonably to comply with ADA and _____ [state statute] requirements in the least expensive reasonable manner, and to create as little disruption as possible to the business operations of Landlord, Tenant and the other tenants of the Property.

(i). Any rules and regulations which would prohibit either party from complying with ADA or _____ [state statute] requirements are deemed by this subparagraph to be modified to the extent necessary to allow compliance.

(j). Non-compliance with the provisions of this Paragraph, after written notice to the non-complying party and an opportunity to cure within a reasonable period, shall be an event of default under the lease. A reasonable period to cure shall mean cure or commencement of efforts to cure within ten days, which efforts are diligently pursued to completion.

ROOMMATE AGREEMENT (ADDENDUM TO THE RENTAL AGREEMENT)

Date: _____

This agreement amends, is incorporated into, and forms a part of the Rental Agreement dated
_____ between _____, Owner(s) and
_____, Tenant(s).

Tenant(s), also known here as "Roommates," desire to rent the premises on a "roommate arrangement." Owner(s) agree to this arrangement under the following terms and conditions:

ROOMMATE APPROVAL AND SUBSTITUTION – Every person who wishes to become a Roommate under this agreement, whether as an original Roommate or as a substituted Roommate, must first submit a Rental Application and be approved by the Owner(s) in writing. The Owner(s) may require substituted Roommates to sign the existing Rental Agreement or may require an entirely new agreement to be signed by the substituted Roommates and the remaining Roommates. Upon substitution of Roommates, Owner(s) may elect to increase the deposit.

FINANCIAL RESPONSIBILITY – Each Roommate agrees to be jointly and severally liable to the Owner(s) for the entire rent and the entire amount of any other charges incurred under the Rental Agreement.

DEPOSITS – Roommates agree to pay deposits to the Owner(s) in the form of a single certified check or money order. The Owner(s) will hold all deposits until the entire dwelling has been vacated completely. Owner(s) may make deposit refunds in the form of a single check made payable jointly to all Roommates with rights to the deposits. This check and the itemized accounting of deposit deductions may be sent to any one of the Roommates with rights to the deposits.

DEPARTING ROOMMATES – Roommates who move out while this Agreement is in effect continue to have financial responsibility under this Agreement unless the Owner(s) release them from this responsibility in writing or unless they are replaced by substituted Roommates approved by the Owner(s). Upon being relieved of financial liability, departing Roommates relinquish all rights to the deposits.

MAXIMUM NUMBER OF ROOMMATES ALLOWED – Without the prior written approval of the Owner(s), Roommates may at no time exceed _____ in number.

GUESTS – Tenant(s) may house any single guest for a maximum period of fourteen days every six months or for whatever period of time the law allows. Guests may at no time exceed _____ in number.

COMMUNICATIONS – Whenever the Owner(s) give a notice to one Roommate, it shall be considered as having been communicated to all Roommates. Whenever one Roommate gives a notice to the Owner(s), it shall be considered as having been communicated from all Roommates.

Owner _____   Roommate _____

                                   Roommate _____

                                   Roommate _____